W9-ABY-473

# SINK YOUR TEETH INTO THESE!

Name ______________________

Use words from the Word Bank to finish the riddle. Then use the same words to complete the puzzle.

**Question**

Why are

(1↓) ___ ___ ___ ___ ___ ___ ___ ___

not very

(4→) ___ ___ ___ ___ ___ ___ ___?

**Answer**

(2↓) ___ ___ ___ ___ ___ ___ ___

they are a (3→) ___ ___ ___ ___

in the (5→) ___ ___ ___ ___.

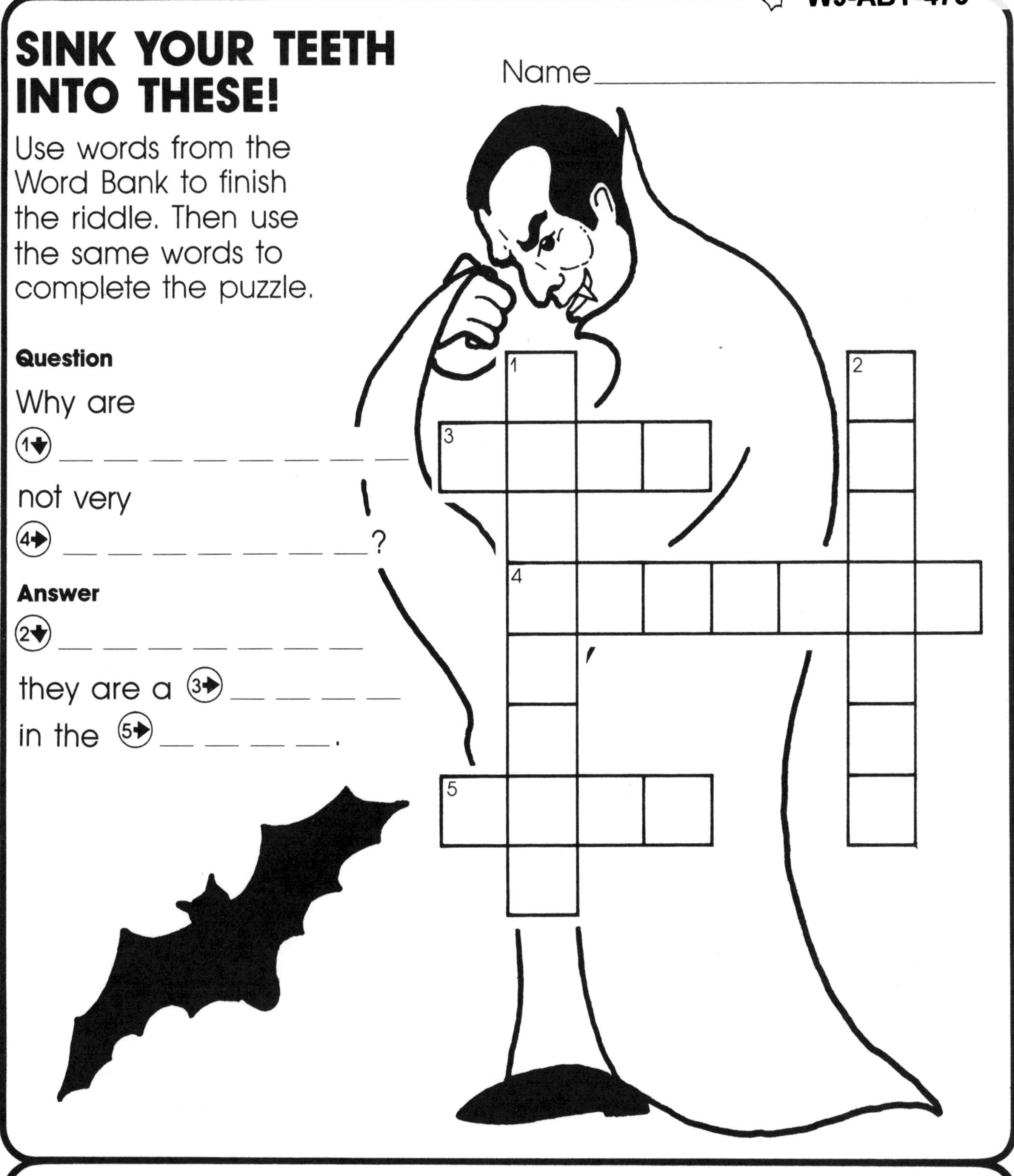


## Word Bank

| beside | vampires | pain | nice |
|---|---|---|---|
| because | ghosts | popular | neck |

 

# GHOST BOOSTERS

Name______________________________

Use words from the Word Bank to finish the riddle. Then use the same words to complete the puzzle.

**Question**

What is the

3→ ___ ___ ___ ___ ___

thing 1↓ ___ ___ ___ ___ ___ ___

do when they get into

their 6→ ___ ___ ___ ___?

**Answer**

They 6→ ___ ___ ___ ___ ___ ___

their 2→ ___ ___ ___ ___ ___

4↓ ___ ___ ___ ___ ___!

1

2

3

4

5

6

Word Bank

| bed | cars | sheet | first |
|---|---|---|---|
| ghosts | black | belts | fasten |

 

# PILGRIM'S PRIDE

Name____________________________

Use words from the Word Bank to finish the riddle. Then use the same words to complete the puzzle.

**Question**

What (1→) _ _ _ _ _

did the

(4→) _ _ _ _ _ _ _ _

do when they came to

(2↓) _ _ _ _ _ _ _ _?

**Answer**

The (3↓) _ _ _ _ _ _ _ _ _

(5↓) _ _ _ _!

1 2 3 4 5

Word Bank

| | | | |
|---|---|---|---|
| Plymouth | dance | Mayflower | America |
| turkeys | corn | Pilgrims | rock |

# REMEMBER NOVEMBER

Name ______________________

Use words from the Word Bank to finish the riddle. Then use the same words to complete the puzzle.

**Question**

What

2→ _ _ _ _ _ _ _

does

3↓ _ _ _ _ _ _ _

celebrate in the

1↓ _ _ _ _ _

of November?

**Answer**

4→ _ _ _ _ _-

5↓ _ _ _ _ _ _!

1

2 3

4 5

Word Bank

| | | | |
|---|---|---|---|
| month | turkey | corn | Dracula |
| holiday | feast | mouth | Fangs-giving |

 

# HAPPY "HO-HO" DAYS

Name____________________________

Use words from the Word Bank to finish the riddle. Then use the same words to complete the puzzle.

**Question**

(4→) __ __ __ __ goes "ho, (5↓) __ __ - __ __ plop"?

**Answer**

(1↓) __ __ __ __ __ Claus

(2→) __ __ __ __ __-ing

his (3↓) __ __ __ __ off.

Word Bank

| | | | |
|---|---|---|---|
| Santa | tree | what | laugh |
| Claus | head | ho-ho | angel |

 

# ALL IS CALM

Name ____________________

Use words from the Word Bank to finish the riddle. Then use the same words to complete the puzzle.

**Question**

(1↓) _ _ _ _

do you call a

(3→) _ _ _ _ _

man who wears

(2↓) _ _ _ _ _ _ _

armor?

**Answer**

A (2→) _ _ _ _ _ _ _

(4→) _ _ _ _ _ _!

1 2 3 4

Word Bank

| night | where | quiet | quick |
|---|---|---|---|
| knight | what | silent | shining |

# HEART THROBS

Name ______________________

Use words from the Word Bank to finish the riddle. Then use the same words to complete the puzzle.

**Question**

What kind of

(1↓) __ __ __ __ __ __ __ __

are (5→) __ __ __ __ __

in the (3→) __ __ __ __ __ __

of February?

**Answer**

(4↓) __ __ __ __ __ __

(2→) __ __ __ __ __ __ __- ists!

Word Bank

| heart | born | cupid | special |
|---|---|---|---|
| valentine | month | doctors | friend |

# "EGGS"-PERTS

Name ____________________

Use words from the Word Bank to finish the riddle. Then use the same words to complete the puzzle.

**Question**

Why did the
(3↓) ___ ___ ___ ___ ___ ___
keeper's (5→) ___ ___ ___ ___
wear a (1→) ___ ___ ___?

**Answer**

She had too (4→) ___ ___ ___ ___
(2↓) ___ ___ ___ ___ hares!

**Word Bank**

| | | | |
|---|---|---|---|
| carry | rabbit | little | eggs |
| many | gray | wife | wig |

 

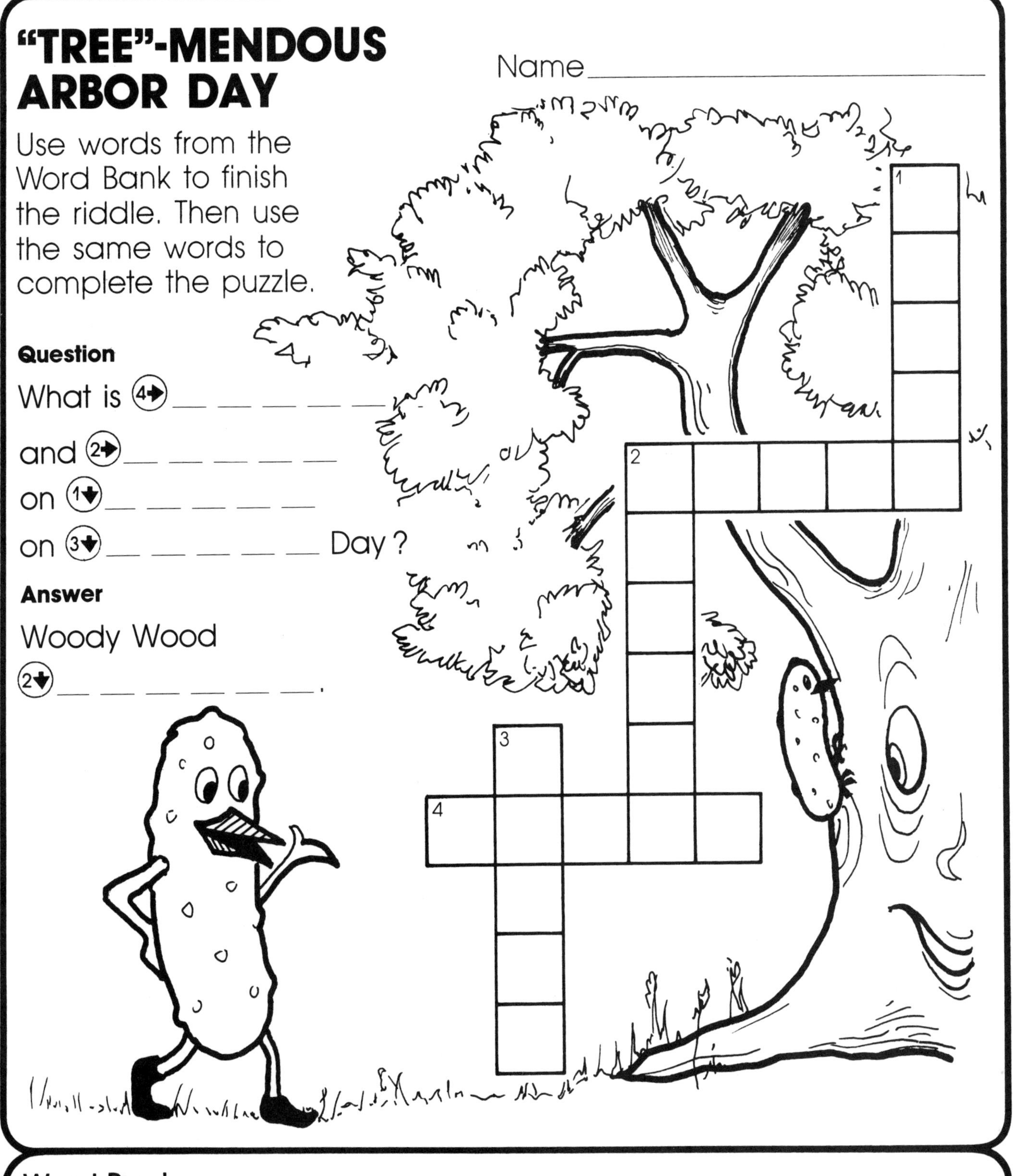

# "TREE"-MENDOUS ARBOR DAY

Name ______________________

Use words from the Word Bank to finish the riddle. Then use the same words to complete the puzzle.

**Question**

What is (4→) _ _ _ _ _ _

and (2→) _ _ _ _ _

on (1↓) _ _ _ _ _

on (3↓) _ _ _ _ _ Day?

**Answer**

Woody Wood (2↓) _ _ _ _ _ _.

Word Bank

| branch | pecks | twig | trees |
|---|---|---|---|
| Arbor | green | pickle | trunks |

# Your Enlightening Library

Name ____________________

**Across**

3. The date your library book must be returned
7. A book about imaginary characters or events
8. The person who writes a book
9. One book in a series of books
10. Looking up information about a topic

**Down**

1. ______ Decimal system
2. Cabinet of cards to help locate a book in the library
4. A set of books containing knowledge on all topics
5. A book about a person's life
6. Facts and information

**Word Bank**

| | | | |
|---|---|---|---|
| media | research | data | encyclopedia |
| books | volume | biography | illustrator |
| reference | fiction | nonfiction | card catalog |
| author | publisher | date due | Dewey |

 

Skill: Parts of speech

# The Grammar Grapevine

Name ______________________________

Identify the part of speech that is underlined.

**Across**

3. He left the library quietly.
5. Ronald Reagan is a ______ noun.
6. A koala lives in Australia.
7. The football and basketball teams traveled by plane.
9. The rocket lifted off at 12:30 p.m.

**Down**

1. He went to the movie with a friend.
2. The word geese is a ______ noun.
3. The brown dog ran after the cat.
4. The word president is a ______ noun.
8. I see, I saw, I have seen. These are examples of verb ______.

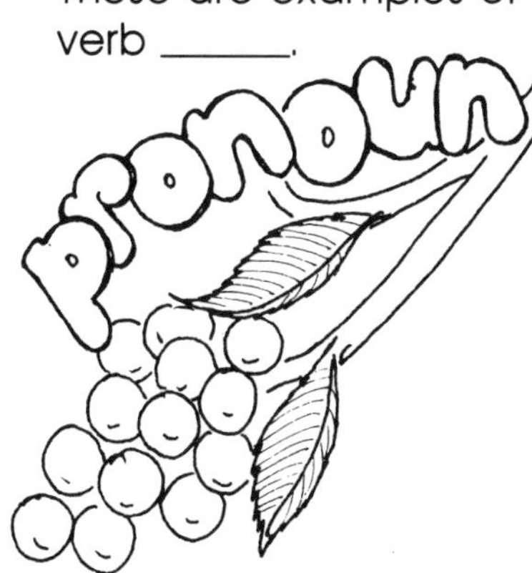


**Word Bank**

| | | | |
|---|---|---|---|
| verb | plural | possessive | pronoun |
| adjective | adverb | negatives | proper |
| common | subject | predicate | helpers |
| noun | tense | singular noun | |

 

# Fighting Disease

Name ______________________

Across
1. Washing your hands with ______ and water helps prevent the spread of diseases.
4. Microscopic organisms that can cause disease
7. Microscopic organisms that can cause disease – includes bacteria
8. A liquid used to prevent or cure a disease
9. A disease that many of us catch – it causes headache, vomiting, and diarrhea.
11. A follow-up dose of a vaccine

Down
2. ______ is the key to good health.
3. Substance that is given to the body to produce immunity to a disease
5. When a disease is spread by contact between two people
6. When your body cannot catch a certain disease, you are __________.
10. A viral disease which causes a stuffed-up nose is the common _________.

germs
virus
disease

Word Bank

| | | | |
|---|---|---|---|
| immune | contagious | soap | chicken pox |
| germs | prevention | water | virus |
| vaccine | booster | flu | antibody |
| serum | bacteria | cold | disease |

 

# Map Mania

Name ______________________

**Across**

3. North America, Asia, and Australia are examples of this land form.
5. The distance north and south of the Equator
7. The earth's shape
9. An imaginary line that divides the earth's surface into the Northern and Southern Hemispheres

**Down**

1. Lines east and west of the Prime Meridian
2. An imaginary, straight line on which the earth rotates
4. Half of the earth
5. A key (or description) accompanying a map
6. The distance above sea level
8. The most accurate model of the earth

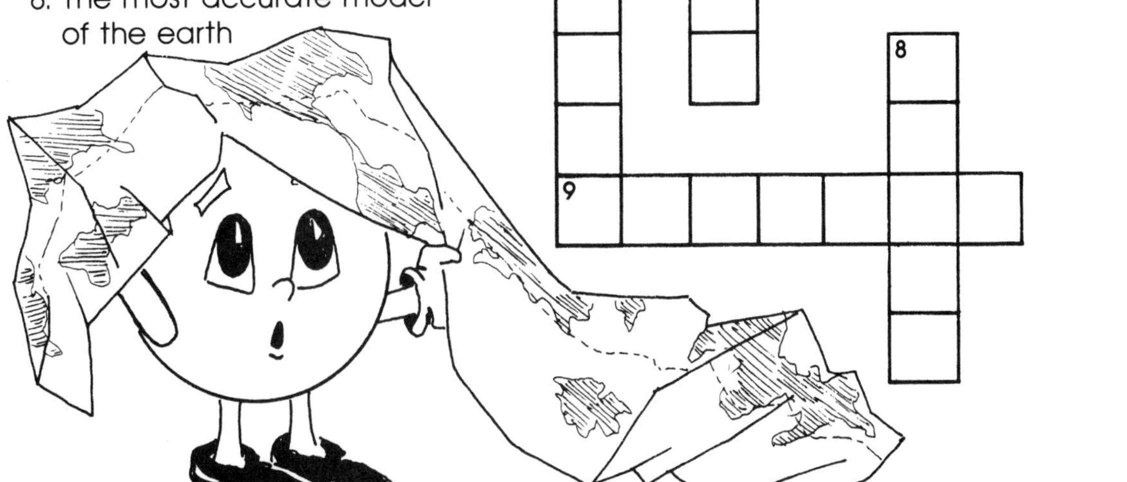

**Word Bank**

| | | | |
|---|---|---|---|
| longitude | compass | North Pole | Great Circle |
| latitude | hemisphere | South Pole | Equator |
| axis | globe | revolution | legend |
| pole | continent | rotation | scale |
| elevation | sphere | ocean | topography |

 

Concept: American colonies

# The Colonies

Name ______________________

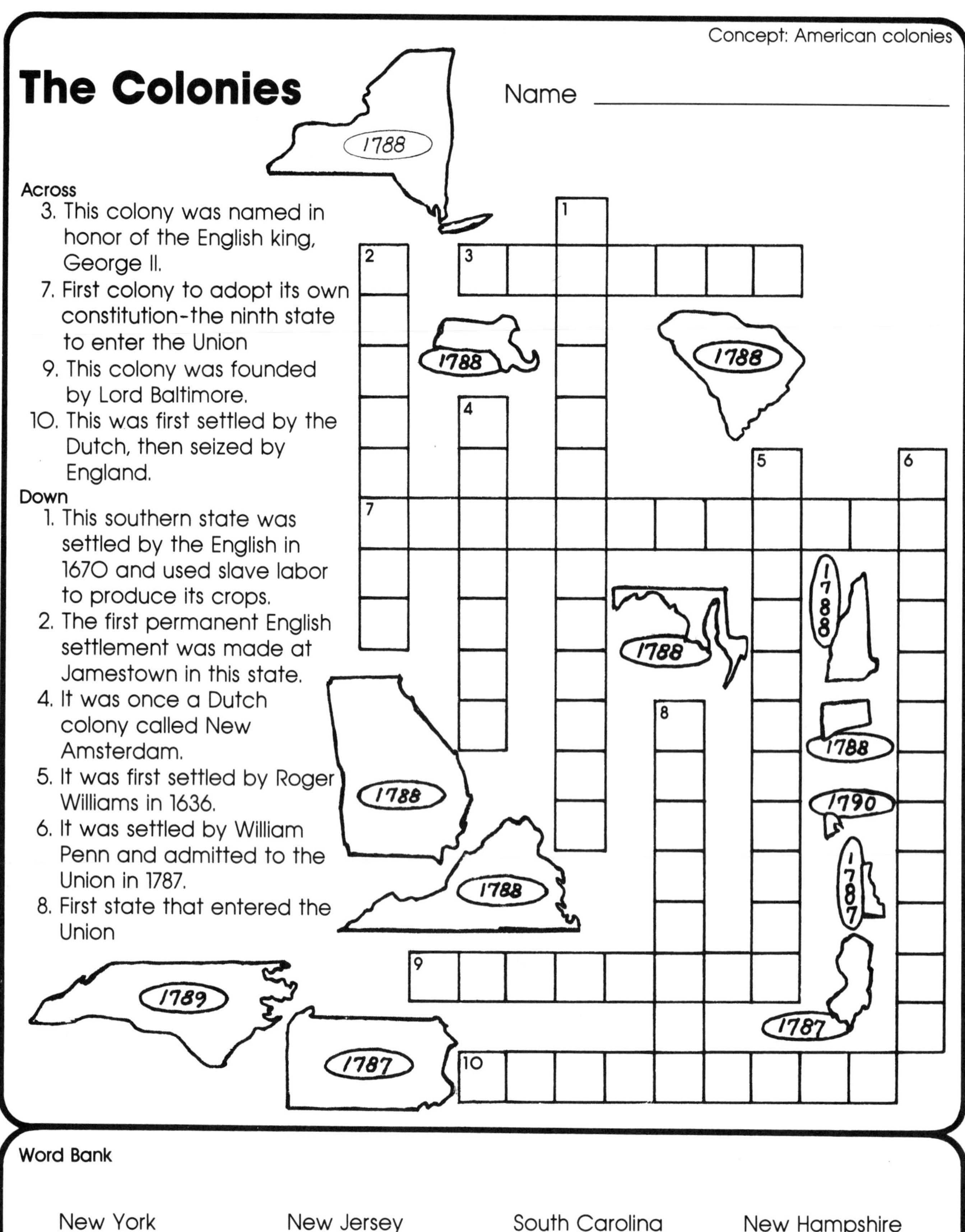


**Across**

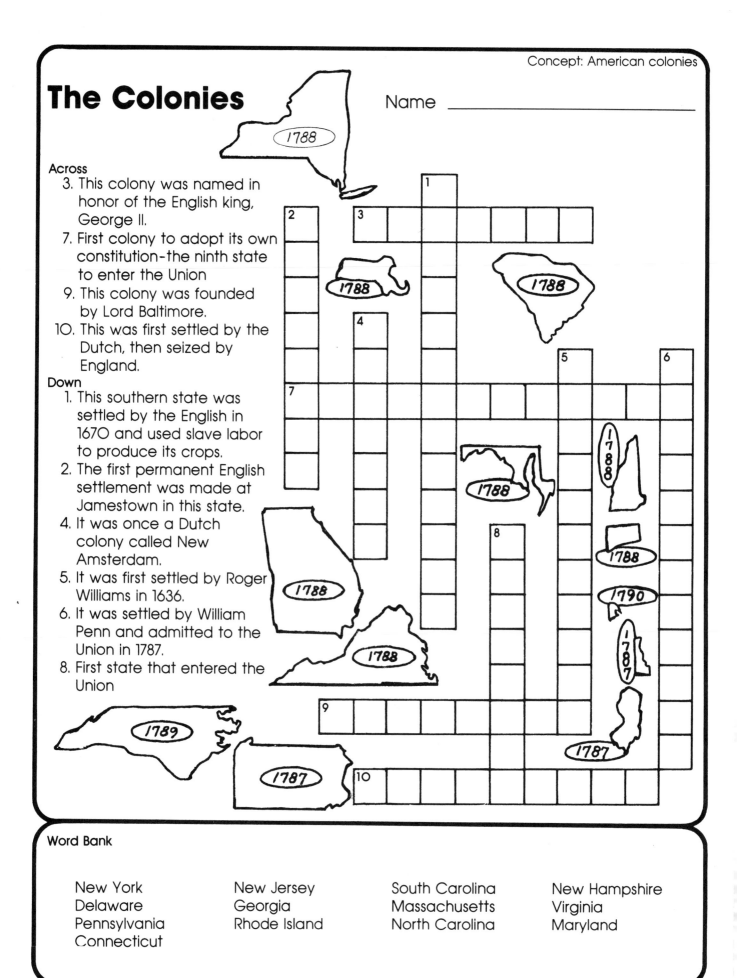

3. This colony was named in honor of the English king, George II.
7. First colony to adopt its own constitution-the ninth state to enter the Union
9. This colony was founded by Lord Baltimore.
10. This was first settled by the Dutch, then seized by England.

**Down**

1. This southern state was settled by the English in 1670 and used slave labor to produce its crops.
2. The first permanent English settlement was made at Jamestown in this state.
4. It was once a Dutch colony called New Amsterdam.
5. It was first settled by Roger Williams in 1636.
6. It was settled by William Penn and admitted to the Union in 1787.
8. First state that entered the Union

**Word Bank**

| | | | |
|---|---|---|---|
| New York | New Jersey | South Carolina | New Hampshire |
| Delaware | Georgia | Massachusetts | Virginia |
| Pennsylvania | Rhode Island | North Carolina | Maryland |
| Connecticut | | | |

 

# Solar Soaring

Name ______________________

**Across**

1. Heavenly bodies seen as small, fixed points of light in the night sky
2. The force that draws all objects toward the center of the earth
4. The ninth and smallest planet in the Solar System
5. The "Red" Planet
6. This planet has nine rings around it.
8. Any heavenly body that revolves around the sun

**Down**

1. The "Great Rings" around this planet are actually pieces of ice and ice-covered rock.
3. Rocky object that orbits the sun
5. Chunks of metal or stone which travel through Earth's atmosphere and burn up
7. The center of our Solar System

**Word Bank**

| | | | |
|---|---|---|---|
| Sun | Mars | Venus | Earth |
| Jupiter | Mercury | Saturn | Neptune |
| Uranus | Pluto | comet | meteor |
| planet | gravity | moon | asteroid |
| stars | astronaut | | |

 

# Rocks

Name ______________________________

Across
2. Rock produced by heat and fire
4. Substances found in the earth, such as coal and gold
5. The hardened remains of a plant or animal
7. A place where stone is excavated to be used for buildings
8. Precious stones
9. A clear, transparent rock

Down
1. The science dealing with the structure of the earth's crust and its various layers
3. Matter that settles to the bottom, often forming rock
4. Rock which has undergone a change in its structure
6. A broken piece of rock

Word Bank

classify
sedimentary
fragment
minerals
streak test
quarry
aggregates
igneous
mineralogist
crystal
gems
fossils
metamorphic
geode
geology

 

Skill: Geometry terms

# Circles and Squares

Name ______________________

Across

2. When 2 halves of a shape are exactly the same, they are said to have ________.
6. The shape made by two straight lines meeting in a point
7. A shape having four equal sides and four right angles
9. Something which has a definite position in space, but no size or shape
10. The outside surface of a figure

Down

1. Part of a line with one end point
3. A three-sided figure
4. A part of a line with two end points
5. The sum of the length of all the sides of a figure
8. A straight line passing through the center of a circle

Word Bank

| | | | |
|---|---|---|---|
| line | line segment | circle | square |
| triangle | cone | point | angle |
| cube | parallel | symmetry | area |
| perimeter | ray | rectangle | diameter |

 

# Holiday Hits

Name ____________________

Across
1. September holiday that honors workers
3. May holiday that honors servicemen who have been killed in wartime
5. We honor our __________ in February.
8. The Jewish Festival of Lights
10. Candy hearts and cute little cards help you celebrate this holiday of love.

Down
2. Your very special day
4. An Irish holiday
6. The day we give thanks
7. The Christian holiday which is a time of giving
9. Trick or treat, jack-o-lanterns, costumes

Word Bank

Christmas
Valentine
Birthday
Presidents
Chanukah
Labor Day
Fourth of July
Columbus Day
Thanksgiving
Memorial Day
New Years Eve
St. Patricks
Halloween
Martin Luther King

 

# Merry Measurement!

Name ______________________

**Across**

2. There are 100 of these in a meter.
3. 4 quarts = 1 __________.
6. There are 60 seconds in 1 __________.
7. 2,000 pounds
9. Equals 2 pints or 4 cups
10. Some have 30 days.

**Down**

1. 10 centiliters = 1 __________.
4. There are 16 in a pound.
5. 1,000 grams = 1 __________.
8. There are 12 in 1 foot.

**Word Bank**

| | | | |
|---|---|---|---|
| second | minute | hour | day |
| week | month | year | inches |
| kilogram | yard | mile | cup |
| deciliter | quart | gallon | ounces |
| centimeter | ton | meter | liter |
| kilometer | | | |

Skill: Library terms

# Librarians Go By the Book!

Name ______________________________

<table>
<tr><td>K</td><td>L</td><td>O</td><td>I</td><td>S</td><td>B</td><td>O</td><td>A</td><td>L</td><td>R</td><td>E</td><td>M</td><td>E</td><td>D</td><td>I</td><td>A</td></tr>
<tr><td>A</td><td>D</td><td>R</td><td>A</td><td>N</td><td>W</td><td>I</td><td>K</td><td>S</td><td>R</td><td>L</td><td>B</td><td>B</td><td>O</td><td>E</td><td>U</td></tr>
<tr><td>P</td><td>E</td><td>N</td><td>C</td><td>Y</td><td>C</td><td>L</td><td>O</td><td>P</td><td>E</td><td>D</td><td>I</td><td>A</td><td>L</td><td>S</td><td>T</td></tr>
<tr><td>E</td><td>W</td><td>O</td><td>L</td><td>I</td><td>F</td><td>G</td><td>N</td><td>A</td><td>F</td><td>M</td><td>O</td><td>E</td><td>F</td><td>R</td><td>H</td></tr>
<tr><td>R</td><td>E</td><td>S</td><td>E</td><td>A</td><td>R</td><td>C</td><td>H</td><td>K</td><td>E</td><td>S</td><td>G</td><td>W</td><td>I</td><td>B</td><td>O</td></tr>
<tr><td>I</td><td>Y</td><td>D</td><td>K</td><td>C</td><td>A</td><td>L</td><td>I</td><td>N</td><td>R</td><td>W</td><td>R</td><td>E</td><td>C</td><td>N</td><td>R</td></tr>
<tr><td>O</td><td>D</td><td>L</td><td>P</td><td>O</td><td>S</td><td>I</td><td>H</td><td>A</td><td>E</td><td>Z</td><td>A</td><td>U</td><td>T</td><td>I</td><td>M</td></tr>
<tr><td>D</td><td>E</td><td>T</td><td>A</td><td>M</td><td>G</td><td>E</td><td>O</td><td>Y</td><td>N</td><td>L</td><td>P</td><td>B</td><td>I</td><td>L</td><td>O</td></tr>
<tr><td>I</td><td>C</td><td>F</td><td>U</td><td>R</td><td>E</td><td>T</td><td>N</td><td>I</td><td>C</td><td>L</td><td>H</td><td>M</td><td>O</td><td>L</td><td>I</td></tr>
<tr><td>C</td><td>I</td><td>Z</td><td>C</td><td>O</td><td>N</td><td>W</td><td>A</td><td>B</td><td>E</td><td>Z</td><td>Y</td><td>X</td><td>N</td><td>U</td><td>A</td></tr>
<tr><td>A</td><td>M</td><td>R</td><td>O</td><td>A</td><td>M</td><td>R</td><td>K</td><td>L</td><td>D</td><td>N</td><td>S</td><td>T</td><td>E</td><td>S</td><td>R</td></tr>
<tr><td>L</td><td>A</td><td>U</td><td>T</td><td>O</td><td>B</td><td>I</td><td>O</td><td>G</td><td>R</td><td>A</td><td>P</td><td>H</td><td>Y</td><td>T</td><td>M</td></tr>
<tr><td>S</td><td>L</td><td>O</td><td>Y</td><td>N</td><td>U</td><td>S</td><td>L</td><td>T</td><td>E</td><td>K</td><td>A</td><td>C</td><td>O</td><td>R</td><td>I</td></tr>
<tr><td>N</td><td>O</td><td>N</td><td>F</td><td>I</td><td>C</td><td>T</td><td>I</td><td>O</td><td>N</td><td>Y</td><td>F</td><td>W</td><td>B</td><td>A</td><td>L</td></tr>
<tr><td>I</td><td>L</td><td>Y</td><td>A</td><td>S</td><td>O</td><td>R</td><td>H</td><td>L</td><td>M</td><td>A</td><td>O</td><td>G</td><td>R</td><td>T</td><td>B</td></tr>
<tr><td>D</td><td>A</td><td>T</td><td>E</td><td>D</td><td>U</td><td>E</td><td>W</td><td>E</td><td>T</td><td>D</td><td>R</td><td>S</td><td>E</td><td>O</td><td>N</td></tr>
<tr><td>M</td><td>H</td><td>I</td><td>C</td><td>A</td><td>E</td><td>B</td><td>F</td><td>O</td><td>L</td><td>G</td><td>Y</td><td>A</td><td>F</td><td>R</td><td>W</td></tr>
<tr><td>S</td><td>T</td><td>U</td><td>V</td><td>O</td><td>L</td><td>U</td><td>M</td><td>E</td><td>S</td><td>O</td><td>I</td><td>G</td><td>L</td><td>E</td><td>C</td></tr>
<tr><td>R</td><td>S</td><td>Y</td><td>E</td><td>L</td><td>W</td><td>O</td><td>D</td><td>O</td><td>R</td><td>E</td><td>S</td><td>D</td><td>T</td><td>A</td><td>S</td></tr>
<tr><td>D</td><td>C</td><td>A</td><td>R</td><td>D</td><td>C</td><td>A</td><td>T</td><td>A</td><td>L</td><td>O</td><td>G</td><td>U</td><td>E</td><td>O</td><td>T</td></tr>
</table>

Sh...You won't need the card catalogue to find these library words. Identify each word.

**Word Bank**

media
encyclopedia
nonfiction
card catalog
date due
author
biography
reference
Dewey Decimal
research
autobiography
periodicals
volumes
fiction
illustrator

 

Skill: Parts of speech

# Grammar Gremlins!

Name ____________________

Parts of speech can be gremlins if not used correctly! Circle these words and identify each.

| L | P | A | O | S | N | I | L | P | U | O | K | E | S | N | C | U | Z | O | N | T | E |
|---|---|---|---|---|---|---|---|---|---|---|---|---|---|---|---|---|---|---|---|---|---|
| S | O | K | I | E | A | R | S | P | L | U | R | A | L | N | O | U | N | I | B | E | L |
| I | S | T | N | O | U | N | O | R | A | I | X | O | L | E | M | W | E | R | L | S | D |
| N | S | O | M | D | I | K | A | E | Z | N | U | A | D | W | M | I | G | O | A | U | B |
| G | E | C | A | D | J | E | C | T | I | V | E | N | E | M | O | R | A | C | L | B | S |
| U | S | A | M | I | B | L | K | E | N | O | Y | A | O | T | N | S | T | E | W | J | A |
| L | S | H | U | L | P | A | R | P | E | F | A | B | I | C | N | A | I | B | O | E | N |
| A | I | E | P | R | O | P | E | R | N | O | U | N | S | H | O | I | V | M | K | C | W |
| R | V | B | A | C | E | W | T | E | H | I | L | Z | O | X | U | B | E | O | T | T | E |
| N | E | N | R | S | A | V | L | D | T | E | A | N | L | D | N | W | S | R | E | W | F |
| O | P | R | S | E | H | A | R | I | C | U | H | O | T | M | S | K | A | W | Y | P | R |
| U | B | I | F | Y | B | A | E | C | R | O | N | E | L | I | L | B | C | B | J | V | O |
| N | M | A | H | P | J | S | N | A | L | T | H | E | L | P | E | R | S | F | D | E | C |
| I | Z | E | G | H | A | P | D | T | C | E | M | J | C | M | A | S | N | W | Y | R | G |
| P | R | O | N | O | U | N | O | E | W | N | K | C | O | E | A | D | V | E | R | B | L |
| A | F | L | E | V | E | R | B | T | E | N | S | E | M | Y | N | S | R | T | P | O | S |

**Word Bank**

verb
adjective
common nouns
noun
plural noun
adverb
subject
verb tense
possessive
negatives
predicate
singular noun
pronoun
proper nouns
helpers

 

# It's Catching!

Name ______________________________

| L | D | S | E | V | I | A | D | V | U | C | M | U | N | I | M |
|---|---|---|---|---|---|---|---|---|---|---|---|---|---|---|---|
| A | B | T | E | H | C | N | O | I | P | K | P | E | L | M | O |
| V | A | C | C | I | N | E | K | R | S | I | R | N | F | I | F |
| O | C | H | O | V | B | I | S | U | E | A | E | L | N | C | K |
| S | T | R | M | T | A | L | O | S | L | E | V | H | S | R | E |
| B | E | U | M | R | X | E | N | F | I | Y | E | T | I | O | F |
| N | R | S | U | O | G | E | R | M | S | T | N | E | L | B | N |
| I | I | G | N | H | B | A | S | I | R | O | T | A | S | E | A |
| P | A | O | I | D | I | N | F | L | U | R | I | G | L | S | V |
| R | S | A | C | O | C | C | E | D | B | O | O | S | T | E | R |
| O | A | P | A | E | L | H | K | W | I | L | N | E | M | O | H |
| T | I | N | B | L | E | I | I | S | G | I | B | R | I | A | E |
| O | Y | S | L | O | M | C | C | E | B | D | O | N | M | G | B |
| Z | A | O | E | H | S | K | U | G | R | I | Y | K | M | S | O |
| O | B | E | O | L | I | E | N | T | O | S | V | A | U | L | L |
| A | I | V | S | Y | C | N | D | E | R | E | Y | O | N | G | Y |
| N | S | R | A | L | B | P | C | L | T | A | S | E | I | R | M |
| S | A | N | T | I | B | O | D | Y | O | S | L | M | T | O | L |
| P | I | L | O | H | N | X | E | K | L | E | N | I | Y | V | S |
| C | O | M | M | O | N | C | O | L | D | S | D | A | V | S | I |

"Catch" these communicable disease words and look up their meanings.

**Word Bank**

flu
booster
protozoans
virus
vaccine
chicken pox
communicable
immunity
bacteria
common cold
diseases
germs
antibody
microbes
prevention

Skill: Map skills

# Map Maze

Name ______________________

| W | H | R | O | T | A | T | I | O | N | I | H | T | D | Y | R |
|---|---|---|---|---|---|---|---|---|---|---|---|---|---|---|---|
| N | A | D | L | O | E | Y | W | H | A | R | M | N | E | O | L |
| H | L | A | D | O | V | A | U | E | Q | U | A | T | O | R | K |
| Y | H | O | E | M | T | R | U | M | Y | E | E | A | T | W | T |
| A | R | E | V | O | L | U | T | I | O | N | A | L | S | R | O |
| T | W | Y | I | C | O | D | E | S | T | A | L | L | E | N | P |
| T | L | Y | O | E | G | A | S | P | H | E | R | E | F | O | O |
| C | O | M | P | A | S | S | R | H | T | C | B | E | V | R | G |
| H | S | O | N | N | U | T | B | E | S | O | R | H | I | T | R |
| Y | A | O | T | V | L | A | U | R | S | N | N | G | I | H | A |
| I | L | A | T | I | T | U | D | E | I | T | O | E | M | P | P |
| P | O | L | E | O | A | O | R | H | N | I | F | R | L | O | H |
| O | N | U | R | E | I | L | E | G | E | N | D | N | E | L | Y |
| N | G | L | O | B | E | M | Y | A | O | E | A | S | L | E | N |
| U | I | U | N | R | L | O | A | C | R | N | P | C | R | T | H |
| G | T | G | V | A | W | D | Y | T | S | T | M | A | E | T | A |
| S | U | S | O | U | T | H | P | O | L | E | N | L | X | A | B |
| A | D | H | A | R | D | R | W | S | I | T | I | E | G | I | N |
| F | E | L | E | V | A | T | I | O | N | C | O | L | T | E | S |
| T | I | G | R | E | A | T | C | I | R | C | L | E | I | R | H |

Work your way through this maze of map study words.

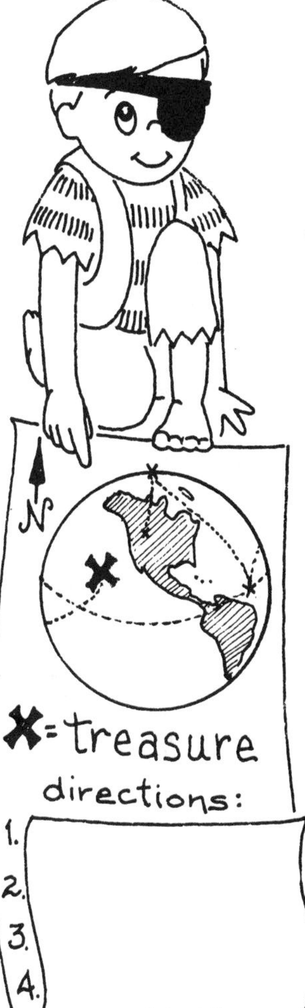


**Word Bank**

longitude
latitude
axis
pole
elevation
compass
hemisphere
globe
continent
sphere
North Pole
South Pole
revolution
rotation
ocean
Great Circle
equator
legend
scale
topography

 

Concept: American colonies

# 13 Strong

Name ____________________

| P | I | E | T | T | L | S | L | I | E | L | N | O | I | P | S |
|---|---|---|---|---|---|---|---|---|---|---|---|---|---|---|---|
| I | L | I | N | E | W | H | A | M | P | S | H | I | R | E | R |
| S | J | M | S | P | S | Y | E | E | O | D | A | T | N | N | T |
| O | O | A | A | N | I | G | T | T | R | L | E | T | R | N | E |
| U | I | R | I | S | D | I | S | A | D | P | N | S | A | S | M |
| T | S | Y | T | E | E | N | A | N | G | S | O | S | H | Y | C |
| H | N | L | N | C | L | N | O | S | D | N | R | F | M | L | A |
| C | M | A | S | S | A | C | H | U | S | E | T | T | S | V | O |
| A | T | N | R | K | W | I | Y | T | N | W | H | E | C | A | S |
| R | G | D | G | R | A | J | N | Y | N | J | C | O | E | N | R |
| O | R | L | A | W | R | D | R | V | I | E | A | H | R | I | H |
| L | H | O | A | R | E | U | G | I | U | R | R | E | F | A | D |
| I | E | S | M | P | N | L | O | R | H | S | O | T | A | S | O |
| N | E | W | Y | O | R | K | A | G | H | E | L | T | W | A | F |
| A | F | B | G | E | O | R | G | I | A | Y | I | O | E | R | U |
| C | B | S | S | Y | C | L | T | N | T | R | N | H | N | L | O |
| Y | L | M | R | H | O | D | E | I | S | L | A | N | D | M | S |
| W | O | E | S | E | M | L | M | A | E | B | R | L | Y | E | W |
| C | O | N | N | E | C | T | I | C | U | T | S | I | A | H | E |
| C | A | O | Y | F | A | Y | S | O | N | E | Y | C | S | S | E |

You've got to start somewhere and that's what the United States did. Locate the thirteen original colonies in this puzzle.

**Word Bank**

New York
New Hampshire
Massachusetts
Rhode Island
Connecticut
New Jersey
Delaware
Virginia
North Carolina
South Carolina
Georgia
Pennsylvania
Maryland

Skill: Astronomy terms

# Soaring Through the Solar System

Name ______________________

Soar through this puzzle and find astronomical words.

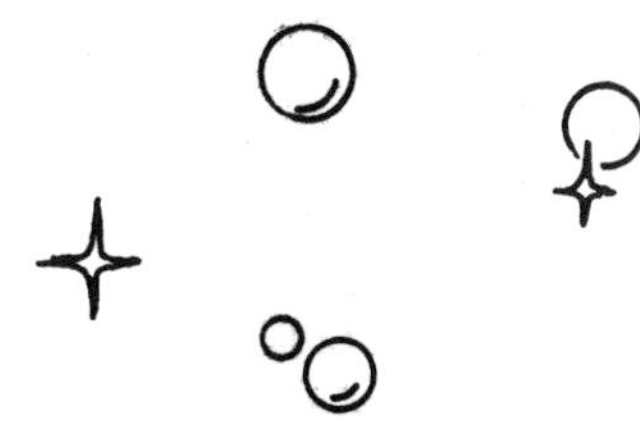

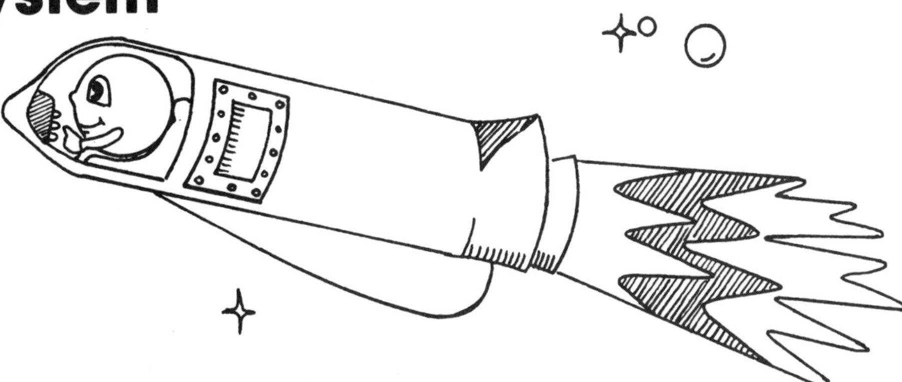

| E | C | L | U | M | K | I | R | P | J | K | S | F | L | E | R | J | E | D | P | B | A |
|---|---|---|---|---|---|---|---|---|---|---|---|---|---|---|---|---|---|---|---|---|---|
| S | A | L | M | C | O | M | E | T | S | U | O | T | V | E | N | U | S | A | L | H | S |
| A | T | R | W | Y | S | E | O | T | U | N | O | Y | U | I | D | P | Y | I | A | N | T |
| S | A | N | T | M | D | I | N | O | E | S | O | S | I | Y | A | I | N | B | N | W | E |
| T | K | T | O | H | E | W | E | T | N | U | P | O | O | N | Y | T | O | O | E | E | R |
| R | S | T | E | A | L | E | V | A | Y | T | L | R | A | U | E | E | A | U | T | H | O |
| O | J | H | S | I | K | T | I | N | A | G | U | U | I | T | M | R | U | Y | S | Y | I |
| N | I | M | E | R | C | U | R | Y | D | L | T | E | P | D | R | I | C | O | B | N | D |
| A | U | A | S | G | R | U | I | S | N | E | O | A | G | H | N | G | I | D | L | E | O |
| U | U | R | A | N | U | S | A | H | I | T | W | N | R | O | E | T | O | U | Y | P | B |
| T | I | S | R | S | U | T | M | Y | E | A | P | R | A | E | I | N | U | E | N | T | R |
| H | I | E | E | V | A | E | T | Y | D | O | T | U | V | T | S | U | N | G | S | U | D |
| M | E | T | E | O | R | H | L | W | E | V | B | E | I | A | H | I | T | V | E | N | M |
| T | G | O | H | A | P | E | M | T | Y | R | E | U | T | T | H | E | L | O | U | E | O |
| I | O | Y | V | T | S | A | T | U | R | N | M | A | Y | S | L | A | S | O | J | G | A |
| U | N | L | E | R | O | E | T | H | Y | E | A | S | L | Y | W | S | T | A | R | S | O |

**Word Bank**

| | | | |
|---|---|---|---|
| sun | Mars | Venus | Earth |
| Jupiter | Mercury | Saturn | Neptune |
| Uranus | Pluto | comet | meteor |
| planets | gravity | moon | asteroid |
| stars | astronaut | | |

Skill: Geology terms

# Rock Hounds!

Name ______________________

This rock and mineral word search is a "gem." Dig out the words and be ready to define them. Look up the names of some rocks and minerals.

| S | E | D | I | M | E | N | T | A | R | Y | I | G | T | O | G | U | H | T | Y | U | L |
|---|---|---|---|---|---|---|---|---|---|---|---|---|---|---|---|---|---|---|---|---|---|
| L | A | T | I | K | R | C | E | Y | C | R | Y | S | T | A | L | S | M | O | T | C | K |
| I | F | N | F | O | M | R | A | M | T | N | O | I | N | G | T | W | I | B | U | L | I |
| M | S | T | R | E | A | K | T | E | S | T | W | A | L | G | O | S | N | E | L | A | E |
| O | N | F | A | E | G | H | K | T | E | S | L | U | O | R | A | H | E | I | R | S | O |
| C | H | I | G | R | A | C | E | A | T | G | E | M | S | E | H | I | R | E | M | S | N |
| B | G | N | M | A | L | I | C | M | A | E | N | T | K | G | J | N | A | M | Y | I | S |
| R | E | T | E | F | Y | G | E | O | D | E | O | N | W | A | E | F | L | A | N | F | E |
| E | O | L | N | S | G | N | I | R | B | E | I | S | E | T | M | A | O | W | G | Y | I |
| C | L | U | T | N | O | K | W | P | L | N | G | O | Y | E | B | G | G | V | Q | B | O |
| F | O | I | S | G | A | I | C | H | L | O | N | I | M | S | E | A | I | B | U | L | G |
| A | G | I | M | B | E | L | A | I | C | Y | E | M | A | S | C | I | S | U | A | D | F |
| H | Y | W | E | N | J | O | L | C | W | V | O | E | N | C | T | R | T | L | R | S | E |
| S | P | R | E | U | S | N | D | E | R | T | U | S | A | R | I | P | L | E | R | N | A |
| J | L | M | I | N | E | R | A | L | S | T | S | O | K | I | G | H | V | U | Y | D | L |
| I | W | D | E | C | B | N | O | M | L | A | S | K | F | O | S | S | I | L | S | J | K |

**Word Bank**

| | | | |
|---|---|---|---|
| classify | streak test | mineralogist | metamorphic |
| sedimentary | quarry | crystals | geode |
| fragments | aggregates | gems | geology |
| minerals | igneous | fossils | |

# Newsworthy!

Name ______________________________

| W | A | B | O | N | I | K | L | S | I | N | D | E | X | N | E |
|---|---|---|---|---|---|---|---|---|---|---|---|---|---|---|---|
| S | E | R | C | B | O | N | W | A | L | W | E | S | K | I | Z |
| A | D | I | O | F | E | A | T | U | R | E | S | D | B | H | E |
| L | I | O | M | B | A | C | G | I | N | A | O | E | L | E | O |
| O | T | M | I | F | N | G | O | R | M | T | S | L | E | A | D |
| S | O | B | C | P | E | A | F | I | O | H | G | F | B | D | I |
| D | R | A | S | L | N | O | S | K | A | E | L | S | N | L | Y |
| R | I | H | D | C | T | Y | U | T | I | R | L | P | O | I | K |
| E | A | E | G | N | E | S | B | A | H | R | O | O | P | N | A |
| H | L | L | W | I | R | L | S | O | L | S | B | R | Y | E | P |
| I | S | P | C | I | T | U | C | S | I | O | N | T | S | W | L |
| K | U | W | R | N | A | O | R | H | P | A | M | S | O | H | A |
| C | L | A | S | S | I | F | I | E | D | A | D | S | A | I | N |
| D | I | N | M | O | N | E | P | S | E | L | M | O | N | L | A |
| M | R | T | A | L | M | A | T | D | P | U | B | L | I | S | H |
| I | W | E | C | H | E | N | I | W | E | Y | C | U | L | B | Y |
| A | U | D | O | E | N | T | O | I | D | A | N | O | R | W | T |
| S | H | O | I | X | T | H | N | Y | C | O | L | U | M | N | S |
| L | M | A | S | T | H | E | A | D | E | M | I | T | S | O | K |
| T | S | Y | W | E | O | A | F | S | K | N | Y | I | M | T | E |

Extra! Extra! Read all about it! Find these newspaper words and be ready to tell what each is. Then find the sections in your paper.

**Word Bank**

| | | | |
|---|---|---|---|
| index | headline | masthead | lead |
| editorial | features | comics | weather |
| classified ads | subscription | publish | help wanted |
| sports | entertainment | columns | |

 

Skill: Geometry terms

# Gangway for Geometry

Name ________________________________

| D | F | E | A | L | N | O | T | I | T | E | N | T | D | I | S |
|---|---|---|---|---|---|---|---|---|---|---|---|---|---|---|---|
| C | P | A | R | A | L | L | E | L | M | K | O | U | A | O | N |
| R | N | U | F | S | E | W | F | W | S | A | R | O | N | I | E |
| E | T | X | T | U | T | N | U | M | R | R | E | C | G | N | A |
| C | O | N | E | G | R | O | O | H | E | E | C | K | L | J | U |
| R | I | N | R | T | I | O | R | R | O | D | T | S | E | T | C |
| L | I | N | E | S | E | G | M | E | N | T | A | E | S | H | T |
| E | O | Y | L | P | E | T | Z | A | R | R | N | W | E | C | E |
| V | A | T | I | O | A | R | B | A | W | I | G | C | L | U | E |
| W | P | E | R | I | M | E | T | E | R | O | L | I | S | A | L |
| E | U | A | E | W | K | R | Z | T | E | M | E | R | N | R | I |
| H | I | S | Q | U | A | R | E | L | A | S | M | C | A | E | N |
| A | O | I | H | I | K | S | U | S | T | S | L | L | D | T | E |
| Y | R | E | A | O | A | E | Y | L | E | C | P | E | S | U | R |
| R | A | E | T | N | S | E | P | O | I | N | T | D | Y | M | P |
| T | B | R | A | L | R | A | D | O | N | A | E | O | M | I | U |
| C | A | U | S | D | I | A | M | E | T | E | R | P | M | E | D |
| U | K | I | O | G | C | M | Y | U | T | H | U | R | E | O | S |
| B | Y | N | R | T | O | L | D | N | I | R | E | L | T | X | N |
| E | L | O | I | T | I | V | Y | R | O | T | T | G | R | T | O |
| A | E | T | R | I | A | N | G | L | E | D | I | E | Y | P | C |

Gangway for the 16 geometric terms hidden in the puzzle. Be a super math student and circle them.

Word Bank

line
triangle
cube
perimeter
line segment
cone
parallel
ray
circle
point
symmetry
rectangle
square
angle
area
diameter

 

# Happy Holidays!

Name ______________________________

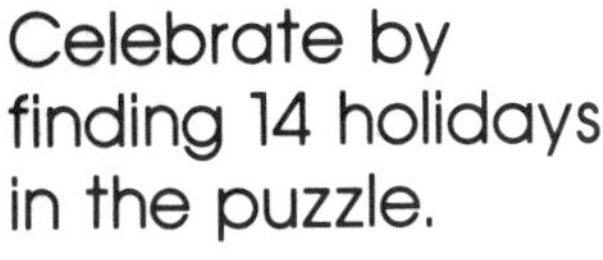

Celebrate by finding 14 holidays in the puzzle.

| A | A | P | R | E | S | I | D | E | N | T | S | D | A | Y | Y | L | A | T | M | F | T |
|---|---|---|---|---|---|---|---|---|---|---|---|---|---|---|---|---|---|---|---|---|---|
| N | I | T | N | C | W | F | E | W | R | B | R | E | T | P | A | V | E | K | A | H | H |
| A | E | J | L | O | N | I | S | T | Y | H | E | I | M | E | O | A | T | O | R | S | A |
| N | E | W | Y | E | A | R | S | E | V | E | S | G | A | T | U | L | W | N | T | O | N |
| L | A | B | O | R | D | A | Y | H | A | I | L | G | N | C | I | E | D | T | I | L | K |
| S | H | I | I | P | O | X | S | R | M | E | B | U | S | H | I | N | N | H | N | E | S |
| B | K | R | M | E | V | U | T | E | M | R | I | H | I | A | L | T | I | O | L | R | G |
| K | S | T | P | A | T | R | I | C | K | S | K | T | R | N | D | I | W | S | U | E | I |
| W | G | H | T | Q | R | L | A | M | O | A | W | U | A | U | H | N | D | T | T | I | V |
| C | A | D | J | U | S | Y | F | E | U | R | S | I | U | K | I | E | C | I | H | M | I |
| E | W | A | L | R | K | Y | R | O | N | D | W | O | H | A | L | L | O | W | E | E | N |
| H | F | Y | L | E | U | F | H | A | G | O | E | N | U | H | E | W | O | U | R | V | G |
| D | O | E | S | S | L | Z | C | H | R | I | S | T | M | A | S | N | Y | T | K | H | S |
| E | M | E | M | O | R | I | A | L | D | A | Y | F | O | R | O | U | I | R | I | E | I |
| N | U | K | F | O | U | R | T | H | O | F | J | U | L | Y | E | T | O | O | N | B | U |
| E | Y | H | U | B | E | W | T | C | O | L | U | M | B | U | S | D | A | Y | G | S | A |

**Word Bank**

| | | | |
|---|---|---|---|
| Christmas | Chanukah | Thanksgiving | St. Patricks |
| Valentine | Labor Day | Memorial Day | Halloween |
| Birthday | Fourth of July | New Years Eve | Martin Luther King |
| President's Day | Columbus Day | | |

 

Concept: Forestry

# Forest Forage

Name ______________________

| M | L | R | O | P | B | C | W | D | C | U | M | P | A | U | F |
|---|---|---|---|---|---|---|---|---|---|---|---|---|---|---|---|
| O | P | U | L | P | M | H | S | A | W | M | I | L | L | R | E |
| L | L | Y | P | Y | A | R | E | U | T | W | L | L | N | C | R |
| C | Y | N | T | E | C | C | N | T | K | A | L | J | L | O | T |
| E | W | D | U | E | H | Y | E | R | I | T | P | A | I | V | I |
| K | O | O | U | T | E | A | O | O | J | E | O | E | O | R | L |
| W | O | A | M | N | T | B | K | P | O | R | N | M | C | K | I |
| I | D | B | G | O | E | E | R | I | H | S | D | I | N | T | Z |
| F | E | G | T | S | U | A | A | C | N | H | P | I | A | N | E |
| O | D | H | S | H | D | D | W | A | G | E | L | D | T | U | R |
| R | O | I | S | B | N | U | B | L | J | D | E | S | I | O | T |
| E | V | E | R | G | R | E | E | N | S | W | M | U | O | R | S |
| S | D | N | L | O | M | B | I | O | H | F | T | L | N | M | O |
| T | O | L | I | D | R | T | S | T | R | E | E | F | A | R | M |
| R | A | I | N | F | O | R | E | S | T | U | N | H | L | I | T |
| A | G | W | A | R | U | Y | G | C | O | E | S | S | F | H | A |
| N | O | I | H | E | A | I | E | R | D | H | O | E | O | S | U |
| G | M | A | N | I | O | C | A | A | H | S | G | C | R | S | V |
| E | B | U | H | F | L | G | U | P | L | O | G | G | E | R | M |
| R | G | T | F | E | G | T | L | B | N | C | R | Q | S | R | T |
| N | W | A | T | E | R | C | Y | C | L | E | P | A | T | E | E |

Forests cover many regions. Forage through this puzzle to find words that will help you get to know the forest regions better.

**Word Bank**

| | | | |
|---|---|---|---|
| evergreens | fertilizer | forest ranger | logger |
| machete | manioc | millpond | national forest |
| plywood | pulp | rain forest | sawmill |
| tree farm | tropical | water cycle | watershed |

# Explorers

Name ______________________

**Across**

1. The New World was named for him.
5. Explored parts of the New World for the Dutch – a river was named for him.
10. Explored the Mississippi River with Jacques Marquette
11. Discovered the North Pole

**Down**

2. Last name of the Portuguese explorer who was the first man to sail around the world
3. Discovered the South Pole
4. Discovered the New World in 1492
6. First man to walk on the moon
7. Member of the first Apollo mission to explore the moon
8. First American to travel in space
9. He discovered New Foundland for England

**Word Bank**

Henry Hudson
Louis Joliet
Robert Peary
Richard Byrd

Neil Armstrong
Edwin Aldrin
Alan Shepard
John Cabot

Christopher Columbus
Ferdinand Magellan
Amerigo Vespucci

 

# It's Called "Politics"! Name ______________________

Across
3. A candidate who already holds the office which he/she is running for
5. A person who tries to get elected to public office
8. The power of the President to refuse to sign a bill passed by Congress
11. A situation where people support a candidate because he/she appears to be the winner
12. The length of service for an elected official

Down
1. The ceremony in which an official takes an oath to carry out the duties of his/her office
2. The formal meeting of a political party
4. Branch of the government which enforces the law
6. Political party represented by a donkey
7. Political party represented by an elephant
9. A formal vote to choose a president, senator, mayor, etc.
10. The goals that a political party establishes and tries to achieve

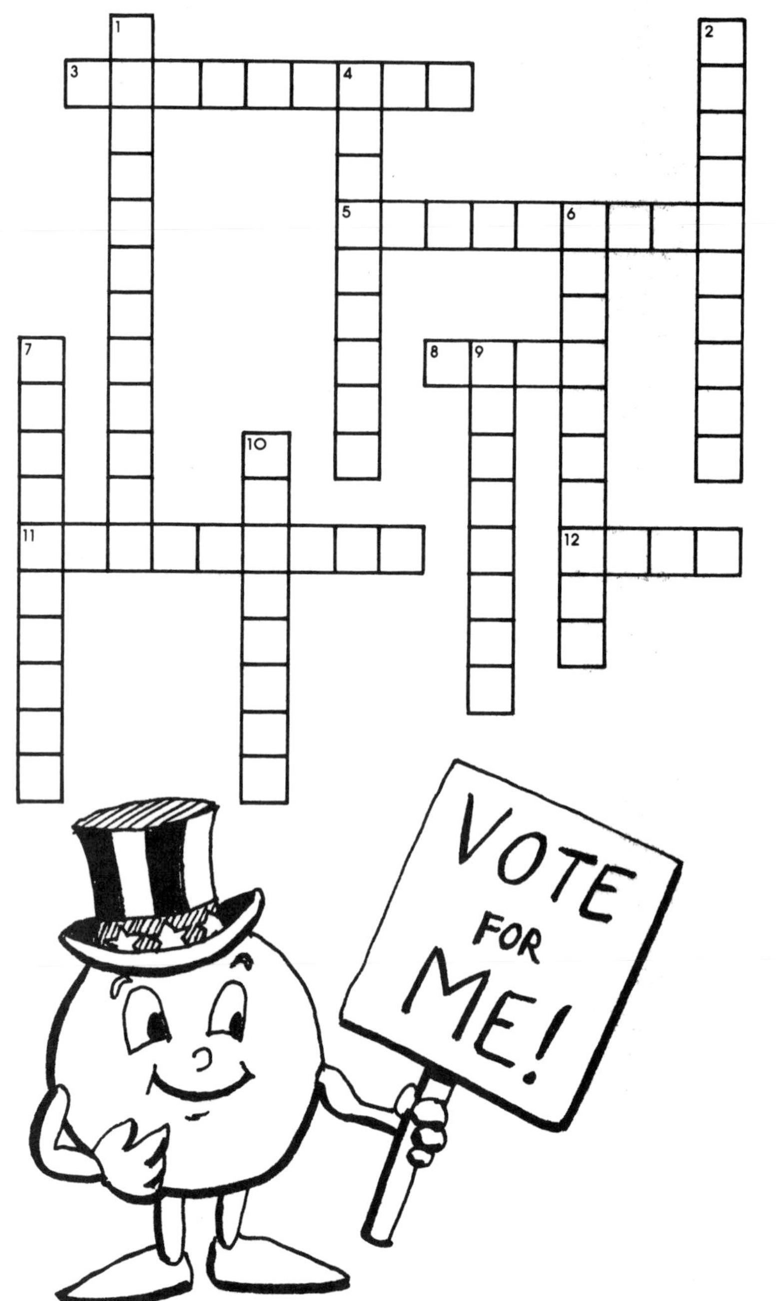


Word Bank

| | | |
|---|---|---|
| convention | candidate | inauguration |
| executive | Democratic | Republican |
| platform | incumbent | bandwagon |
| election | veto | term |

 

# Amazing Mammals

Name ______________________

**Across**

1. A small, North American mammal–it climbs trees, is active at night, and has yellow-black fur with a long black-ringed tail.
6. A large ape–it has shaggy, reddish hair, long arms, and a hairless face.
7. Any of various mammals that feed on ants
10. A large African antelope with long, twisted horns
11. Related to the monkey, it has large eyes and soft, wooly fur.
12. A wild African hog–it has large tusks and warts under its eyes.

**Down**

2. This South American mammal is prized for its pale-gray fur.
3. This is a wolf-like predator with a shrill cry.
4. This mammal resembles a horse with dark stripes.
5. An African anteater
8. This mammal makes burrows–it has thick, short legs and long claws on the forefeet.
9. Any of several slow-moving, tree-dwelling, South American mammals.

**Word Bank**

| | | |
|---|---|---|
| lemur | chinchilla | hyena |
| badger | anteater | eland |
| sloth | warthog | raccoon |
| zebra | aardvark | orangutan |

 

Skill: Metrics

# Measuring the Metric Way

Name ______________________

**Across**

2. Another name for centigrade
5. 100 centimeters = 1 ______
9. 10 ______ = 1 meter
10. 1,000 grams = 1 ______
11. A surface measure which equals 10,000 square meters

**Down**

1. 100 liters = ______
3. A metric measure of area
4. There are 100 in a meter.
5. Metric equivalent of 2,204.62 pounds
6. Liquids are measured in ______ in the metric system.
7. Weight is measured in ______ in the metric system.
8. 10 milliliters = 1 ______



Word Bank

| | | |
|---|---|---|
| centiliter | celsius | metric ton |
| decimeters | kilogram | meter |
| hectoliter | grams | liters |
| centimeter | square meter | hectare |

 

# The First Presidents

Name ____________________________

**Across**

2. 13th President–he signed the "Fugitive Slave Bill."
3. 1st President–he was a General in the Revolutionary War.
9. 6th President–he was first to live in the President's house in Washington, D.C.
11. 10th President–he signed the bill to admit Texas as a state.

**Down**

1. 11th President–he signed a peace treaty with Mexico that gave us California.
4. 7th President–he was nicknamed "Old Hickory."
5. 3rd President–his home was called Monticello.
6. 2nd President–his son later became President.
7. 8th President–he failed in his bid for re-election.
8. 4th President–he served two terms.
10. 5th President–a famous doctrine was named after him which warned Europe not to engage in any colonization of North and South America.

**Word Bank**

| | | |
|---|---|---|
| George Washington | Zachary Taylor | James Monroe |
| Thomas Jefferson | John Adams | James Polk |
| Andrew Jackson | John Q. Adams | Martin Van Buren |
| Millard Fillmore | William Harrison | John Tyler |
| James Madison | | |

 

# The Middle Presidents

Name ______________________

**Across**

1. 25th President–he was assassinated.
6. 19th President–he worked to restore the Union after the Civil War and to guarantee the rights of the freed slaves.
12. 23rd President–he was defeated by Grover Cleveland in his attempt to win a second term in office.

**Down**

2. 17th President–he was the Vice-President who became President when Abraham Lincoln died.
3. 21st President–he signed the bill providing for civil service exams.
4. 16th President–he held office during the Civil War and was later assassinated.
5. This man was our 22nd and 24th President.
7. 14th President–he was not a popular President.
8. 18th President–he was a General for the Union Army during the Civil War.
9. 26th President–he said, "Speak softly and carry a big stick."
10. 27th President–he became Chief Justice of the Supreme Court after leaving office.
11. 20th President–he was assassinated before serving one year in office.

**Word Bank**

| | | |
|---|---|---|
| Benjamin Harrison | Abraham Lincoln | Rutherford Hayes |
| William McKinley | James Buchanan | James Garfield |
| Theodore Roosevelt | Grover Cleveland | William Taft |
| Franklin Pierce | Ulysses Grant | Andrew Johnson |
| Chester Arthur | | |

 

# The Later Presidents

Name ______________________________

**Across**

2. 33rd President–he ended World War II by dropping the bomb on Japan.
3. 32nd President–he was the only president elected to serve four terms.
5. 38th President–he became President when Richard Nixon resigned.
8. 40th President–this President used to be an actor.
11. 29th President–Teapot Dome scandal happened during this President's term.

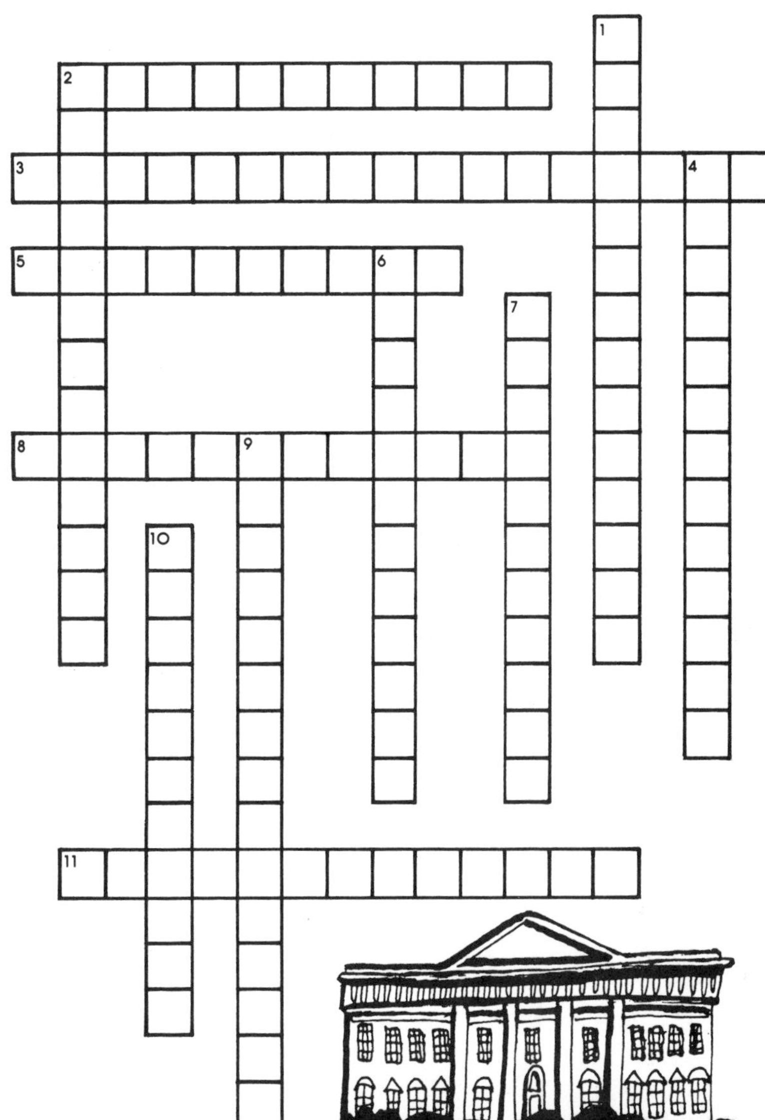


**Down**

1. Vice-President who became the 30th President of the U.S. at the death of President Harding.
2. 31st President–many people blamed him for the Great Depression.
4. 36th President–he became President when John Kennedy was assassinated.
6. 37th President–he resigned rather than face impeachment.
7. 35th President–he was very popular but was assassinated on November 22, 1963.
9. 34th President–he served as a General in the Army before his election.
10. 39th President–he was respected for his attempts to bring peace to the Middle East.

**Word Bank**

Gerald Ford
Dwight Eisenhower
Jimmy Carter
Ronald Reagan
Herbert Hoover
Woodrow Wilson
John Kennedy
Calvin Coolidge
Harry Truman
Franklin Roosevelt
Warren Harding
Lyndon Johnson
Richard Nixon

 

Skill: Geography terms

# Land and Water

Name ______________________________

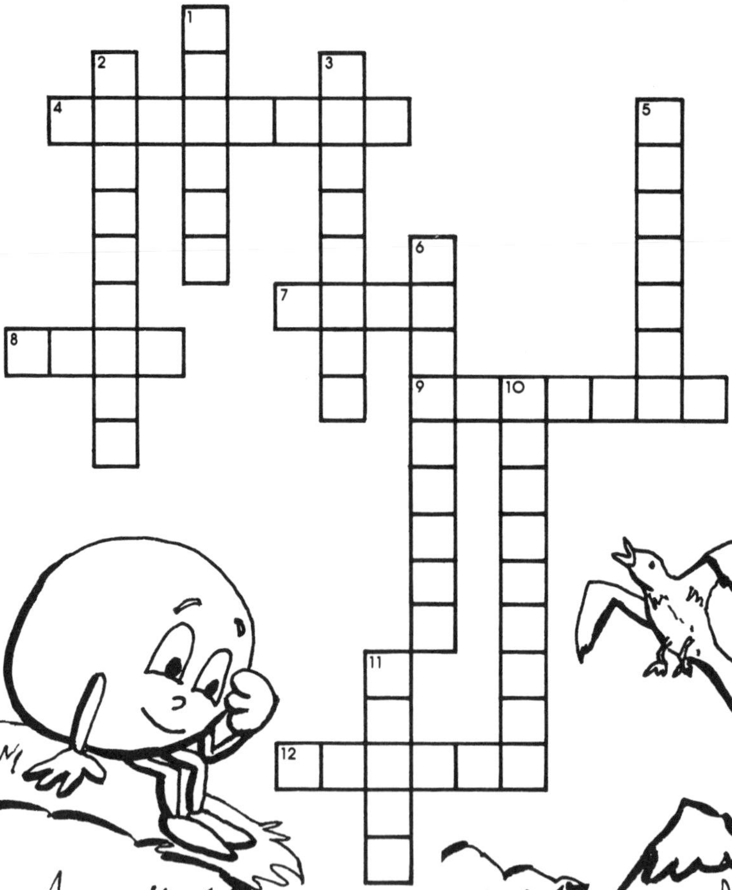

**Across**

4. High, rocky land, usually with steep sides and round or pointed top
7. A point of land sticking out into a body of water
8. A ridge of rock or sand at or near the surface of water
9. A narrow strip of land that connects two larger bodies of land
12. Low land between hills or mountains

**Down**

1. A long, narrow valley between high cliffs
2. One of seven large bodies of land on the Earth
3. Hills, mountains, or plateaus
5. A level area of land found in the mountains
6. A body of land almost surrounded by water
10. A river or stream that flows into a larger river
11. Land deposited at the mouth of a river

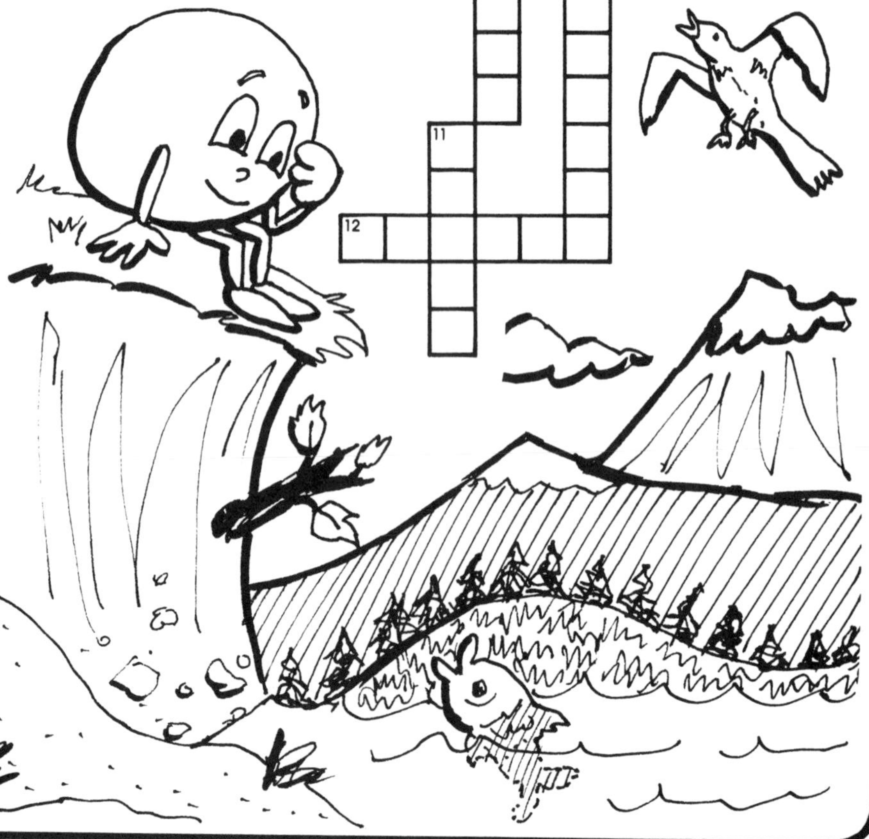

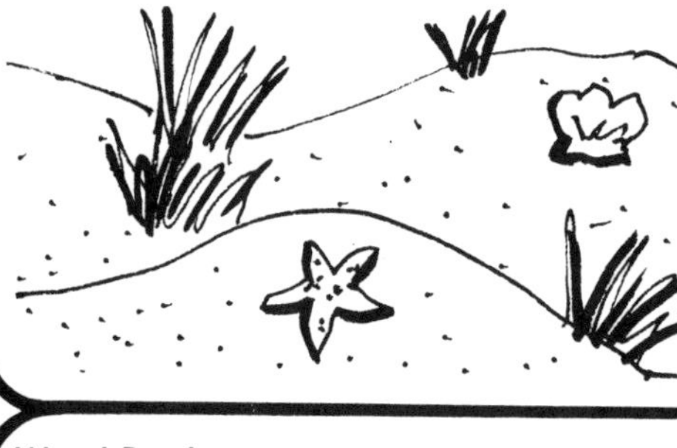

**Word Bank**

| | | | |
|---|---|---|---|
| isthmus | strait | divide | continent |
| canyon | peninsula | tributary | highland |
| reef | cliff | lake | cape |
| delta | valley | mountain | island |
| channel | plain | canal | desert |
| plateau | | | |

# Plant Life

Name ____________________

**Across**

2. The process by which a leaf uses sunlight and chlorophyll to turn water and carbon dioxide into food
4. These plants have two cotyledons, or food parts.
7. Plants that live more than two years before completing a life cycle
11. A colorless, odorless gas that passes out of the lungs and is absorbed by plants
12. Cone-bearing plants that stay green all year long

**Down**

1. Green-colored matter in plants
3. Plants that complete a life cycle within two years
5. Plants with tubes in their leaves, stems, and roots
6. Layer of wood on a tree showing one year of growth
8. Plants that stay green all year long
9. Scientists who study plants
10. These plants have one cotyledon, or food part.

**Word Bank**

| | | | |
|---|---|---|---|
| annual | biennials | perennials | annual ring |
| stomata | deciduous plants | evergreen | chlorophyll |
| photosynthesis | carbon dioxide | botanists | nonvascular |
| vascular | spores | conifers | dicots |
| monocots | | | |

Skill: Classifying animals

# The Animal World

Name ______________________________

Across
5. Animals without backbones
7. Warm-blooded vertebrates with feathers
8. Animals that maintain a constant body temperature with the help of hair or feathers as insulation
11. Cold-blooded vertebrate that lives part of its life in the water and part on land
12. Animals with a body temperature that varies according to the temperature of their environment

Down
1. Soft-bodied invertebrates that are classified into three groups: flat, round, or segmented
2. Invertebrates with soft bodies–many have shells.
3. Simplest group of vertebrates having scales, fins, and gills
4. Alligators, lizards, snakes, turtles
6. Animals with backbones
9. Warm-blooded vertebrates with fur or hair–females can produce milk for their young.
10. Plant-like sea animals

Word Bank

| | | | |
|---|---|---|---|
| vertebrates | birds | fish | amphibian |
| reptiles | worms | mammals | sponges |
| hollow-boned | invertebrates | mollusks | warm-blooded |
| arthropods | spiny-skinned | classifying | cold-blooded |

 

Skill: Computer terms

# Be Computer Wise!

Name ______________________

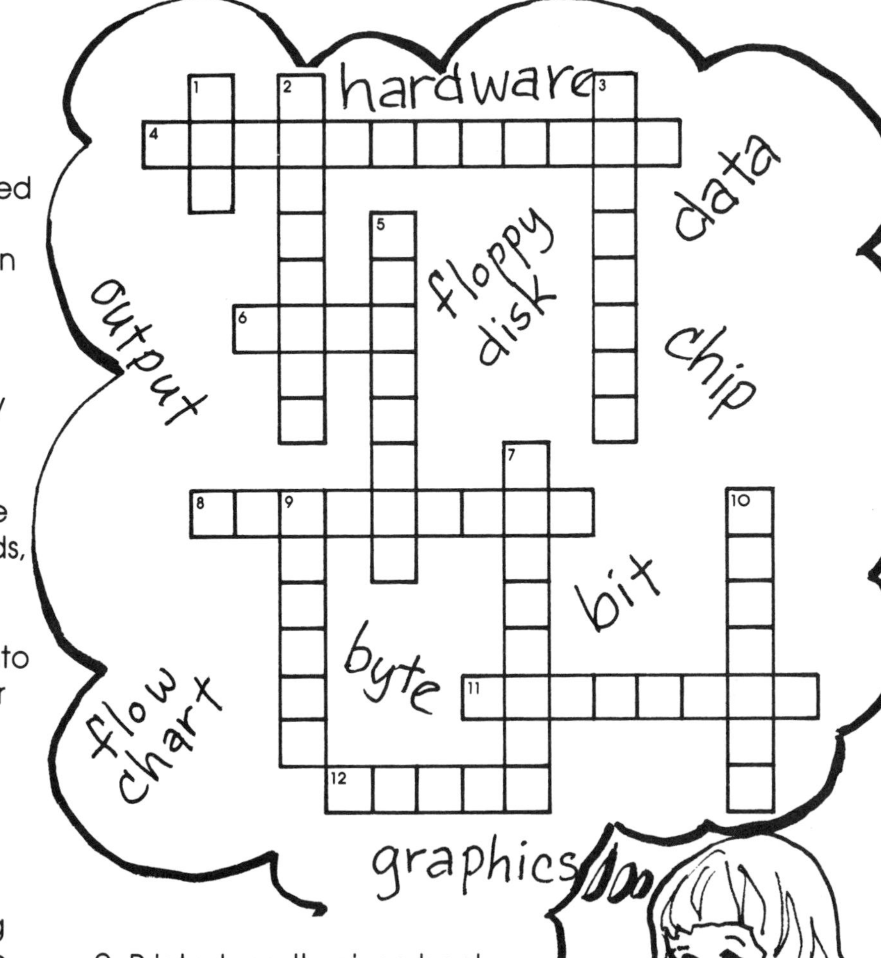


**Across**

4. A system in which the digits O and 1 are used, and numbers are grouped by powers of two.
6. Numbers and information that are given to a computer
8. A graphic outline of the steps that are necessary to do a specific job
11. Any program used on a computer which may be stored on punched cards, floppy discs, cassette tapes, or reels of tape
12. Information that is put into a computer in any order

**Down**

1. A storage cell in the computer's memory
2. The working parts of a computer including a video screen, processing unit, keyboard, disc drive, and printer
3. Hardware that looks like a typewriter and is used to give information to the computer
5. Pictures and colors that can be programmed to appear on a screen
7. Computer output that is typed, or printed out, on paper
9. Printed results given back by a computer
10. The sequence of operations to be performed by a computer in processing data

**Word Bank**

| | | | |
|---|---|---|---|
| binary system | program | hardware | data |
| input | software | byte | keyboard |
| printout | graphics | character | bit |
| flow chart | chip | floppy disc | cursor |
| output | | | |

 

Skill: Measurement terms

# Measuring – Let's Compare!

Name ______________________

**Across**

3. 3 teaspoons = 1 ______
5. Equals 4 pecks or 8 gallons
7. ⅛ of a mile or 220 yards
8. 2,000 pounds
11. A measure of land which equals 43,560 square feet
12. 4 cups = 1 ______

**Down**

1. A unit of weight for precious stones which equals .2 of a gram
2. A measure of length equal to 1/12 of a foot
4. Liquid measure in the metric system
6. 12 inches or ⅓ of a yard
9. $\frac{1}{16}$ of a pound
10. Length measure in the metric system

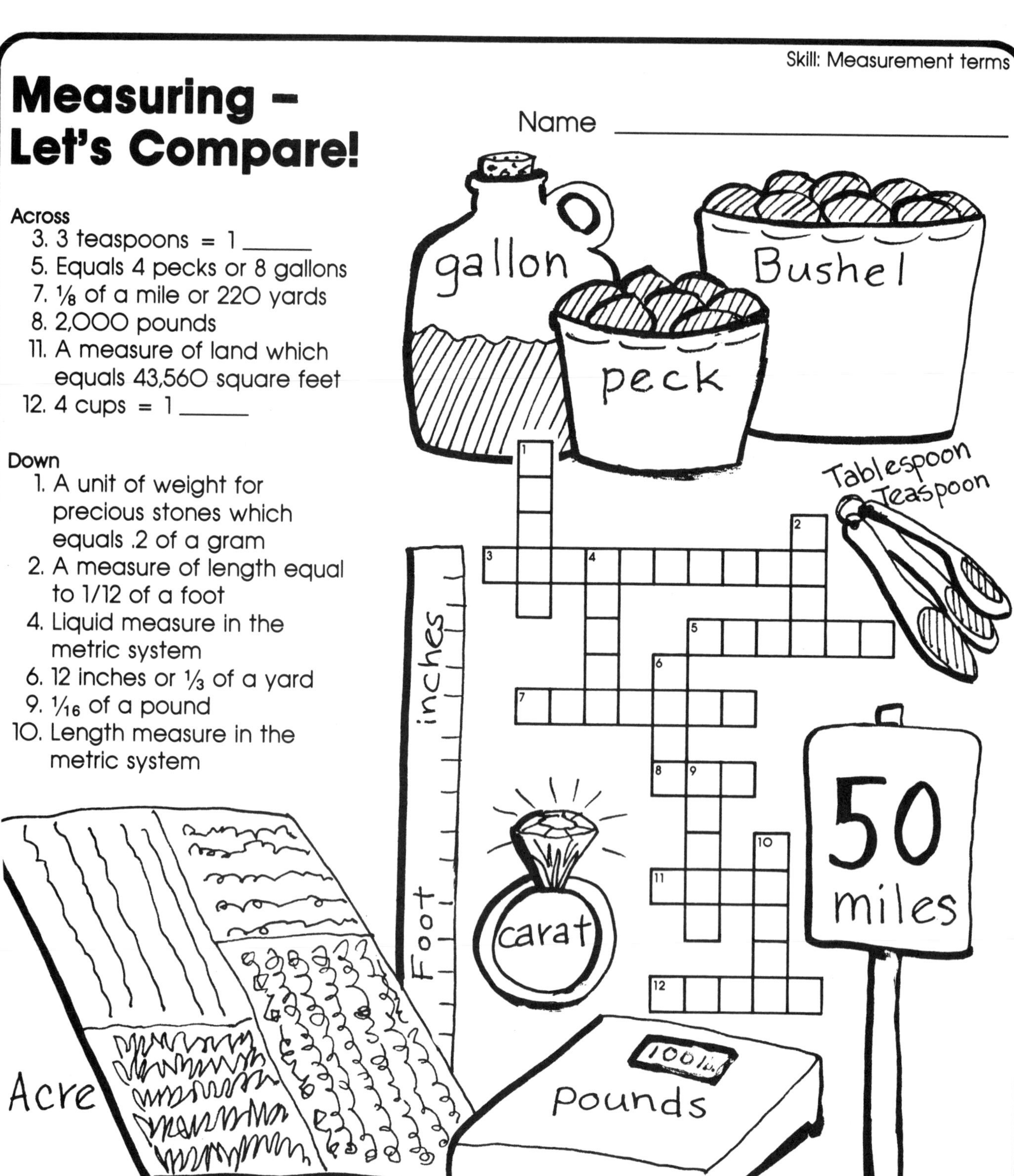


**Word Bank**

| | | | |
|---|---|---|---|
| meter | furlong | bushel | liter |
| teaspoon | ounce | gram | tablespoon |
| pound | foot | pint | ton |
| yard | quart | dram | peck |
| inch | gallon | carat | mile |

 

# Now for the Nouns

Name ____________________

Find the nouns. But be careful–sometimes there is more than one.

**Across**

2. Plants make food by photosynthesis.
5. I can name the capital of every state.
9. Our leaders have had awesome responsibilities.
10. A citizen has many rights and responsibilities.
11. What is the capital of your state?
12. What will be your occupation when you grow up?

**Down**

1. The President met with members of the Press.
3. Many U.S. Presidents have earned a place in history.
4. A vertebrate is an animal with a backbone.
6. What does this abbreviation stand for?
7. We will choose a new Mayor in the next election.
8. Geography is Cindy's favorite subject.

NOUNS

persons

places

things

**Word Bank**

| | | | |
|---|---|---|---|
| President | state | occupation | geography |
| Press | food | history | leaders |
| Mayor | photosynthesis | backbone | responsibilities |
| election | rights | vertebrate | abbreviation |
| capital | citizen | subject | |

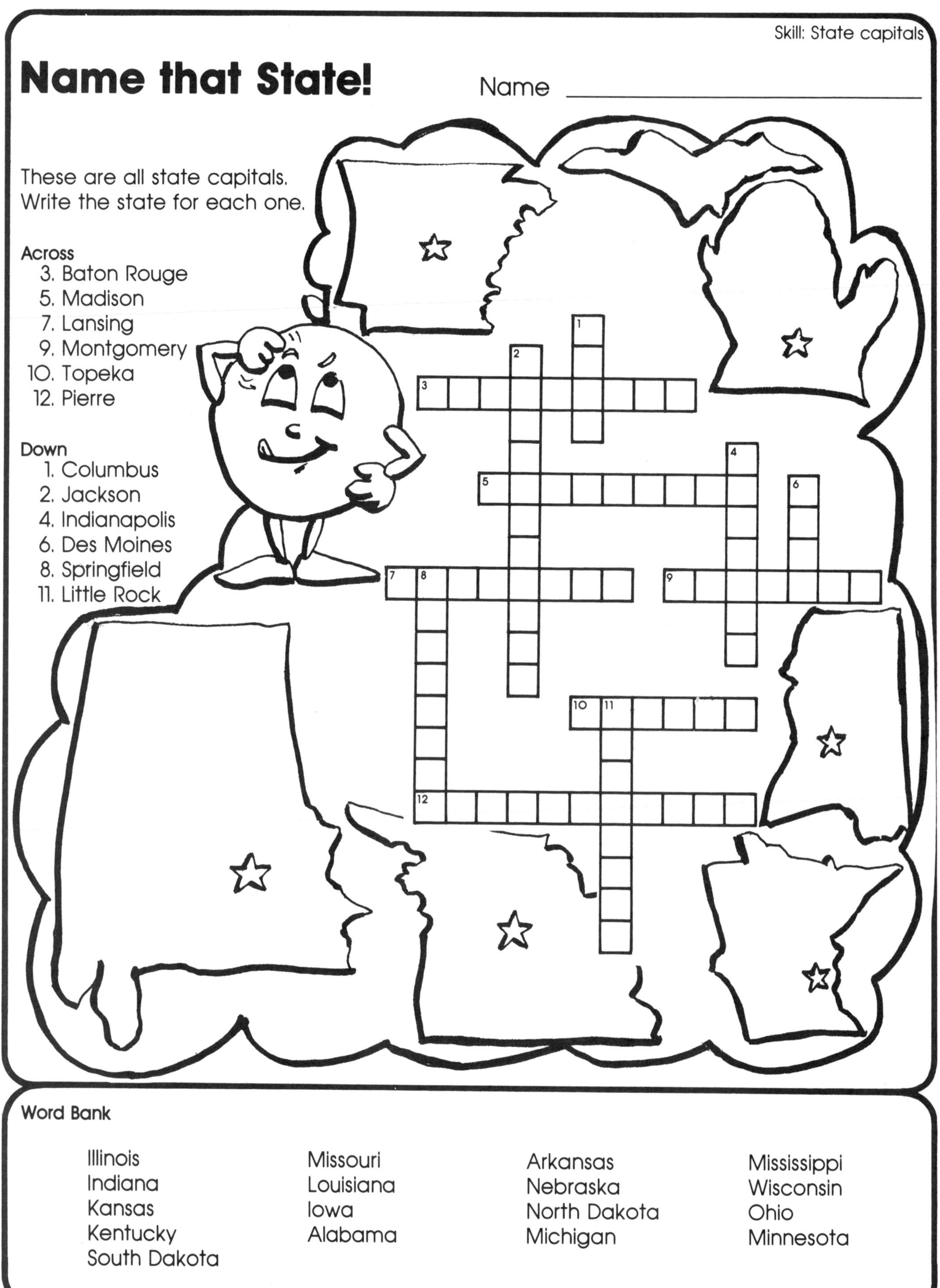


Word Bank

Illinois
Indiana
Kansas
Kentucky
South Dakota
Missouri
Louisiana
Iowa
Alabama
Arkansas
Nebraska
North Dakota
Michigan
Mississippi
Wisconsin
Ohio
Minnesota

 

# The World of Work

Name ____________________

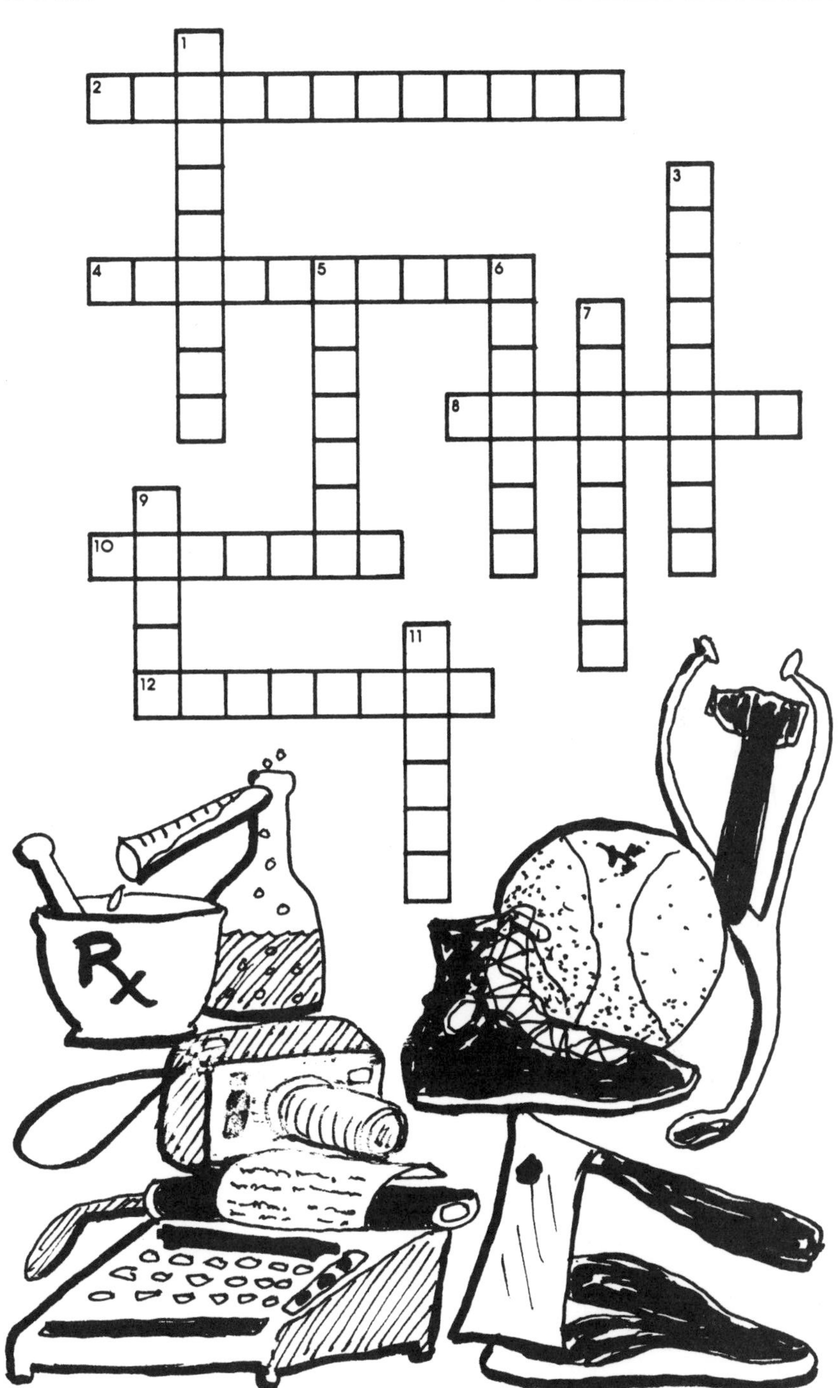

**Across**

2. A person who earns a living taking pictures
4. One who is trained to prepare prescriptions
8. An artist who carves figures of clay, stone, and wood
10. A person who cuts up and sells meat
12. The driver of a train

**Down**

1. A person who takes care of a home
3. A person whose job is keeping records and doing clerical work for a person or organization
5. A person who plays games requiring physical strength and skill
6. Someone who helps other people learn about math, English, and other subjects
7. A man who sells things either in a store or door-to-door
9. A person trained to take care of the sick, injured, or aged
11. A person who makes metal objects by melting pieces of metal together

**Word Bank**

| | | | |
|---|---|---|---|
| actor | teacher | pharmacist | computer operator |
| salesman | psychiatrist | engineer | secretary |
| homemaker | butcher | miner | welder |
| nurse | athlete | photographer | sculptor |

 

Concept: Prominent Black Americans

# Prominent Blacks

Name ____________________

**Across**

3. A civil rights leader and winner of the Nobel Peace Prize in 1964
5. Former heavyweight boxing champion of the world
8. First black congresswoman–she was elected in 1969.
10. Former top-seeded tennis player
12. Former football running back–he set a record for most yards gained in a season.

**Down**

1. A young television actor
2. Superstar of the 80's–a real "thriller"
4. First black candidate for U.S. Presidency
6. The creator of "Fat Albert"
7. First black member of the U.S. Supreme Court
9. American operatic soprano
11. She was an early Civil Rights activist who was arrested for refusing to sit in the black section in the rear of a segregated bus.



**Word Bank**

| | | |
|---|---|---|
| Booker T. Washington | Shirley Chisholm | Gary Coleman |
| Muhammed Ali | Arthur Ashe | Barbara Jordan |
| Martin Luther King, Jr. | Jesse Owens | O.J. Simpson |
| Constance Baker Motley | Jesse Jackson | Thurgood Marshall |
| Benjamin Bannekar | Leontyne Price | Rosa Parks |
| Michael Jackson | Bill Cosby | Diana Ross |

Concept: Prominent women

# You've Come a Long Way!

Name ______________________________

**Across**

2. Throughout her life and her husband's presidency, she worked for the betterment of people.
4. She was a leader in the Suffrage Movement of the early 1900's.
6. First woman to run for Vice-President of the United States
10. She taught others to overcome their handicaps by overcoming her own.
11. First woman astronaut for the United States

**Down**

1. Known as the "First Lady of the American Theater"
3. First black to play national indoor tennis tournaments–she won at Wimbledon in 1957.
4. First woman to serve on the U.S. Supreme Court
5. Gold medal gymnast in the 1984 Olympics
7. She won the Nobel Peace Prize in 1979 for her work in Calcutta, India.
8. Once a member of the Supremes, she has become one of the most talented singers of the 70's and 80's.

9. Former Prime Minister of Israel

**Word Bank**

| | | |
|---|---|---|
| Diana Ross | Margaret Mead | Sally Ride |
| Coretta Scott King | Geraldine Ferraro | Althea Gibson |
| Sandra Day O'Connor | Harriet Tubman | Golda Meir |
| Eleanor Roosevelt | Mother Teresa | Helen Keller |
| Mary Lou Retton | Susan B. Anthony | Helen Hayes |

Skill: State Capitals

# Name that Capital!

Name ______________________________

What are the capitals of these states?

**Across**
2. Florida
7. Vermont
8. Delaware
9. New Jersey
11. West Virginia
12. Massachusetts

**Down**
1. North Carolina
3. Georgia
4. Connecticut
5. New York
6. Rhode Island
10. Virginia

UNITED STATES

Denver
Boston
Lansing
Albany
Providence

**Word Bank**

Tallahassee
Lansing
Jefferson City
Denver
Montpelier
Atlanta
Providence
Dover
Raleigh
Charleston
Albany
Sacramento
Hartford
Richmond
Trenton
Boston

Skill: State Nicknames

# What's in a Nickname?

Name ______________________

**Across**
3. The Golden State
5. The Lone Star State
8. The Silver State
9. The Last Frontier
12. The Land of Enchantment

**Down**
1. The Beehive State
2. The Evergreen State
4. The Beaver State
6. The Aloha State
7. The Sooner State
10. The Sunshine State
11. The Wolverine State

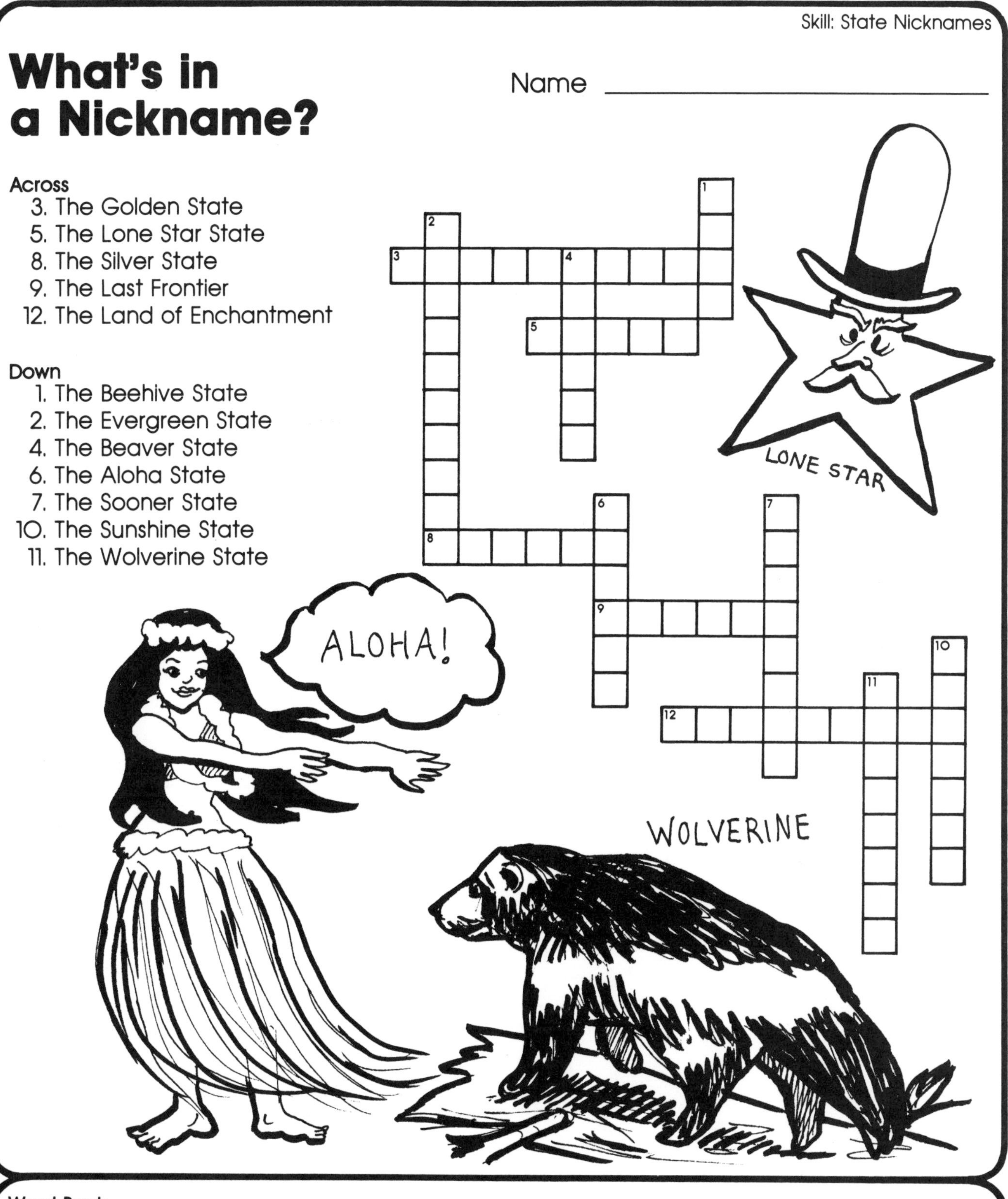


**Word Bank**

| | | | |
|---|---|---|---|
| Alaska | Utah | Michigan | Ohio |
| Hawaii | Oregon | Nevada | California |
| New York | Texas | Washington | New Mexico |
| Florida | Oklahoma | Illinois | Colorado |

 

# Explorers

Name ____________________

| C | O | F | E | D | W | I | N | A | L | D | R | I | N | T | R |
|---|---|---|---|---|---|---|---|---|---|---|---|---|---|---|---|
| H | E | R | N | A | N | D | O | D | E | S | O | T | O | P | F |
| R | V | A | T | N | S | J | A | Q | M | E | I | Z | C | W | E |
| I | R | N | E | I | L | A | R | M | S | T | R | O | N | G | R |
| S | V | C | U | P | O | F | O | L | B | O | D | T | H | X | D |
| T | S | I | Q | R | K | D | N | G | Y | J | V | I | L | S | I |
| O | C | S | U | J | O | H | N | C | A | B | O | T | O | H | N |
| P | A | C | A | Q | M | U | K | C | P | X | E | D | U | O | A |
| H | P | O | N | C | E | D | E | L | E | O | N | H | I | F | N |
| E | B | C | K | O | I | M | A | N | B | O | K | G | S | I | D |
| R | H | O | J | Y | L | G | H | J | L | G | G | E | J | F | M |
| C | B | R | I | C | H | A | R | D | B | Y | R | D | O | D | A |
| O | I | O | P | N | E | L | T | I | M | R | S | Q | L | E | G |
| L | Z | N | V | M | U | B | W | C | V | C | F | O | I | D | E |
| U | J | A | C | Q | U | E | S | C | A | R | T | I | E | R | L |
| M | I | D | O | A | J | N | D | L | P | C | D | U | T | R | L |
| B | Q | O | R | L | V | A | S | C | O | D | E | G | A | M | A |
| U | P | B | S | M | K | O | T | A | W | S | J | B | X | I | N |
| S | U | R | O | B | E | R | T | P | E | A | R | Y | F | V | G |
| O | L | N | R | A | Q | T | E | L | Z | K | Y | R | A | F | T |
| A | M | E | R | I | G | O | V | E | S | P | U | C | C | I | H |

Discover the fourteen explorers hidden in the puzzle. Then choose four of them and find four facts about each one.

**Word Bank**

- Ferdinand Magellan
- Hernando deSoto
- Christopher Columbus
- Francisco Coronado
- Amerigo Vespucci
- Vasca deGama
- Neil Armstrong
- Jacques Cartier
- Ponce de Leon
- Louis Joliet
- John Cabot
- Edwin Aldrin
- Richard Byrd
- Robert Peary

 

Skill: Government

# Elections

Name ______________________

Get on the bandwagon! Circle these 15 words that you hear when election time rolls around.

| A | O | R | B | U | G | L | A | S | D | D | C | O | N | V | E | N | T | I | O | N | B |
|---|---|---|---|---|---|---|---|---|---|---|---|---|---|---|---|---|---|---|---|---|---|
| D | I | N | C | U | M | B | E | N | T | E | G | G | S | R | L | T | E | I | P | I | X |
| J | N | O | R | E | S | U | T | C | M | M | R | S | H | V | E | E | R | N | O | M | W |
| R | B | M | G | O | H | E | H | R | I | O | V | A | R | O | C | G | A | S | L | S | O |
| L | S | I | R | E | P | U | B | L | I | C | A | N | T | S | T | U | B | L | I | O | S |
| E | V | N | O | A | B | L | E | N | L | R | H | T | A | D | I | O | L | A | T | E | S |
| P | L | A | T | F | O | R | M | Y | L | A | K | V | V | M | O | R | C | R | I | E | T |
| H | L | T | C | A | N | D | I | D | A | T | E | B | S | O | N | A | E | Y | C | T | H |
| D | R | I | W | H | K | A | E | A | N | E | P | O | L | I | T | I | C | I | A | N | S |
| N | I | O | E | C | A | M | P | A | I | G | N | T | Q | F | T | E | B | H | L | E | W |
| T | O | N | G | A | R | Z | T | R | D | A | B | R | U | H | A | C | R | E | P | E | A |
| E | W | D | S | N | V | B | A | N | D | W | A | G | O | N | E | E | R | I | A | M | O |
| E | L | E | G | T | O | D | A | V | C | O | L | B | E | T | E | R | D | G | R | K | R |
| C | A | N | O | N | E | Q | B | R | E | A | L | T | R | S | B | A | N | O | T | O | W |
| T | A | G | I | O | Y | V | S | U | R | D | O | M | K | I | Y | M | N | G | Y | S | N |
| I | V | E | I | N | A | U | G | U | R | A | T | I | O | N | A | L | G | N | D | M | Y |

**Word Bank**

| | | | | |
|---|---|---|---|---|
| platform | convention | incumbent | Democrat | election |
| bandwagon | ballot | voter | politicians | campaign |
| nomination | candidate | Republican | political party | inauguration |

 

# Metric Madness

Name ______________________

Find the 16 metric math terms in this puzzle.

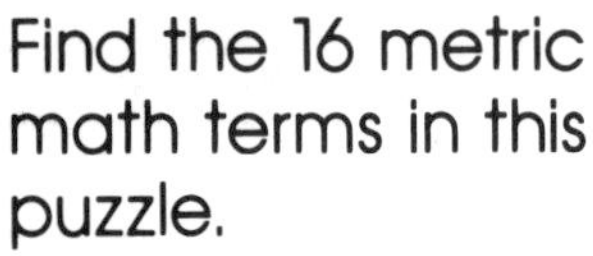

| B | E | G | A | K | I | L | O | M | E | T | E | R | N | A | D | N | H | N | G | T | O |
|---|---|---|---|---|---|---|---|---|---|---|---|---|---|---|---|---|---|---|---|---|---|
| S | O | M | H | U | K | S | F | T | R | I | L | E | W | O | E | M | E | S | M | L | E |
| A | D | E | C | I | M | E | T | E | R | O | L | I | P | I | C | E | L | S | I | U | S |
| C | O | J | E | Y | O | Y | S | L | E | R | E | A | L | V | I | T | F | O | L | I | Q |
| Z | B | E | N | E | R | C | O | M | T | M | C | G | A | Z | G | R | E | P | L | R | U |
| E | V | A | T | K | T | D | A | E | E | N | L | S | R | A | R | I | O | F | I | C | A |
| Z | O | K | I | L | O | G | R | A | M | T | A | R | N | A | A | C | R | A | M | I | R |
| N | E | S | L | T | E | O | H | S | E | N | E | O | B | E | M | T | R | L | E | K | E |
| A | R | L | I | T | E | R | S | G | H | A | O | R | T | L | I | O | W | L | T | W | M |
| E | O | T | T | E | M | C | L | O | D | T | R | I | T | M | O | N | T | S | E | L | E |
| A | P | S | E | T | L | M | J | E | R | M | E | T | U | E | V | M | N | S | R | U | T |
| W | I | N | R | R | N | D | A | B | E | N | H | E | C | T | A | R | E | O | L | M | E |
| R | H | W | R | D | O | E | A | B | O | L | A | F | M | R | L | G | F | N | O | L | R |
| H | E | C | T | O | L | I | T | E | R | G | S | O | M | I | Y | I | W | M | I | T | S |
| I | L | L | A | H | S | A | L | F | N | E | H | D | E | C | A | M | E | T | E | R | O |
| W | T | U | G | A | C | L | H | A | M | C | R | Y | W | L | E | Z | L | N | A | E | M |

**Word Bank**

kilogram
hectoliter
decameter
decigram
centiliter
millimeter
meter
liter
gram
metric
Celsius
hectare
metric ton
kilometer
square meters
decimeter

 

# First Presidents

Name ______________________________

The first 13 presidents of the U.S. are hidden in this puzzle. Circle them. Then find the dates they were in office.

| J | A | M | E | S | M | O | N | R | O | E | I | C | G | E | D | O | A | B | L | A | J |
|---|---|---|---|---|---|---|---|---|---|---|---|---|---|---|---|---|---|---|---|---|---|
| O | N | U | M | I | L | L | A | R | D | F | I | L | L | M | O | R | E | N | M | C | A |
| H | D | I | C | D | B | M | K | I | E | U | N | E | F | C | H | E | D | B | A | B | M |
| N | R | R | E | A | S | I | N | K | R | N | B | L | A | D | B | I | C | D | R | O | E |
| A | E | S | T | R | O | L | A | B | S | M | D | P | M | R | A | D | B | A | T | E | S |
| D | W | O | J | A | M | E | S | P | O | L | K | B | H | C | D | R | I | F | I | D | M |
| A | J | F | O | D | B | I | R | H | U | S | O | C | N | A | L | E | L | A | N | D | A |
| M | A | D | H | E | F | A | C | A | T | O | G | D | G | E | A | N | J | K | V | C | D |
| S | C | U | N | C | T | N | F | O | B | F | Y | I | E | B | Q | M | N | H | A | S | I |
| F | K | B | T | H | O | M | A | S | J | E | F | F | E | R | S | O | N | O | N | U | S |
| C | S | C | Y | F | G | D | N | A | I | D | G | U | V | I | W | R | G | X | B | D | O |
| B | O | A | L | Z | A | C | H | A | R | Y | T | A | Y | L | O | R | A | G | U | Z | N |
| E | N | B | E | W | I | L | L | I | A | M | H | A | R | R | I | S | O | N | R | T | X |
| D | W | M | R | C | W | E | I | F | B | I | N | S | A | I | E | U | C | W | E | H | B |
| G | E | O | R | G | E | W | A | S | H | I | N | G | T | O | N | H | I | F | N | Y | Z |
| L | B | T | H | R | J | O | H | N | Q | U | I | N | C | Y | A | D | A | M | S | E | B |

**Word Bank**

Zachary Taylor
John Adams
William Harrison
James Madison
James Monroe
Martin VanBuren
John Quincy Adams
George Washington
James Polk
Thomas Jefferson
Millard Fillmore
John Tyler
Andrew Jackson

Skill: U.S. Presidents

# America's Best

Name ______________________

We've been lucky to have so many outstanding presidents. Show your patriotism by circling 13 presidents in red crayon or red pen.

| B | W | B | E | L | D | R | U | T | H | E | R | F | O | R | D | H | A | Y | E | S | G |
|---|---|---|---|---|---|---|---|---|---|---|---|---|---|---|---|---|---|---|---|---|---|
| A | F | A | K | C | W | I | L | L | I | A | M | T | A | F | T | S | Z | C | W | A | R |
| F | E | B | E | L | E | M | Y | P | O | L | C | I | N | Y | S | J | I | V | I | C | O |
| G | O | R | J | A | M | E | S | B | U | C | H | A | N | A | N | A | T | L | L | B | V |
| H | R | A | F | N | H | O | S | S | W | P | D | A | O | R | M | M | D | G | L | E | E |
| A | H | H | A | N | D | R | E | W | J | O | H | N | S | O | N | E | O | A | I | U | R |
| I | T | A | F | P | J | O | S | V | E | D | E | L | P | O | M | S | S | I | A | Y | C |
| J | I | M | E | O | T | R | G | L | F | E | I | L | D | B | L | G | N | A | M | A | L |
| L | Y | L | T | D | O | S | R | G | L | H | O | D | Q | M | A | A | I | N | M | E | E |
| J | B | I | C | I | F | R | A | N | K | L | I | N | P | I | E | R | C | E | C | K | V |
| B | E | N | J | A | M | I | N | H | A | R | R | I | S | O | N | F | E | L | K | L | E |
| A | E | C | Q | U | L | U | T | N | E | R | P | Q | C | R | C | I | T | S | I | Q | L |
| I | Z | O | C | H | E | S | T | E | R | A | R | T | H | U | R | E | L | D | N | R | A |
| A | K | L | M | A | D | A | N | I | M | W | D | O | A | R | T | L | S | H | L | V | N |
| G | H | N | D | C | U | A | V | S | A | N | B | E | A | Y | D | D | A | H | E | I | D |
| A | T | H | E | O | D | O | R | E | R | O | O | S | E | V | E | L | T | I | Y | N | L |

**Word Bank**

Benjamin Harrison
William McKinley
Theodore Roosevelt
Franklin Pierce
Chester Arthur

Abraham Lincoln
James Buchanan
Grover Cleveland
Ulysses Grant

Rutherford Hayes
James Garfield
William Taft
Andrew Johnson

# America's Leaders

Name ______________________________

America is only as great as its people and its leaders! Circle 13 of America's presidents.

| D | W | I | G | H | T | E | I | S | E | N | H | O | W | E | R | Q | R | J | A | R | B |
|---|---|---|---|---|---|---|---|---|---|---|---|---|---|---|---|---|---|---|---|---|---|
| E | C | P | A | S | N | G | O | E | O | R | U | R | U | N | M | E | A | O | U | F | D |
| H | A | R | R | Y | T | R | U | M | A | N | S | A | T | H | I | E | G | H | M | R | L |
| U | L | S | N | H | A | N | V | E | P | N | A | T | R | U | O | S | T | N | B | W | C |
| R | V | A | L | E | D | O | E | D | U | T | M | A | E | W | N | V | E | K | O | A | L |
| U | I | O | R | O | N | A | L | D | R | E | A | G | A | N | O | T | I | E | C | R | E |
| S | N | U | S | T | M | A | O | N | S | T | U | L | Y | I | M | R | A | N | A | R | S |
| O | C | H | E | R | B | E | R | T | H | O | O | V | E | R | E | T | H | N | S | E | E |
| W | O | O | D | R | O | W | W | I | L | S | O | N | A | H | M | N | K | E | Q | N | B |
| C | O | T | S | A | S | H | E | W | R | G | T | I | F | H | E | I | C | D | E | H | U |
| L | L | Y | N | D | O | N | J | O | H | N | S | O | N | C | E | A | S | Y | T | A | B |
| R | I | C | H | A | R | D | N | I | X | O | N | O | A | R | H | N | B | O | E | R | S |
| T | D | E | L | I | O | N | Y | P | G | E | R | A | L | D | F | O | R | D | C | D | P |
| R | G | E | L | D | G | A | E | N | U | B | L | M | B | R | Y | E | T | T | N | I | W |
| S | E | D | E | O | T | R | J | I | M | M | Y | C | A | R | T | E | R | B | A | N | F |
| F | R | A | N | K | L | I | N | R | O | O | S | E | V | E | L | T | S | N | E | G | R |

**Word Bank**

Gerald Ford
Woodrow Wilson
Franklin Roosevelt
Dwight Eisenhower
John Kennedy
Warren Harding
Jimmy Carter
Calvin Coolidge
Lyndon Johnson
Ronald Reagan
Harry Truman
Richard Nixon
Herbert Hoover

# Gangway for Geography

Name ______________________

Clear the way for geographical words! Find 21 words related to the earth's surface.

| A | R | I | X | Y | T | O | D | I | V | I | D | E | O | V | R | E | R | I | C | J | Y | N |
|---|---|---|---|---|---|---|---|---|---|---|---|---|---|---|---|---|---|---|---|---|---|---|
| J | W | A | K | I | R | D | E | L | T | A | A | O | R | N | O | S | C | A | Z | C | T | U |
| V | R | G | T | S | I | Y | S | E | P | L | A | T | E | A | U | A | L | T | H | O | E | L |
| O | B | C | R | O | B | A | E | S | R | M | L | A | C | P | C | M | I | U | E | N | A | B |
| U | Z | A | J | Q | U | E | R | T | S | I | S | L | A | N | D | E | F | E | B | T | O | E |
| E | C | N | P | E | T | G | T | R | T | E | P | O | P | I | N | M | F | N | T | I | A | J |
| C | H | A | R | U | A | L | A | E | O | E | B | M | E | O | I | B | A | H | A | N | E | D |
| S | N | L | I | H | R | R | S | Q | P | S | H | C | R | N | D | U | D | R | E | E | F | T |
| W | U | M | S | A | Y | E | R | I | S | T | H | M | U | S | M | E | H | M | A | N | S | A |
| P | L | A | I | N | R | M | G | N | U | R | E | G | R | H | Y | V | I | T | O | T | L | U |
| J | D | E | H | O | F | S | T | P | V | A | L | L | E | Y | O | N | G | A | E | N | G | M |
| A | I | O | I | S | O | E | N | S | A | I | M | Z | E | O | S | R | H | L | R | M | S | U |
| E | M | H | C | A | N | Y | O | N | V | T | A | T | B | A | I | A | L | A | T | O | A | M |
| O | S | G | R | E | M | O | U | N | T | A | I | N | Y | S | T | U | A | K | I | L | I | Y |
| S | F | R | O | J | G | N | O | O | W | G | E | I | C | H | A | N | N | E | L | L | U | A |
| I | P | E | N | I | N | S | U | L | A | T | X | B | O | E | Z | T | D | A | A | G | L | J |

**Word Bank**

- isthmus
- canyon
- reef
- delta
- channel
- plateau
- strait
- peninsula
- cliff
- valley
- plain
- divide
- tributary
- lake
- mountain
- canal
- continent
- highland
- cape
- island
- desert

 

Skill: Plant terms

# Dig Into These!

Name ______________________________

| S | N | I | T | O | Y | T | R | L | O | N | S | F | D | S | I |
|---|---|---|---|---|---|---|---|---|---|---|---|---|---|---|---|
| O | P | E | R | E | N | N | I | A | L | S | A | B | E | B | G |
| I | H | Z | N | Y | D | I | C | O | T | S | E | D | C | H | C |
| C | O | N | I | F | E | R | S | O | M | T | E | L | I | F | N |
| H | T | I | V | E | I | O | O | N | I | H | O | G | D | E | O |
| L | O | H | E | V | A | S | C | U | L | A | R | O | U | L | N |
| O | S | P | O | R | E | S | B | G | E | H | J | K | O | R | V |
| R | Y | I | T | A | T | W | O | A | I | N | S | O | U | M | A |
| O | N | S | T | R | A | P | B | O | T | A | N | I | S | T | S |
| P | T | N | I | R | Q | N | I | T | S | N | E | D | P | S | C |
| H | H | G | S | I | E | R | E | T | S | N | H | E | L | X | U |
| Y | E | G | M | B | H | S | N | E | U | U | Y | E | A | H | L |
| L | S | I | O | N | I | N | N | Z | Y | A | G | T | N | C | A |
| L | I | Y | N | U | S | J | I | K | U | L | S | D | T | E | R |
| X | S | T | O | M | A | T | A | N | D | R | I | A | S | B | E |
| D | E | R | C | T | V | E | L | E | T | I | I | T | L | A | I |
| A | T | E | O | E | N | E | S | T | E | N | H | I | S | N | I |
| D | I | L | T | W | C | E | V | E | R | G | R | E | E | N | S |
| N | D | A | S | D | E | I | H | N | E | E | A | H | T | U | R |
| I | G | T | R | H | N | C | G | A | N | T | S | C | I | A | O |
| C | A | R | B | O | N | D | I | O | X | I | D | E | H | L | R |

Planted in this puzzle are 17 plant-related words. Dig them out and circle in green.

**Word Bank**

annual
stomata
photosynthesis
vascular
monocots
biennials
deciduous plants
carbon dioxide
spores
perennials
evergreens
botanists
conifers
annual ring
chlorophyll
nonvascular
dicots

Skill: Classifying animals

# Be Wise — Analyze!

Name ______________________________

| F | W | A | R | M | B | L | O | O | D | E | D | E | L | D |
|---|---|---|---|---|---|---|---|---|---|---|---|---|---|---|
| H | S | T | N | G | R | V | S | S | I | Y | N | L | T | H |
| I | A | R | T | H | R | O | P | O | D | S | N | T | I | O |
| O | M | U | I | S | A | I | I | A | T | U | O | L | F | L |
| S | P | O | N | G | E | S | N | L | W | A | O | R | M | L |
| L | H | N | T | E | H | S | Y | E | N | D | O | S | U | O |
| A | I | V | C | L | A | S | S | I | F | Y | I | N | G | W |
| M | B | E | A | N | O | I | K | T | O | O | N | N | G | B |
| B | I | R | D | S | T | T | I | W | O | R | M | S | I | O |
| R | A | T | R | A | O | B | N | E | O | S | O | R | M | N |
| O | N | E | S | T | R | O | N | N | E | T | L | F | O | E |
| H | S | B | T | U | B | R | E | P | T | I | L | E | S | D |
| N | T | R | A | M | A | E | D | I | S | T | U | P | E | F |
| O | G | A | A | H | M | R | T | P | D | K | S | L | S | R |
| F | N | T | X | U | E | A | O | L | E | S | K | A | C | N |
| H | I | E | H | S | A | H | R | P | M | A | S | R | I | E |
| U | G | S | E | M | A | M | M | A | L | S | E | M | E | T |
| A | I | I | H | T | B | O | Q | C | A | E | O | C | O | O |
| S | B | C | O | L | D | B | L | O | O | D | E | D | O | L |
| N | E | I | N | V | E | R | T | E | B | R | A | T | E | S |
| D | I | T | W | B | P | S | R | S | Y | W | R | T | W | L |

Help this wise old owl find the 16 animal classification terms hidden in the puzzle.

**Word Bank**

| | | | |
|---|---|---|---|
| vertebrates | invertebrates | fish | amphibians |
| reptiles | birds | mammals | sponges |
| hollow-boned | worms | mollusks | warm-blooded |
| arthropods | spiny-skinned | classifying | cold-blooded |

 

# The Long and Short of It

Name ______________________

| U | I | L | T | N | E | D | O | P | O | U | N | D | S | T | W |
|---|---|---|---|---|---|---|---|---|---|---|---|---|---|---|---|
| N | O | S | E | N | I | O | R | I | C | G | E | H | Y | T | B |
| I | B | P | E | O | J | U | N | I | O | R | R | A | O | S | A |
| T | M | O | N | V | U | N | B | P | H | S | U | L | F | T | N |
| E | D | S | N | E | S | R | E | A | Y | T | C | O | L | E | N |
| D | H | P | B | E | F | O | R | E | N | O | O | N | A | G | O |
| S | F | O | I | R | I | N | O | R | U | L | E | C | S | R | D |
| T | N | S | O | R | N | U | I | L | M | F | I | N | E | R | O |
| A | N | T | E | M | I | S | O | T | B | R | A | S | P | O | M |
| T | O | S | N | T | E | A | L | R | E | A | I | L | E | T | I |
| E | T | C | E | T | E | R | A | M | R | P | O | T | A | S | N |
| S | I | R | O | L | R | S | V | L | T | A | D | S | O | C | I |
| O | N | I | P | B | D | Y | E | H | R | F | E | A | S | K | U |
| F | E | P | L | U | H | R | N | E | L | T | O | K | U | L | J |
| A | R | T | A | C | D | X | U | Y | L | E | M | N | S | Y | R |
| M | O | B | E | F | O | R | E | C | H | R | I | S | T | U | K |
| E | L | I | H | N | E | D | W | I | C | N | R | E | R | L | M |
| R | V | M | I | C | O | N | A | L | U | O | R | M | E | L | T |
| I | Q | U | O | L | R | S | F | R | A | O | N | T | E | M | K |
| C | E | N | T | I | M | E | T | E | R | N | E | O | T | L | I |
| A | S | T | R | U | T | E | L | E | V | I | S | I | O | N | O |

Here are 15 abbreviations of words or phrases. Now, you find the words they are abbreviated for.

**Clue Bank**

p.s. etc. lbs. ave. no. t.v. B.C. A.D.
cm U.S.A. jr. a.m. p.m. sr. st.

 

Skill: Computer terms

# Do You Compute?

Name ______________________________

| C | E | N | T | I | G | E | B | U | V | B | V | C | R | E | B |
|---|---|---|---|---|---|---|---|---|---|---|---|---|---|---|---|
| R | H | G | A | P | R | O | G | R | A | M | S | E | L | M | I |
| H | U | N | C | R | U | D | U | H | N | E | E | B | I | R | N |
| F | Y | C | H | A | R | A | C | T | E | R | T | N | A | T | A |
| L | E | L | I | Y | B | T | N | E | P | G | G | D | L | E | R |
| O | M | O | P | P | I | A | U | B | E | U | O | S | L | T | Y |
| P | S | N | Y | O | Y | E | S | A | N | O | T | E | T | C | S |
| P | R | I | N | T | O | U | T | L | V | I | N | I | S | P | Y |
| Y | E | H | F | E | R | I | O | R | N | O | W | G | Y | R | S |
| D | I | A | E | G | R | A | P | H | I | C | S | L | B | I | T |
| I | R | R | R | V | D | Y | T | O | T | O | L | R | A | N | E |
| S | B | D | U | K | E | Y | B | O | A | R | D | U | S | T | M |
| C | K | W | N | L | L | A | S | U | O | C | Y | A | N | E | I |
| E | A | A | D | S | E | C | U | R | S | O | R | O | C | R | T |
| A | R | R | B | I | L | H | O | T | R | T | Y | N | S | W | H |
| R | J | E | O | N | K | H | I | M | A | O | O | H | U | E | A |
| A | B | S | M | P | S | S | O | F | T | W | A | R | E | A | S |
| B | Y | T | E | U | H | T | C | W | E | E | C | P | E | L | O |
| E | D | I | E | T | N | F | L | O | W | C | H | A | R | T | B |
| H | I | V | Q | E | T | I | E | R | W | O | T | N | I | T | Y |
| G | T | K | E | U | S | O | K | I | S | O | H | D | E | T | U |

Are you computer wise? Sort through these letters and circle 18 words related to computers.

**Word Bank**

binary system
input
printout
flow chart
output
program
software
graphics
chip
printer
hardware
byte
character
floppy disc
data
keyboard
bit
cursor

Skill: Measurement terms

# Can You Measure Up?

Name ______________________________

| H | P | G | H | I | E | D | R | S | S | Y | A | A | W | L | T |
|---|---|---|---|---|---|---|---|---|---|---|---|---|---|---|---|
| I | Y | A | R | D | S | R | U | A | S | L | C | P | L | A | E |
| S | L | A | T | T | P | A | U | R | M | I | L | E | Y | C | L |
| L | N | O | C | N | Y | M | A | Y | D | L | I | C | I | R | Z |
| I | W | G | O | U | H | W | T | F | O | O | T | K | U | E | O |
| Y | S | A | M | M | P | U | T | U | P | A | E | E | S | M | N |
| P | T | I | D | R | I | H | Y | R | I | O | R | S | T | P | I |
| S | E | B | S | U | R | A | O | L | O | M | K | R | L | I | Y |
| T | A | B | L | E | S | P | O | O | N | Y | E | T | U | P | N |
| R | S | U | O | A | R | N | O | N | E | L | O | E | N | I | L |
| B | P | I | A | T | O | T | H | G | R | S | B | H | I | N | E |
| T | O | A | W | T | I | M | N | Y | A | O | E | V | M | T | Z |
| C | O | T | O | O | B | M | B | U | S | H | E | L | B | E | L |
| I | N | C | H | D | O | T | O | L | G | H | W | Z | U | S | C |
| E | A | A | N | N | D | G | A | L | L | O | N | U | E | O | P |
| S | A | R | S | M | T | I | A | V | T | A | G | L | H | U | O |
| C | T | A | H | U | I | R | N | H | E | S | R | N | U | N | O |
| B | O | T | O | N | S | S | C | Y | S | A | A | D | W | C | R |
| N | O | N | N | E | Y | E | Y | O | E | T | M | E | T | E | R |
| E | A | Q | U | A | R | T | F | N | F | I | U | N | B | C | A |
| L | S | O | Z | L | I | E | M | P | O | U | N | D | A | Q | O |

You can measure up by finding these 22 measurement terms. Circle them.

**Word Bank**

| | | | |
|---|---|---|---|
| meter | liter | gram | foot |
| yard | inch | mile | furlong |
| teaspoon | tablespoon | pint | quart |
| cup | gallon | peck | bushel |
| ounce | pound | ton | dram |
| carat | acre | | |

Skill: Recognizing nouns

# A Nose for Nouns

Name ______________________

| I | Y | M | A | A | T | U | P | R | E | S | I | D | E | N | T |
|---|---|---|---|---|---|---|---|---|---|---|---|---|---|---|---|
| L | A | R | O | E | P | S | E | N | O | H | Y | P | L | D | E |
| E | L | S | Y | R | U | B | D | F | I | L | T | M | E | Q | A |
| H | T | O | C | C | U | P | A | T | I | O | N | O | C | Z | F |
| C | U | F | E | N | M | A | M | O | N | C | N | K | T | H | A |
| C | I | T | I | Z | E | N | G | D | S | A | U | A | I | O | R |
| E | K | W | U | R | F | S | E | R | K | A | M | P | O | R | B |
| Z | E | A | B | B | R | E | V | I | A | T | I | O | N | R | O |
| O | E | R | D | M | N | T | O | R | Z | A | Q | E | I | L | M |
| G | G | E | U | D | S | T | S | I | Y | O | I | J | N | P | D |
| H | L | Q | S | O | R | T | I | T | A | E | D | V | H | D | I |
| S | I | O | L | O | L | E | A | D | E | R | L | E | M | T | S |
| M | I | S | J | O | P | I | M | T | E | L | G | R | S | O | C |
| A | C | N | T | E | A | O | E | Z | E | S | T | T | L | H | O |
| M | I | A | N | O | A | S | O | N | O | P | U | E | R | L | V |
| M | E | A | S | U | R | E | M | E | N | T | D | B | L | K | E |
| A | C | T | E | R | F | Y | T | R | M | N | O | R | T | B | R |
| L | M | H | O | T | E | R | G | E | O | G | R | A | P | H | Y |
| E | O | L | O | M | A | E | S | A | H | K | C | T | U | V | R |
| G | O | P | H | O | T | O | S | Y | N | T | H | E | S | I | S |
| C | A | T | O | C | A | P | I | T | A | L | S | T | E | L | I |

There are 16 nouns hidden in the puzzle. If you can sniff them out, you will have a nose for nouns.

NOUNS

persons

places

things

Word Bank

leader
state
history
president

abbreviation
mammal
discovery
software

election
citizen
geography
occupation

measurement
photosynthesis
capital
vertebrate

 

# Hats Off to You!

Name ______________________

What kind of hat will you wear when you grow up? Maybe it will be one of the 16 hidden in this puzzle.

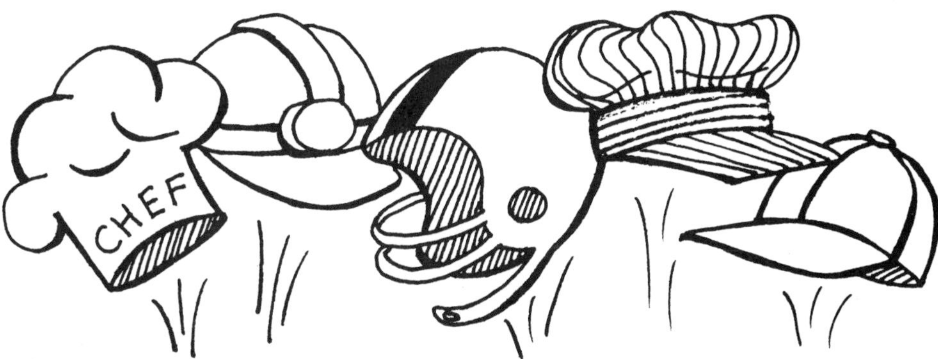


| | | | | | | | | | | | | | | | | | | | | | |
|---|---|---|---|---|---|---|---|---|---|---|---|---|---|---|---|---|---|---|---|---|---|
| W | S | H | E | U | M | R | B | U | T | C | H | E | R | X | U | I | P | R | Y | C | B |
| S | A | A | P | N | Z | Q | G | S | A | Z | X | E | N | G | I | N | E | E | R | O | E |
| E | I | P | H | O | T | O | G | R | A | P | H | E | R | W | H | M | P | S | V | M | E |
| C | B | Y | A | T | Q | R | R | A | O | W | I | V | A | G | A | J | S | O | U | P | L |
| R | N | G | R | Z | W | S | E | R | H | S | I | Z | W | V | F | L | Y | T | I | U | G |
| E | H | O | M | E | M | A | K | E | R | C | U | Y | B | E | B | K | C | G | T | T | E |
| T | C | O | A | Z | P | S | Z | G | M | U | Z | A | X | U | D | K | H | E | D | E | R |
| A | A | F | C | O | E | T | E | H | E | L | U | X | C | T | C | L | I | C | S | R | F |
| R | D | M | I | N | E | R | B | G | T | P | S | A | L | E | S | M | A | N | B | O | E |
| Y | C | N | S | O | W | T | B | E | M | T | I | Z | D | A | C | J | T | I | R | P | A |
| S | E | A | T | H | L | E | T | E | S | O | V | W | Y | C | D | M | R | B | M | E | F |
| E | T | C | I | V | N | U | L | W | O | R | B | X | E | H | A | I | I | X | T | R | W |
| O | U | T | M | K | W | X | E | D | R | V | W | U | Z | E | E | N | S | R | O | A | R |
| I | A | O | O | E | N | V | A | B | E | U | G | T | R | R | B | H | T | S | R | T | U |
| W | H | R | J | M | M | Z | G | N | U | R | S | E | O | I | A | N | O | I | R | O | I |
| G | H | E | M | L | E | W | Z | E | S | T | R | S | S | T | F | G | P | Q | U | R | V |

**Word Bank**

| | | | |
|---|---|---|---|
| actor | teacher | computer operator | pharmacist |
| salesman | engineer | psychiatrist | secretary |
| homemaker | butcher | miner | welder |
| nurse | athlete | photographer | sculptor |

 

Concept: Prominent Black Americans

# Prominent Blacks

Name ____________________

Find the 16 outstanding Black Americans hidden in this puzzle.

| S | R | C | O | N | S | T | A | N | C | E | B | A | K | E | R | M | O | T | L | E | Y |
|---|---|---|---|---|---|---|---|---|---|---|---|---|---|---|---|---|---|---|---|---|---|
| T | I | W | E | J | R | E | D | O | V | C | L | N | P | E | R | L | T | H | E | S | O |
| B | O | O | K | E | R | T | W | A | S | H | I | N | G | T | O | N | B | O | O | H | M |
| A | J | J | T | S | L | Y | N | G | P | A | L | T | Y | L | S | H | I | M | N | I | I |
| R | E | S | N | S | D | H | F | B | L | R | E | C | P | R | A | E | O | A | T | R | C |
| B | S | I | U | E | L | S | D | N | R | L | I | L | E | G | P | S | L | S | Y | L | H |
| A | S | M | F | O | R | N | T | O | D | I | M | O | R | T | A | F | S | B | N | E | A |
| R | E | P | C | W | E | M | L | A | F | E | R | C | F | H | R | T | E | R | E | Y | E |
| A | J | S | H | E | S | N | D | B | R | P | O | Y | M | E | K | I | P | A | P | C | L |
| J | A | O | M | N | A | L | R | M | T | R | U | P | H | D | S | C | T | D | R | H | J |
| O | C | N | A | S | N | O | L | U | N | I | H | I | T | V | B | R | O | L | I | I | A |
| R | K | A | M | U | H | A | M | M | E | D | A | L | I | J | E | T | F | E | C | S | C |
| D | S | P | O | N | S | A | N | D | R | E | W | Y | O | U | N | G | L | Y | E | H | K |
| A | O | L | G | L | P | C | E | M | L | O | M | P | E | R | T | D | G | C | P | O | S |
| N | N | R | T | H | U | R | G | O | O | D | M | A | R | S | H | A | L | L | A | L | O |
| U | M | A | R | T | I | N | L | U | T | H | E | R | K | I | N | G | J | R | T | M | N |

**Word Bank**

Booker T. Washington
Muhammed Ali
Martin Luther King, Jr.
Constance Baker Motley
Charlie Pride
Michael Jackson
Shirley Chisholm
Andrew Young
Jesse Owens
Jesse Jackson
Leontyne Price
Thomas Bradley
Barbara Jordan
O.J. Simpson
Thurgood Marshall
Rosa Parks

Concept: Prominent women

# You've Come a Long Way!

Name ______________________________

There have been many outstanding women in history. Find the 15 hidden in this puzzle and circle them.

| C | F | L | E | L | E | A | N | O | R | R | O | O | S | E | V | E | L | T | O | R | M |
|---|---|---|---|---|---|---|---|---|---|---|---|---|---|---|---|---|---|---|---|---|---|
| O | B | R | M | A | R | G | A | R | E | T | M | E | A | D | K | O | T | R | M | S | O |
| R | I | T | I | M | O | N | T | R | A | K | E | M | L | P | Q | U | A | Z | E | U | T |
| E | H | E | L | E | N | H | A | Y | E | S | F | R | L | N | S | U | M | Y | C | S | H |
| T | E | F | Y | R | N | S | I | N | Y | C | T | A | Y | B | C | O | T | S | O | A | E |
| T | L | J | D | T | E | M | A | R | Y | L | O | U | R | E | T | T | O | N | T | N | R |
| A | E | C | I | V | M | E | C | L | B | R | E | A | I | Y | R | G | E | A | S | B | T |
| S | N | L | C | P | E | F | Y | R | L | G | O | L | D | A | M | E | I | R | M | A | E |
| C | K | V | K | F | O | L | S | W | Z | T | E | F | E | H | U | R | L | M | O | N | R |
| O | E | G | E | R | A | L | D | I | N | E | F | E | R | R | A | R | O | J | R | T | E |
| T | L | K | N | A | J | L | O | P | H | T | G | Z | Y | K | L | C | G | N | O | H | S |
| T | L | M | S | A | N | D | R | A | D | A | Y | O | C | O | N | N | O | R | G | O | A |
| K | E | G | O | M | Y | G | E | O | L | E | R | F | N | O | P | R | I | S | T | N | K |
| I | R | U | N | R | M | B | T | A | M | R | O | S | T | R | A | K | L | E | S | Y | F |
| N | T | S | P | H | A | R | R | I | E | T | T | U | B | M | A | N | T | C | U | R | L |
| G | B | R | G | Q | L | Y | A | L | T | H | E | A | G | I | B | S | O | N | F | G | O |

**Word Bank**

- Emily Dickenson
- Coretta Scott King
- Sandra Day O'Connor
- Eleanor Roosevelt
- Mary Lou Retton
- Margaret Mead
- Geraldine Ferraro
- Harriet Tubman
- Mother Teresa
- Susan B. Anthony
- Sally Ride
- Althea Gibson
- Golda Meir
- Helen Keller
- Helen Hayes

 

Skill: State Nicknames

# Nicknaming the States

Name ______________________

Whew! We found you in the nick of time! See if you can locate the states whose nicknames are listed here.

| S | E | T | A | U | K | V | S | W | A | S | B | P | D | C | E | N | Y | A | N | Z | M |
|---|---|---|---|---|---|---|---|---|---|---|---|---|---|---|---|---|---|---|---|---|---|
| T | E | X | A | S | T | T | G | A | E | M | W | C | A | N | X | A | M | B | L | C | I |
| E | E | R | H | E | S | L | P | S | K | O | K | L | A | H | O | M | A | N | O | O | P |
| N | U | M | R | R | R | M | U | H | O | N | E | V | B | R | R | O | P | B | E | C | L |
| N | Q | E | I | D | A | H | O | I | J | T | H | U | I | F | E | T | O | S | R | O | Q |
| E | E | O | S | Q | C | P | L | N | C | A | P | V | H | Q | G | P | V | U | G | L | K |
| S | H | W | P | F | I | E | O | G | I | N | W | M | N | G | O | M | N | C | T | O | F |
| S | C | G | M | T | D | N | A | T | H | A | W | A | I | I | N | Q | L | R | E | R | J |
| E | E | O | O | E | R | A | M | O | R | P | B | E | C | S | A | L | A | S | K | A | J |
| E | N | S | C | U | X | K | S | N | U | H | J | A | S | B | G | R | C | C | H | D | I |
| A | O | B | M | I | L | I | R | K | O | I | E | H | R | S | F | S | E | D | G | O | E |
| I | C | N | J | N | T | L | C | A | L | I | F | O | R | N | I | A | D | U | O | D | I |
| T | C | I | U | T | G | J | I | O | R | O | N | E | V | A | D | A | U | E | T | T | C |
| U | A | R | I | Z | O | N | A | N | Y | U | T | U | A | T | V | A | W | V | L | A | Q |
| D | O | B | F | E | F | I | P | O | E | Q | W | Y | O | M | I | N | G | F | P | S | H |
| R | A | E | G | H | V | J | M | Z | S | N | X | T | O | U | M | V | X | W | N | G | R |

**Clue Bank**

The Sooner State
The Grand Canyon State
The Treasure State
The Beehive State
The Golden State
The Evergreen State
The Volunteer State
The Centennial State
The Silver State
The Equality State
The Aloha State
The Lone Star State
The Gem State
Land of Enchantment
The Last Frontier
The Beaver State

Skill: Atomic terms

# Understanding Atoms

Name________________________________

**Across**

3. Matter made of only one kind of atom
4. What is formed when atoms combine by sharing electrons
8. Positive electric charge within the nucleus of an atom
10. Small pieces of matter
11. Letter or letters
12. What a thing is made up of; it occupies space.

**Down**

1. An uncharged particle within the nucleus of an atom
2. Very tiny part that makes up matter
5. Tiny negative electrical charges that move around the nucleus of an atom
6. An atom that has lost or gained electrons
7. Characteristics or qualities of a thing
8. Chart that shows all of the elements classified by similar properties
9. Symbols put together to show the elements which make a compound

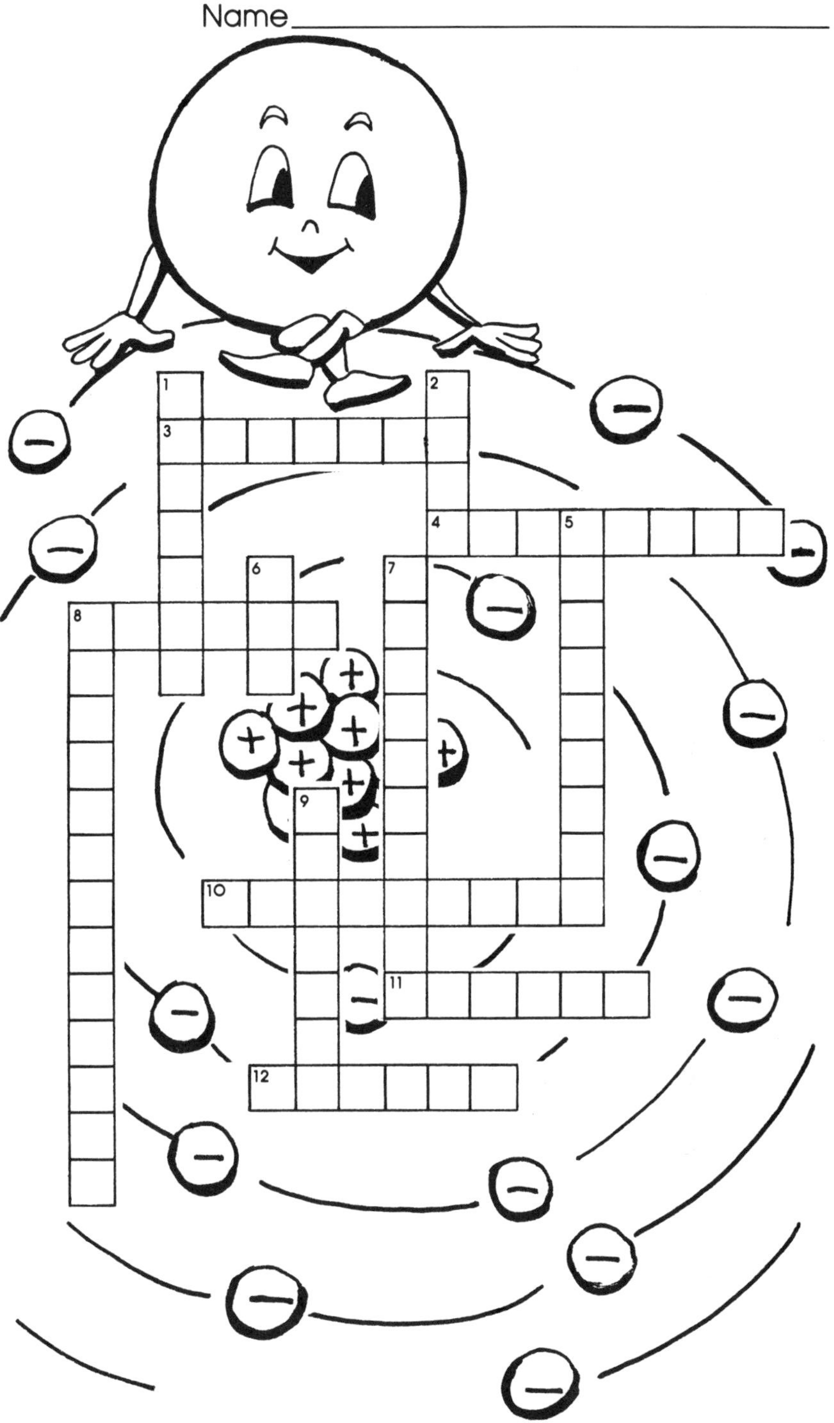


**Word Bank**

| | | | |
|---|---|---|---|
| neutron | proton | electrons | negative charge |
| atom | matter | particles | positive charge |
| element | symbol | properties | electron cloud |
| molecule | ion | compound | periodic table |
| formula | | | |

# Put the Plug on Drugs

Name______________________________

**Across**

4. Drug used for relaxation and sleep, could cause drug dependence if misused
6. To use wrongly, misuse
8. Drug that produces altered sensations, or the seeing or hearing of things that do not exist
10. A dangerous, habit-forming drug made from opium
11. Narcotics are taken from this plant.

**Down**

1. A drug that may be prescribed by doctors to relieve tension or lower blood pressure
2. A stimulating drug present in coffee and tea
3. An unwanted effect in drugs
5. A drug that is capable of causing drowsiness, sleep, unconsciousness, or stupor
6. Drug used medically to increase the activity of the brain or some other part of the body
7. Food or drug that increases the activity of the brain or other part of the body
9. A depressant

**Word Bank**

| | | | |
|---|---|---|---|
| abuse | stimulant | amphetamine | narcotic |
| placebo | addiction | barbiturate | opium |
| pharmacy | hallucinogen | caffeine | sedative |
| depressant | prescription | heroin | side effect |
| tranquilizer | dependence | | |

 

Skill: Math terms

# Math Is It!

Name_______________________________

Across
1. The answer in subtraction
4. The total of two addends
6. A quantity less than a whole
8. The number by which the dividend is divided
10. The bottom number of a fraction
12. Numbers expressed in the decimal system

Down
1. The number the divisor is divided into
2. An example is: $A + B = B + A$
3. One of two numbers added to get the sum
5. The answer in multiplication
7. The answer in division
9. The number from which another is to be subtracted
11. That branch of math which deals with points, lines, shapes, and solids

Word Bank

| | | | |
|---|---|---|---|
| addend | minuend | quotient | geometry |
| sum | subtrahend | remainder | decimals |
| multiplicand | difference | numerator | Commutative Law |
| multiplier | divisor | denominator | Distributive Law |
| product | dividend | fraction | Associative Law |

 

Skill: European countries and capitals

# Embark on Europe

Name____________________

**Across**

2. Bern is this country's capital.
4. Bucharest is the capital of this country.
5. This country shares the Iberian Peninsula with Portugal.
8. Belgrade is its capital.
10. Russian is the chief language of this country.
11. Amsterdam is this country's capital.
12. This is Sweden's capital and home of Alfred Nobel, founder of the Nobel Peace Prize.

**Down**

1. Liechtenstein is this country's capital.
3. Poland's capital
6. Oslo is its capital. It was the first European country to given women voting rights.
7. Portugal's capital
9. This country and its capital have the same name.

**Word Bank**

| | | |
|---|---|---|
| Malta | Spain | Switzerland |
| Soviet Union | Warsaw | Vaduz |
| Yugoslavia | Luxembourg | Lisbon |
| Norway | Stockholm | San Marino |
| Netherlands | Moraco | Rumania |

 

# Gallantly Greek

Name____________________________________________

What Greek letters do these symbols represent?

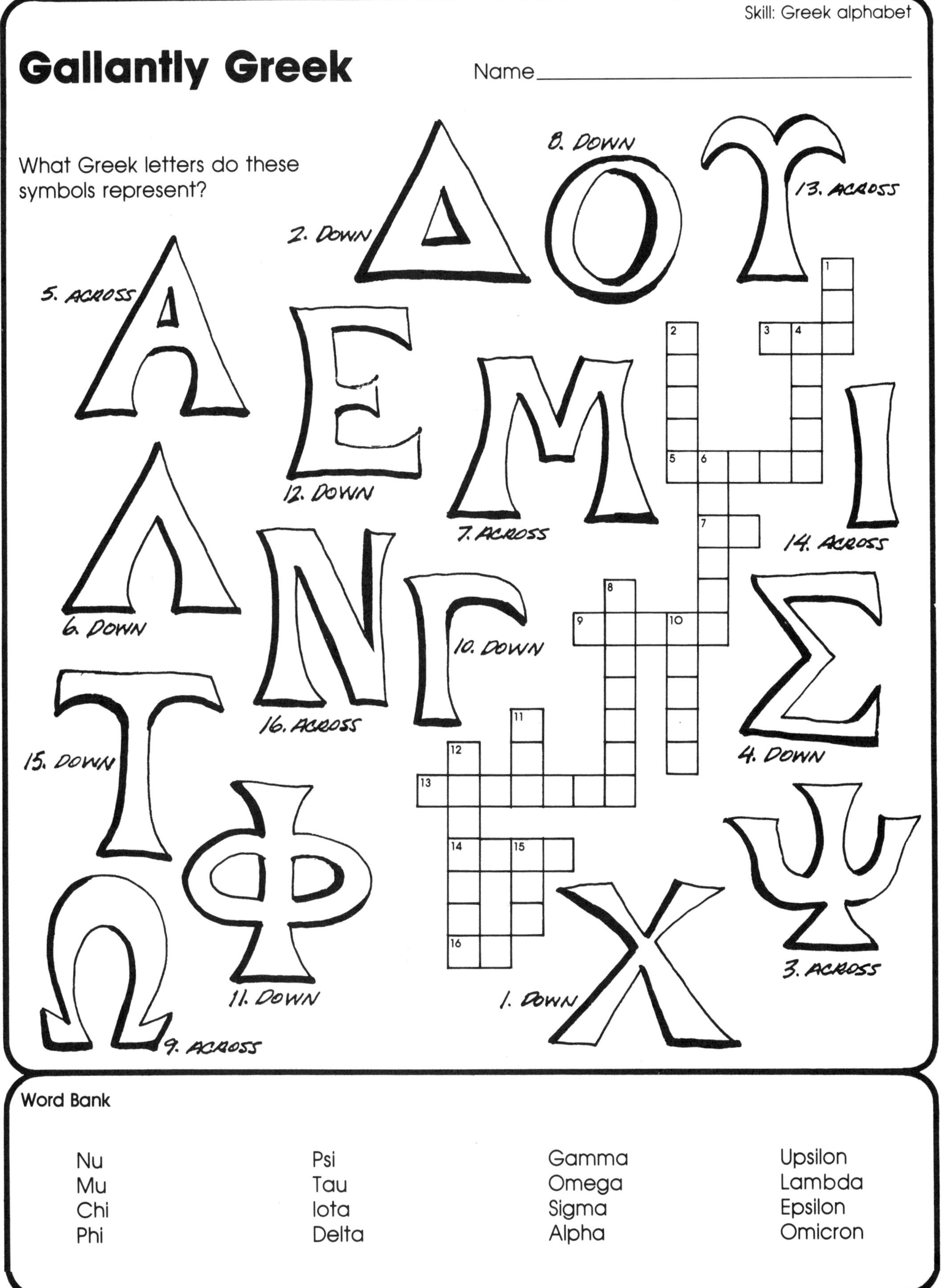


**Word Bank**

| | | | |
|---|---|---|---|
| Nu | Psi | Gamma | Upsilon |
| Mu | Tau | Omega | Lambda |
| Chi | Iota | Sigma | Epsilon |
| Phi | Delta | Alpha | Omicron |

 

Skill: Prepositions

# Preposition Patch

Name ______________________________

Find the preposition in each sentence.

**Across**

2. The dog ran after the cat.
6. The kite went above the trees.
7. The colt walked behind his mother.
8. The ladder leaned against the wall.
9. Do not go swimming without a buddy.
12. Look for the ball under the pile of leaves.
13. Harold and Sandy went to the store together.

**Down**

1. The child may not go beyond the gate.
3. Stacey went with her friend.
4. Your turn to bat is before his.
5. Pirates must have hidden the gold beneath this spot.
6. Jim just went around the corner.
10. Put the book upon the table.
11. Grandfather's farm is just over the next hill.
12. Practice your piano until the hour is finished.

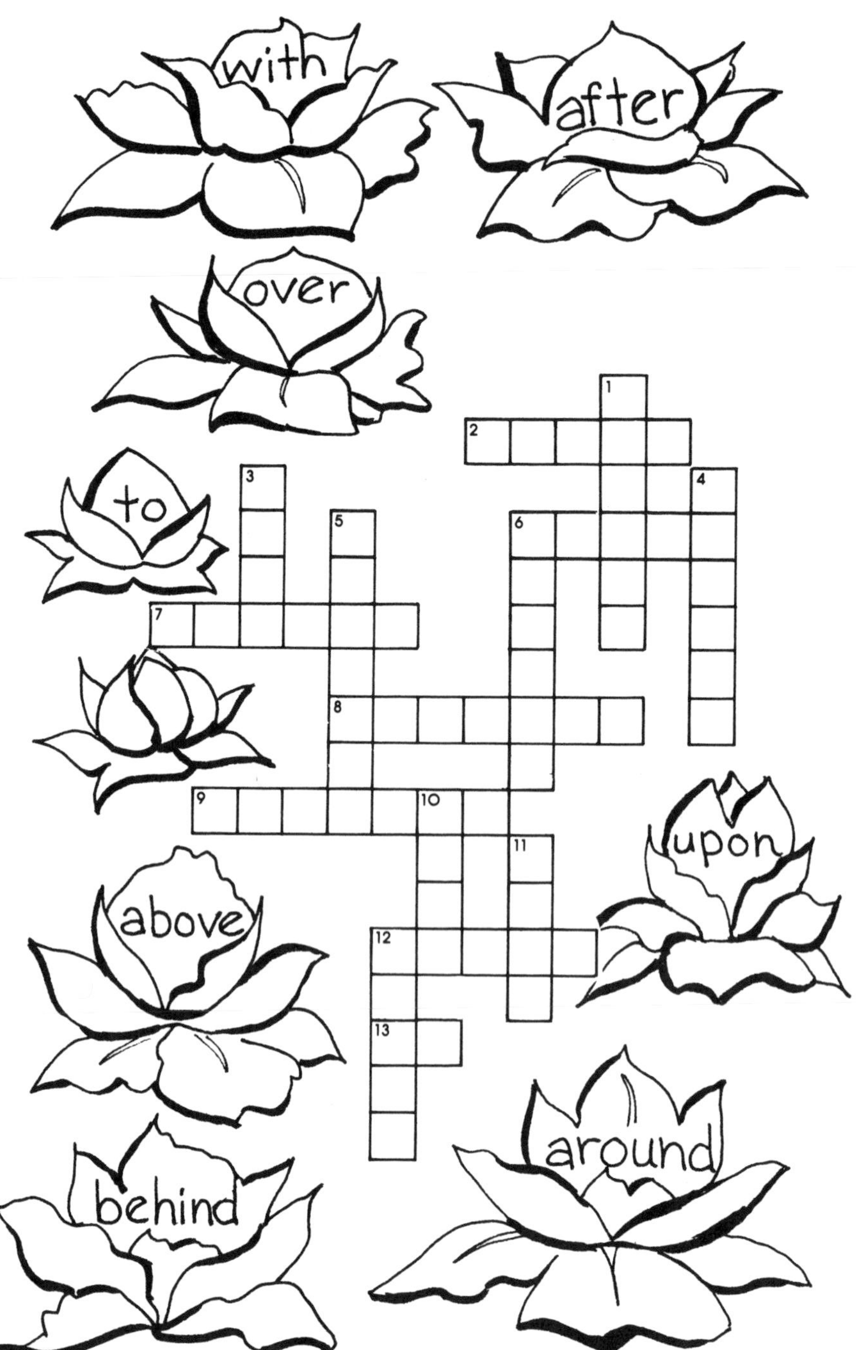


**Word Bank**

| | | | | |
|---|---|---|---|---|
| beyond | under | after | until | upon |
| with | before | to | behind | beneath |
| against | without | around | above | over |

Skill: Geometry terms

# Gung-Ho for Geometry

Name____________________________________

**Across**

2. The distance across a circle through its center
7. A many-sided figure
11. The distance from the center of a circle to its edge
12. A triangle with no congruent sides
13. A figure formed by two rays with the same end point

**Down**

1. An angle whose measure is less than 90°
3. A triangle with two congruent sides
4. Lines which have only one end point
5. A quadrilateral with two parallel sides
6. A part of a line with two end points
8. An angle whose measure is greater than 90°
9. The point at the "corner" of an angle, plane or solid figure
10. Lines in a plane that will never meet

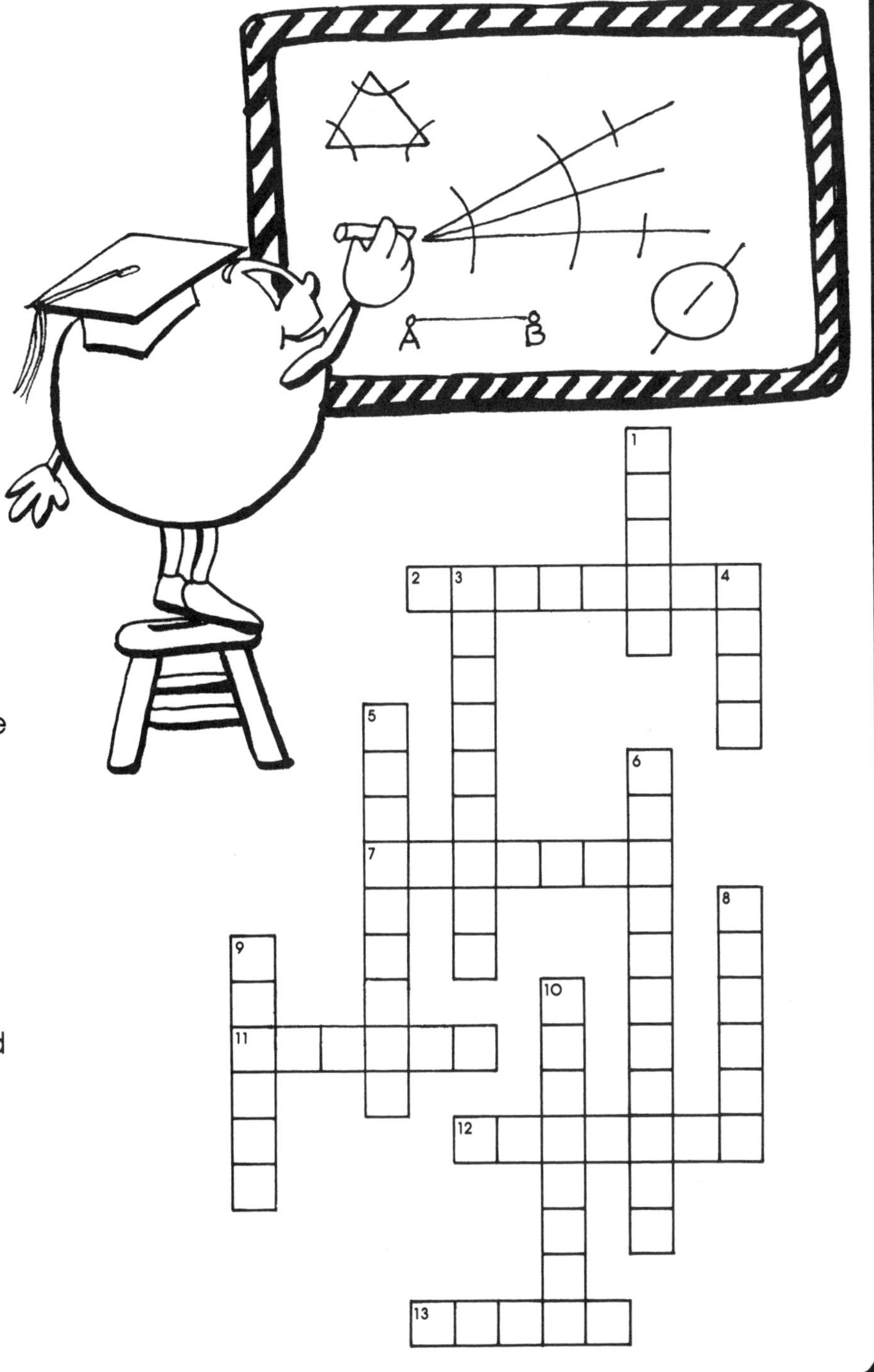


**Word Bank**

| | | | |
|---|---|---|---|
| trapezoid | polygon | radius | acute |
| diameter | isosceles | scalene | rays |
| parallel | vertex | obtuse | angle |
| line segment | | | |

 

# We're Studying These!

Name________________________________

**Across**

2. Dermatology is the study of ______.
4. Hydrology studies this.
7. The study of feet
10. The study of birds
11. Anthropology is the study of this mammal.
12. Ophthalmology studies this part of the body.

**Down**

1. Graphology studies this human skill.
3. The study of the heart
5. The study of fossils
6. Mammalogy is the study of ______.
8. This is the study of fish.
9. Osteology studies the ______.

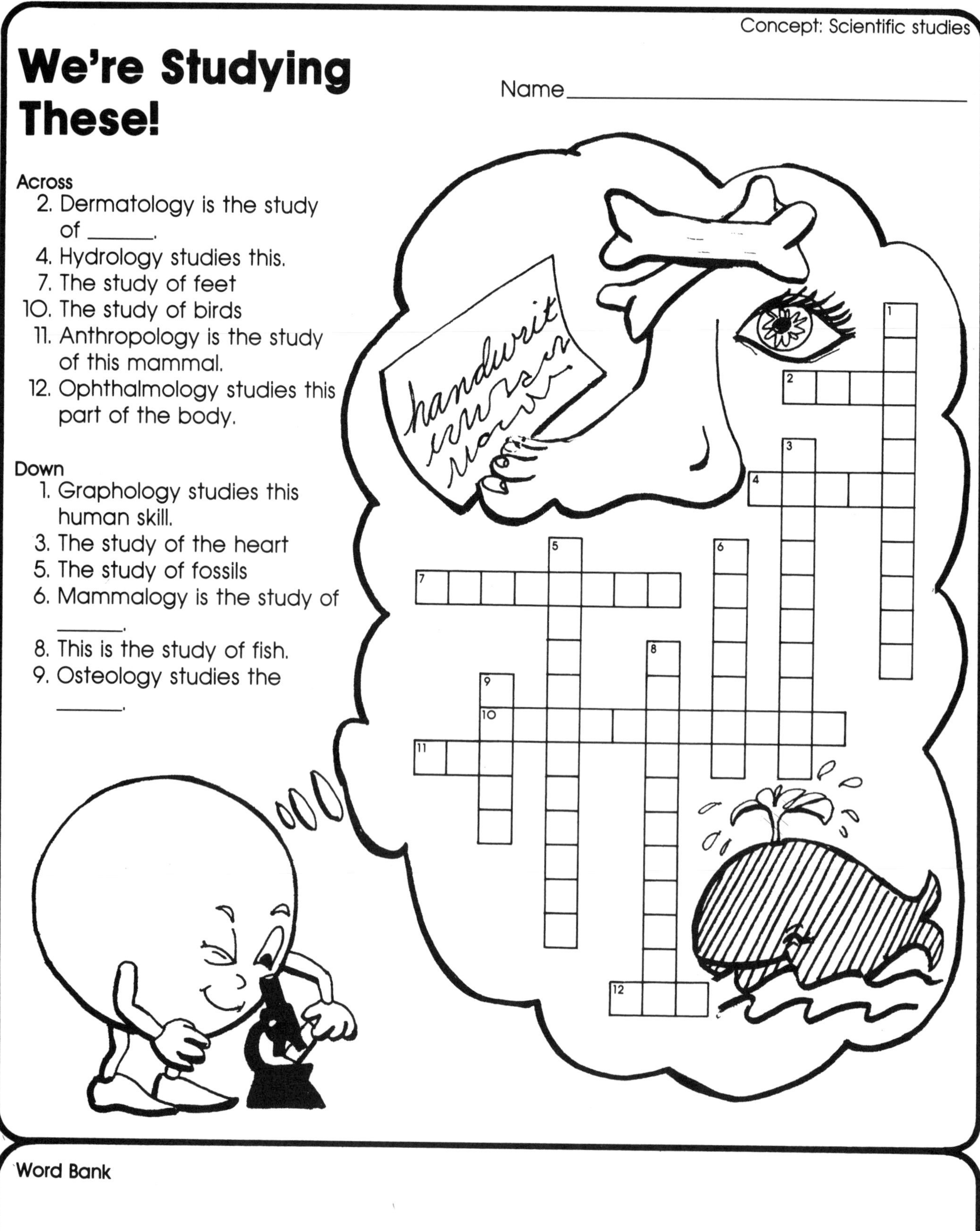


**Word Bank**

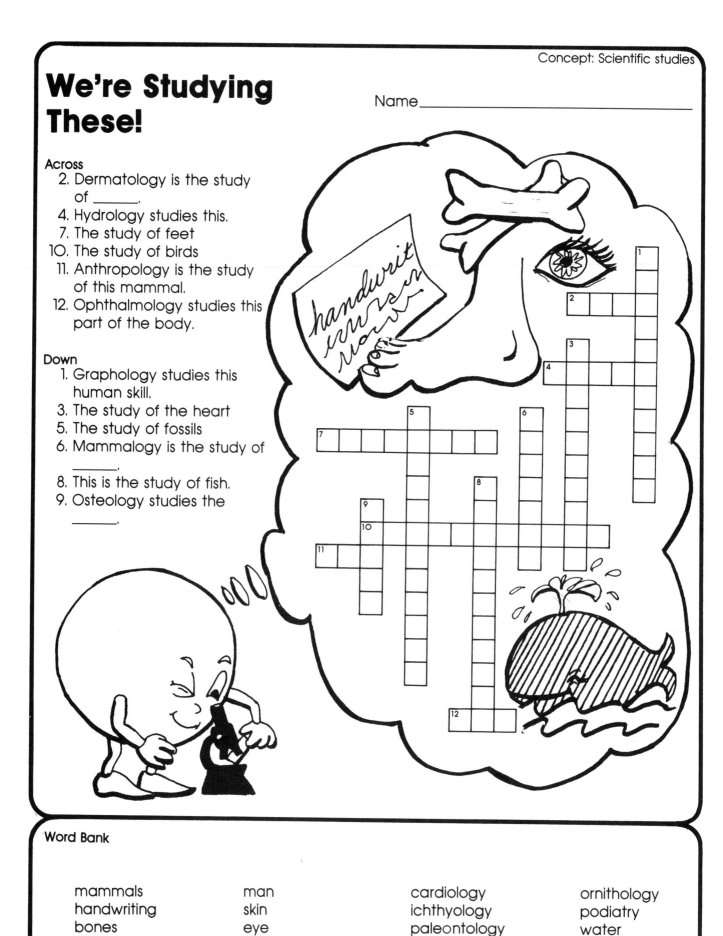

| | | | |
|---|---|---|---|
| mammals | man | cardiology | ornithology |
| handwriting | skin | ichthyology | podiatry |
| bones | eye | paleontology | water |

Concept: Frequently misspelled words

# Spelling Demons

Name________________________________

**Across**

2. A feeling or knowledge of right and wrong
4. That which is known or learned
5. The sum of 29 and 11
9. An army officer
10. A non-professional
11. The ordinal number before ninth
12. To inhale and exhale air

**Down**

1. People admired for courage
3. A chart that shows the days of the year
5. When something is well known to you, it is ____________.
6. Person who keeps a systematic record of business
7. Something accomplished by skill or work
8. Funny, amusing

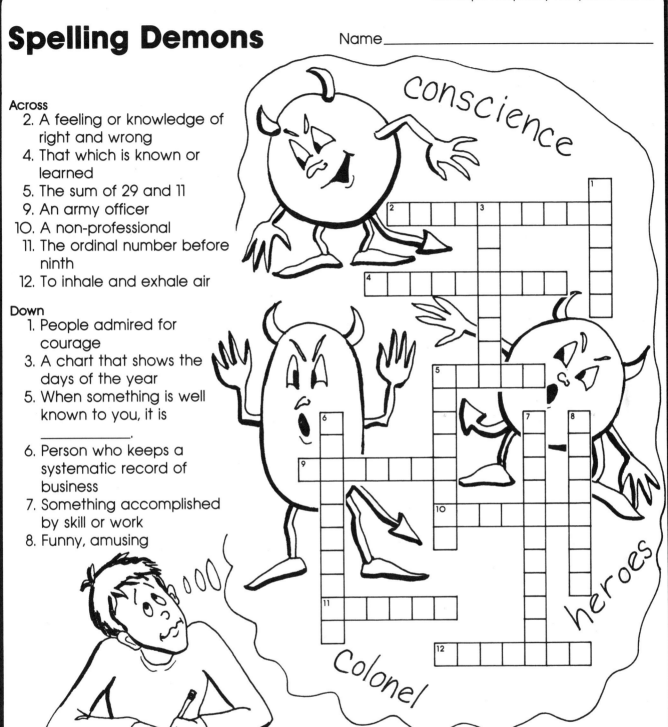

**Word Bank**

achievement
eighth
knowledge
amateur
familiar
bookkeeper
immediately
breathe
calendar
forty
humorous
colonel
conscience
heroes

Skill: Geology terms

# Geological Journey

Name______________________________

**Across**

3. A rock formed by layers of sediment
5. Scientists who study the earth's structure
7. Land deposited at the mouth of a river
8. The removal of soil by wind, ice, and water
11. Rock formed from cooled lava
12. Deep, narrow valleys with steep sides
13. An underwater mass made up of the stony skeletons of certain ocean animals
14. Loose material covering the bedrock of the earth

**Down**

1. Rock formed by heat and pressure
2. The outer part of the earth
4. The lowlands between hills or mountains
6. Earth substances deposited by water or wind
9. A break in the layers of rock which causes a section of it to become dislocated
10. A large mass of earth or rock rising high above the rest of the land

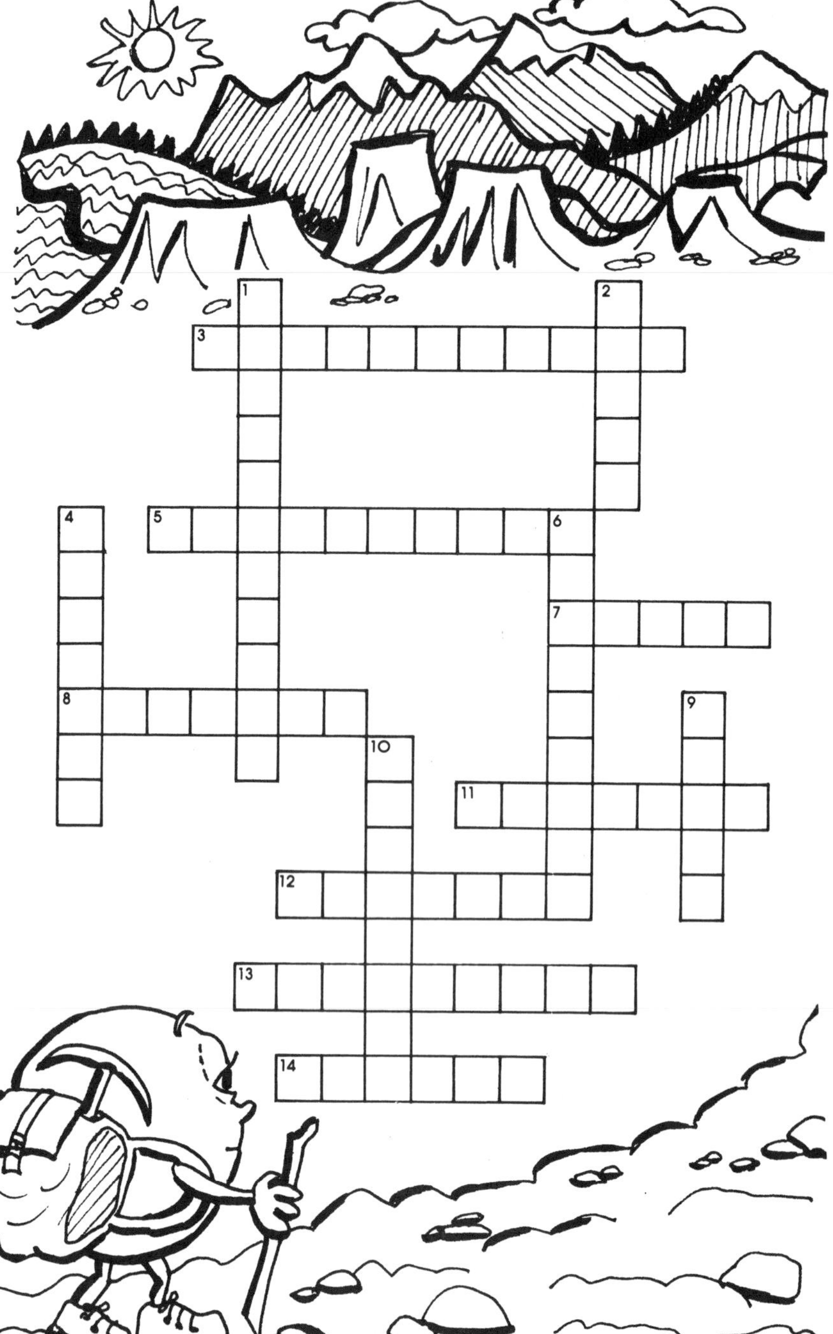


**Word Bank**

| | | | |
|---|---|---|---|
| crust | metamorphic | geologists | delta |
| fault | mountain | igneous | erosion |
| mantle | sedimentary | sediments | canyons |
| valleys | coral reef | | |

 

Skill: Chemical elements and symbols

# Chemical Cohesion

Name______________________________

Which element does each symbol stand for?

**Across**
1. Cu
3. N
4. He
6. K
9. Mg
11. B
13. Au

**Down**
2. P
5. Ag
7. Na
8. Hg
10. Ne
12. O

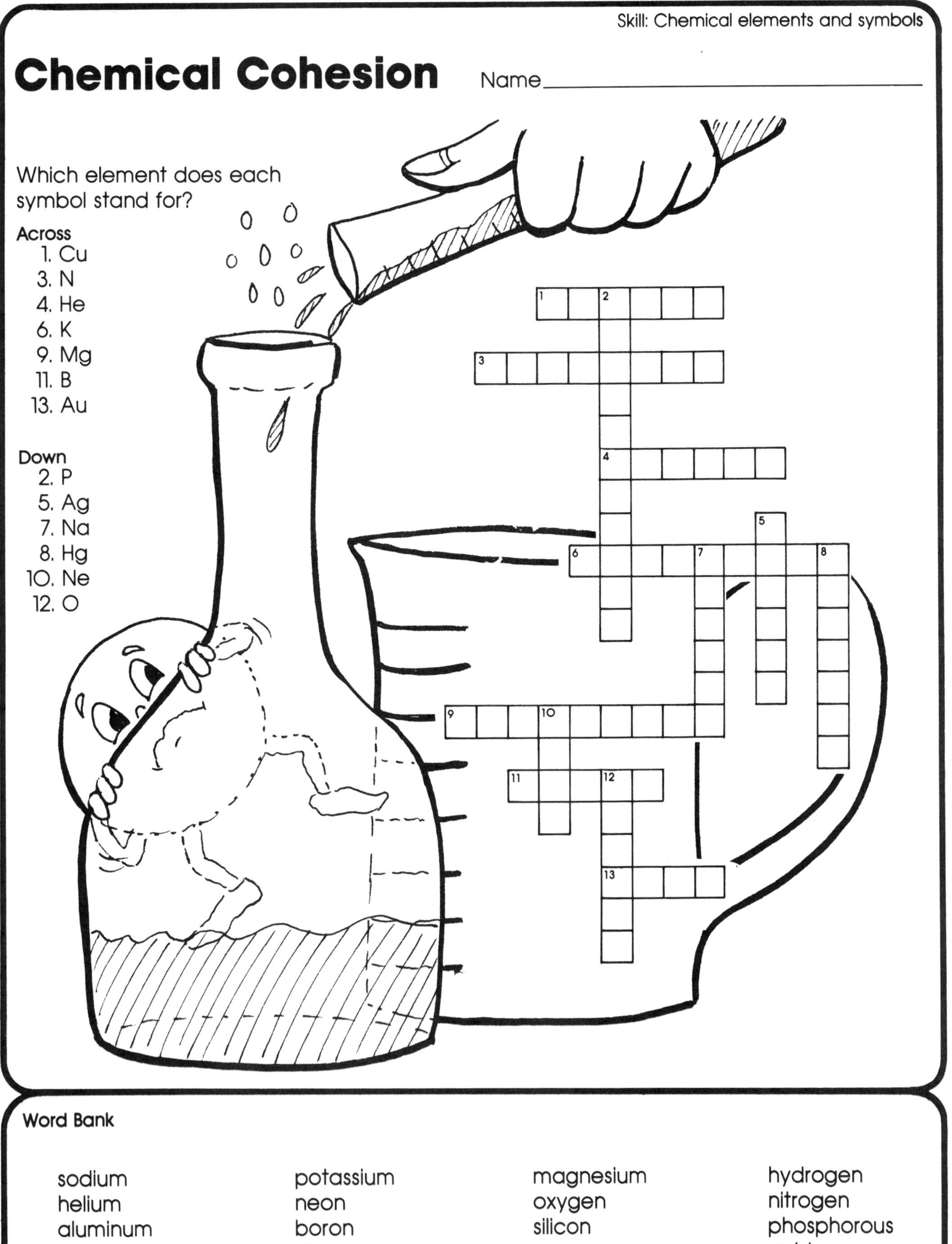

**Word Bank**

| | | | |
|---|---|---|---|
| sodium | potassium | magnesium | hydrogen |
| helium | neon | oxygen | nitrogen |
| aluminum | boron | silicon | phosphorous |
| copper | silver | mercury | gold |

# Pick 'em Out

Name____________________________

What part of speech is underlined?

**Across**

3. Jane went with Jim and her.
4. Geoffrey ate the apple.
7. Run for your life!
10. Happiness is two kinds of ice cream.
11. Cindy will help her mother.
12. Norma and Bruce live in Chicago.

**Down**

1. Suddenly, Aaron ran out of the house.
2. Wow! This is fun!
5. Those flowers are beautiful.
6. The broom closet is full.
8. Put the dishes in the dishwasher.
9. The chubby bear ate the marshmallows.

**Word Bank**

| | | | |
|---|---|---|---|
| nouns | pronoun | complement | possessive pronoun |
| verb | subject | preposition | linking verb |
| adverb | article | conjunction | helping verb |
| adjective | predicate | interjection | prepositional phrase |

 

Concept: Ecology-related terms

# Ecology Wise

Name ______________________________

Across

2. Items that decompose and become part of the environment
6. Substances that make something unclean
7. The removal of soil by wind, water, or ice
8. Smoke and fog
9. A vaporous matter rising from something which is burning
10. Organic wastes and wastewater from the kitchen, bathroom, or laundry
12. That which makes our environment dirty and unhealthy

Down

1. Organisms which prevent other organisms from harming crops
3. Organisms that cause dead organisms to decay
4. A substance added to soil to replace minerals
5. Reusing items or resources
11. The natural, living part of our world

Word Bank

| | | | |
|---|---|---|---|
| decomposers | erosion | crop rotation | biodegradable |
| fertilizer | pollution | hazardous wastes | environment |
| biocontrols | sewage | thermal pollution | smog |
| smoke | impurities | recycling | |

 

Skill: Homonyms

# Which Is Which?

Name_____________________________________________________________________

Don't be confused by these homonyms.

**Across**

3a. a passageway
3b. a small island
5a. a built-in bed
5b. born or produced
6a. going from place to place to sell things
6b. a foot-operated lever
8a. mature
8b. a deep sound expressing pain
9a. a person who digs coal
9b. someone under the legal age

**Down**

1a. cried
1b. having no hair
2a. the ringing of bells
2b. to cut away the skin or rind of a fruit
4a. published in several continuous parts
4b. a breakfast food made with grains
7a. to cover something in a deep hole
7b. a small, juicy fruit with seeds

MIRACLE POTION

pedal and peddle

TV Serial Drama

cereal

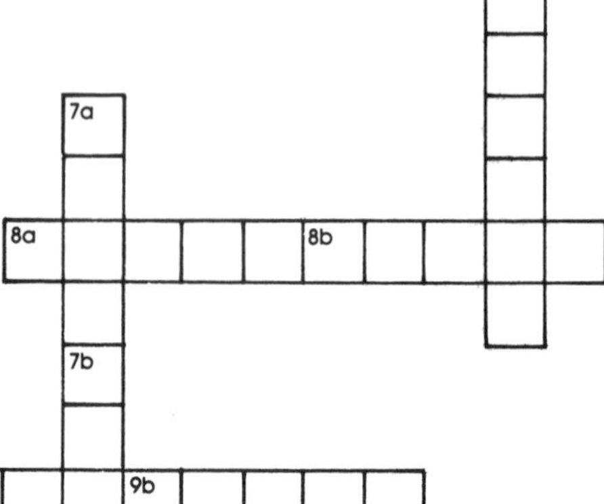

bury and berry

**Word Bank**

| | | | |
|---|---|---|---|
| aisle | minor | pedal | birth |
| miner | grown | bald | serial |
| groan | peddle | isle | bury |
| berth | peel | berry | peal |
| bawled | cereal | | |

 

# Star Light, Star Bright

Name________________________________

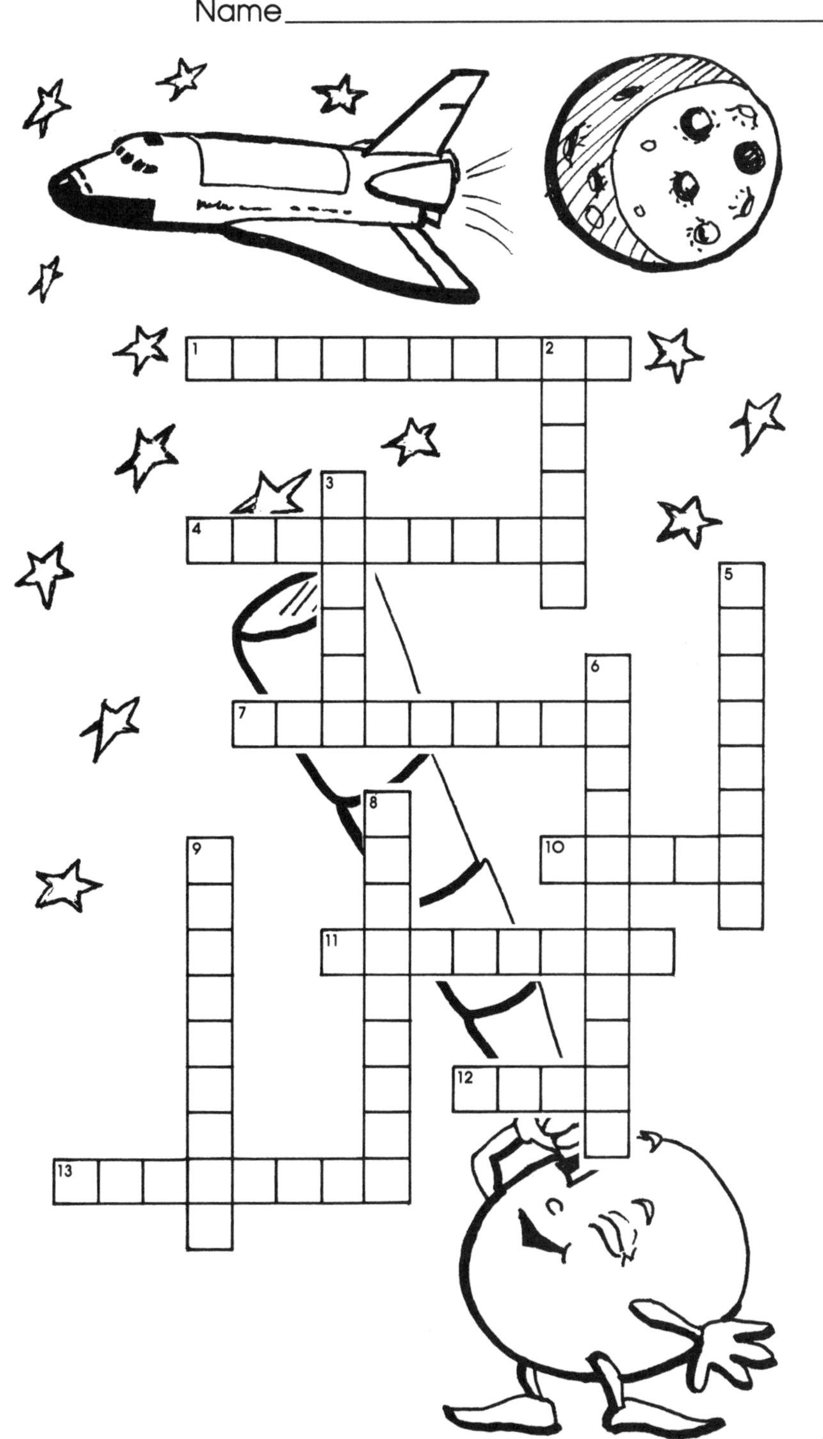

Across

1. The collapsed core of a star that is left before it becomes a black hole
4. Any object in space that orbits a larger object
7. An area of strong gravity in space where a very large star used to be
10. A spacecraft not in orbit around the earth
11. The time in a star's life when most of the hydrogen is changed to helium and the star gets large and red
12. Stars that suddenly become very bright and then slowly become dim
13. Space and all the objects in it

Down

2. A device used to launch objects into space
3. A large cloud of dust and gas in space
5. A grouping of millions of stars
6. Small, dense core of a star that remains after a supernova occurs
8. Instrument used when viewing space
9. A very large exploding star

Word Bank

| | | | |
|---|---|---|---|
| rocket | astronomer | satellite | probe |
| astronaut | space shuttle | universe | galaxies |
| telescope | nebula | red giant | white dwarf |
| nova | supernova | neutron star | black hole |

 

Concept: Frequently misspelled words

# Spell It Right!

Name______________________________

Don't let these spellings get the best of you.

nineth or ninth? vacuum or vacume? pursue or persue similar or similer?

**Across**

1. Something kept as a reminder of a person, place, or event
4. Free time
5. To skillfully manage something
6. Spelled incorrectly
8. Something which helps make the time pass pleasurably
10. Lines that are extended in the same direction and will never meet
12. The smallest quantity possible

**Down**

1. The officer just above a corporal
2. An officer who takes the place of a superior when he/she is absent
3. An empty space
7. Same as
9. The Middle Ages
11. To follow someone or something in order to capture

**Word Bank**

| | | | |
|---|---|---|---|
| laboratory | leisure | lieutenant | maneuver |
| medieval | minimum | misspelled | ninth |
| parallel | pastime | pursue | sergeant |
| similar | souvenir | vacuum | |

 

Skill: Irregular plurals

# More, More— Lots More!

Name________________________________

What is the plural of these words? Write the definitions next to the singular form.

**Across**

2. larva ____________________
5. datum ____________________
6. sheep ____________________
7. louse ____________________
10. graffito ____________________
12. die ____________________

**Down**

1. oasis ____________________
3. alga ____________________
4. alumnus ____________________
8. cactus ____________________
9. trivium ____________________
11. fungus ____________________
13. crisis ____________________

**Word Bank**

| | | | |
|---|---|---|---|
| data | fungi | cacti | algae |
| dice | larvae | trivia | alumni |
| lice | oases | graffiti | crises |
| sheep | | | |

Skill: Names of skeletal bones

# Find Those Bones!

Name____________________________

**Across**
2. toes or fingers
3. breastbone
4. collarbone
8. heel bone
9. wrist bones
12. ankle bones

**Down**
1. kneecap
4. tailbone
5. shorter forearm bone
6. shoulder bone
7. upper arm bone
10. larger forearm bone
11. thigh bone

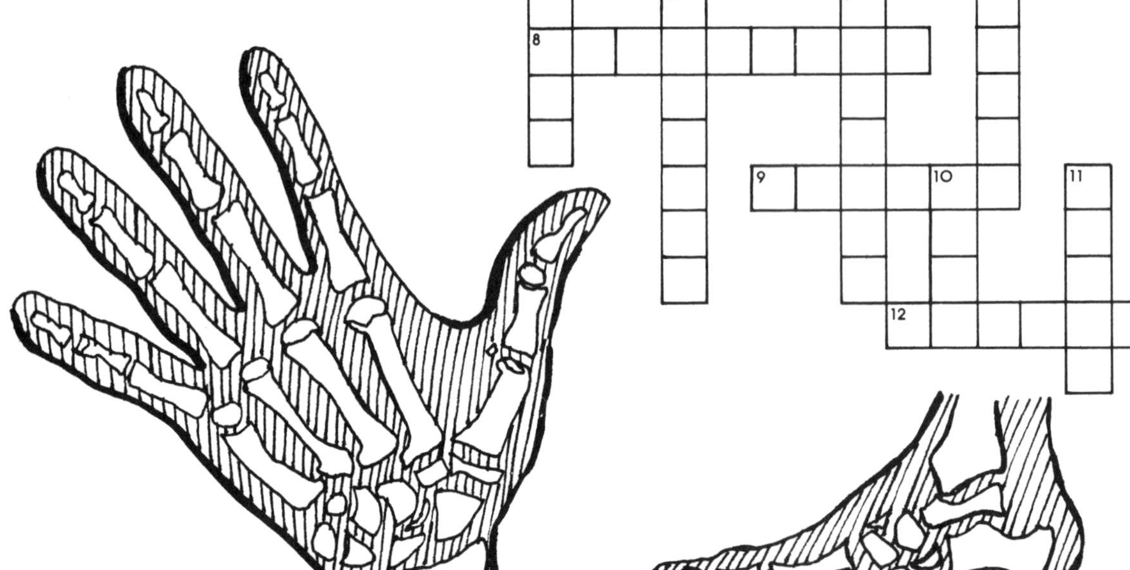

**Word Bank**

| | | | |
|---|---|---|---|
| sternum | femur | calcaneus | mandible |
| coccyx | scapula | clavicle | humerus |
| patella | phalanges | tarsus | radius |
| ulna | tibia | fibula | carpus |

 

Skill: Map terminology

# Map Mania!

Name ____________________

**Across**

1. A social scientist who studies the earth and its surface
7. Distance east or west of an imaginary line running through Greenwich, England
8. The representation of distance on a map
10. An imaginary line on the earth's surface running between the North and South Poles
11. Distance above sea level
12. The most accurate models of the earth

**Down**

2. 0° latitude
3. The distance of any place on the globe north or south of the equator
4. One of the seven large bodies of land on the earth
5. A key accompanying a map
6. Half of the earth
9. Lines on a globe that run east and west around the earth

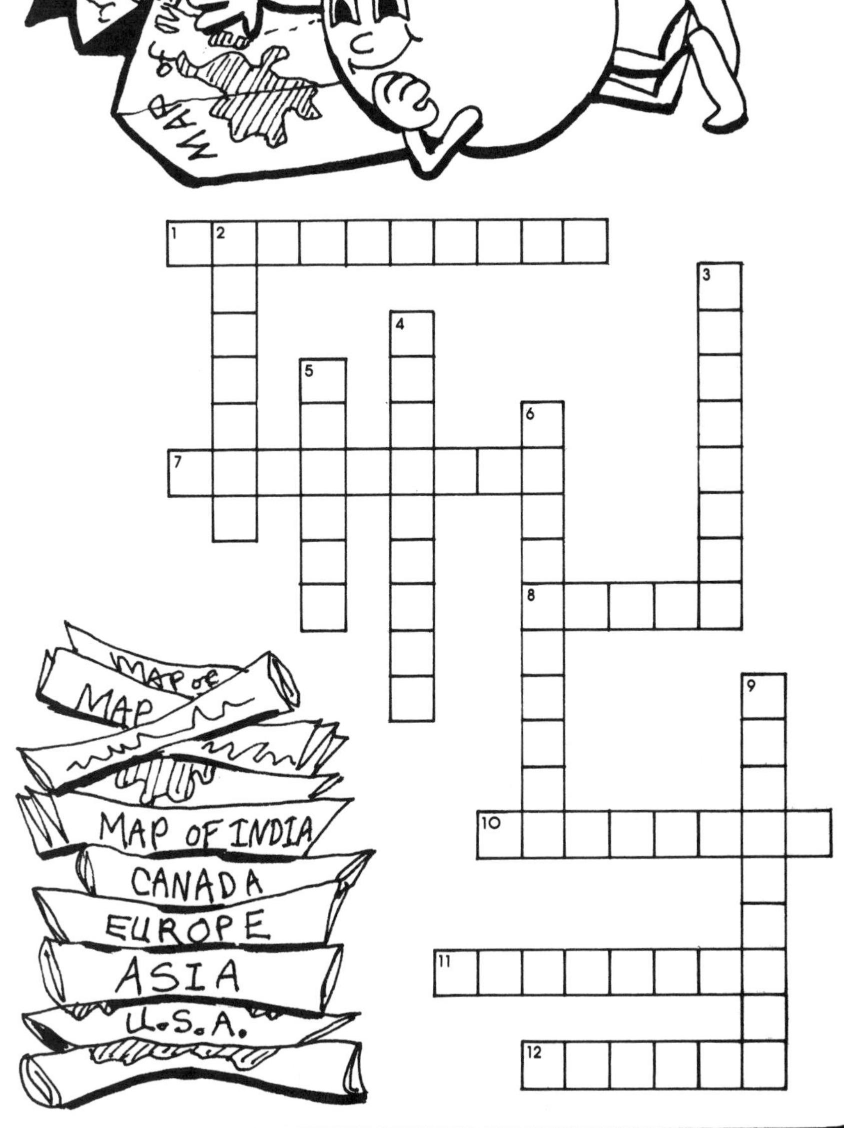


**Word Bank**

| | | | |
|---|---|---|---|
| altitude | longitude | meridian | topographic map |
| globes | model | legend | scale |
| equator | altitude | continent | contour lines |
| hemisphere | geographer | parallels | prime meridian |
| latitude | | | |

 

# Amazing Atoms!

Name ____________________________

| T | R | I | L | N | E | R | N | S | A | S | M | A | P | O | R |
|---|---|---|---|---|---|---|---|---|---|---|---|---|---|---|---|
| N | E | D | E | I | S | P | A | R | T | I | C | L | E | S | I |
| H | A | S | L | N | K | S | Y | M | B | O | L | D | P | U | B |
| L | T | E | E | G | M | A | R | O | A | N | N | T | R | F | G |
| I | H | C | C | F | P | U | I | L | F | E | N | E | O | V | A |
| T | E | F | T | O | R | Y | E | E | M | N | I | T | P | E | T |
| S | P | E | R | I | O | D | I | C | T | A | B | L | E | N | B |
| O | V | L | O | N | T | P | T | U | E | N | A | M | R | R | M |
| C | T | E | N | Z | O | E | T | L | S | E | A | A | T | O | M |
| I | E | C | P | S | N | R | W | E | R | E | T | H | I | N | M |
| A | H | T | M | O | S | V | N | I | T | K | E | N | E | E | A |
| A | I | R | A | F | A | E | A | G | R | O | R | W | S | I | T |
| F | L | O | A | R | M | A | E | N | I | R | N | T | E | H | T |
| O | L | N | E | G | A | T | I | V | E | C | H | A | R | G | E |
| R | U | C | O | M | P | O | U | N | D | T | E | V | A | W | R |
| M | E | L | H | I | L | N | E | T | H | Y | I | R | E | Y | I |
| U | P | O | S | I | T | I | V | E | C | H | A | R | G | E | T |
| L | C | U | N | L | D | R | O | S | G | E | N | F | T | R | E |
| A | B | D | E | E | N | T | A | E | N | E | U | T | R | O | N |
| N | A | N | D | O | E | L | E | M | E | N | T | S | V | L | S |
| R | T | A | B | A | W | G | A | N | A | M | T | Y | T | E | N |

Atoms make up everything in this world. Locate and circle 17 terms related to the atom.

**Word Bank**

- neutron
- positive charge
- elements
- molecule
- electron cloud

- proton
- atom
- periodic table
- ion

- electron
- matter
- symbol
- compound

- negative charge
- particles
- properties
- formula

 

# Drug-free Is the Way to Be

Name ______________________________

When you're happy about yourself, you don't need drugs to get high. Circle 19 drug-related words. Then, write 10 things you like about yourself.

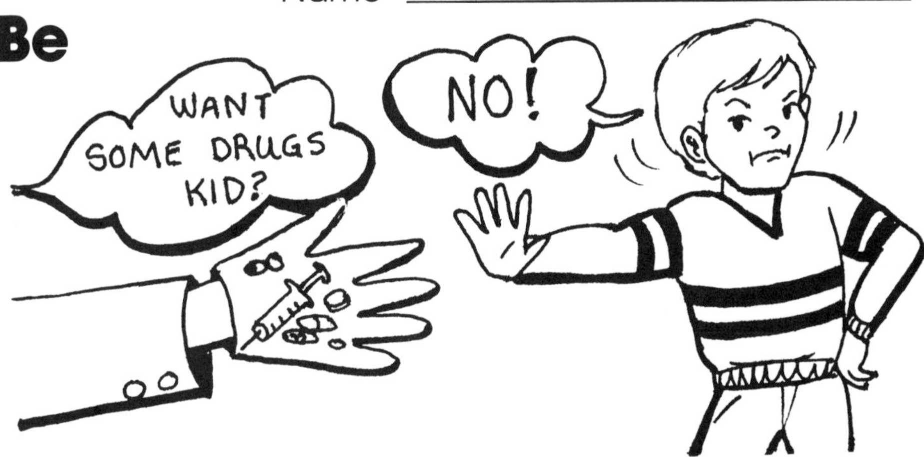


| S | O | H | A | L | L | U | C | I | N | O | G | E | N | S | O | N | T | I | E | T | P |
|---|---|---|---|---|---|---|---|---|---|---|---|---|---|---|---|---|---|---|---|---|---|
| R | H | T | M | N | I | L | T | L | A | N | I | A | S | C | T | E | P | E | D | O | H |
| E | S | R | P | E | B | O | T | S | R | V | B | L | E | H | A | L | R | O | S | S | A |
| H | S | U | H | G | D | E | P | E | N | D | E | N | C | E | H | R | E | L | T | S | R |
| A | N | O | E | R | E | B | R | D | S | M | A | R | T | R | Q | U | S | U | I | I | M |
| B | A | C | T | L | R | I | H | A | T | S | E | Y | D | O | R | S | C | O | M | D | A |
| I | R | Y | A | D | D | I | C | T | I | O | N | L | R | I | Y | O | R | Y | U | E | C |
| L | C | E | M | I | H | E | R | I | R | A | O | M | A | N | E | R | I | E | L | E | Y |
| I | O | P | I | U | M | S | U | V | C | E | R | Y | H | T | H | E | P | O | A | F | V |
| T | T | R | N | P | L | A | C | E | B | O | F | A | U | K | S | A | T | I | N | F | L |
| A | I | F | E | S | O | B | T | R | M | U | N | H | A | N | L | T | I | L | T | E | L |
| T | C | F | H | A | R | U | N | O | R | M | A | O | H | V | A | I | O | B | I | C | Y |
| I | D | E | P | R | E | S | S | A | N | T | C | A | F | F | E | I | N | E | D | T | A |
| O | O | E | G | Y | C | E | Y | D | N | E | L | J | R | O | N | Y | Q | E | N | H | E |
| N | B | A | R | B | I | T | U | R | A | T | E | L | E | A | R | M | U | E | O | F | T |
| R | O | N | S | T | A | L | D | S | A | T | R | A | N | Q | U | I | L | I | Z | E | R |

**Word Bank**

abuse
stimulant
amphetamine
narcotic
tranquilizer
placebo
addiction
barbiturate
opium
dependence
pharmacy
hallucinogen
caffeine
sedative
rehabilitation
depressant
prescription
heroin
side effect

 

# Math Counts Too!

Name ______________________________

| | | | | | | | | | | | | | | | |
|---|---|---|---|---|---|---|---|---|---|---|---|---|---|---|---|
| M | Q | R | E | M | A | I | N | D | E | R | L | A | U | W | M |
| P | U | O | Y | Z | B | O | B | R | P | C | E | S | I | Q | I |
| A | N | X | M | D | E | C | I | M | A | L | S | S | P | E | N |
| N | B | Q | U | O | T | I | E | N | T | I | L | O | D | U | U |
| U | C | W | L | F | R | A | C | T | I | O | N | C | D | D | E |
| M | U | L | T | I | P | L | I | C | A | N | D | I | E | E | N |
| E | A | W | I | C | A | M | S | S | M | P | I | A | O | N | D |
| R | N | V | P | E | G | R | E | F | E | N | F | T | I | O | E |
| A | J | D | L | R | E | T | L | O | U | T | F | I | U | M | S |
| T | K | A | I | T | O | A | O | T | T | L | E | V | F | I | M |
| O | A | C | E | A | M | D | D | N | A | T | R | E | R | N | T |
| R | R | I | R | A | E | R | U | O | A | M | E | L | E | A | R |
| L | G | B | H | D | T | N | R | C | T | W | N | A | A | T | O |
| W | D | I | S | N | R | A | A | H | T | H | C | W | L | O | O |
| T | I | V | T | A | Y | D | T | C | I | E | E | F | F | R | T |
| H | V | O | U | I | M | G | E | T | A | D | D | E | N | D | O |
| D | I | V | I | S | O | R | I | S | E | T | L | H | P | O | S |
| Y | D | C | O | M | M | U | T | A | T | I | V | E | L | A | W |
| S | E | U | S | Y | A | Z | N | C | E | E | X | T | A | K | T |
| U | N | S | T | A | S | U | B | T | R | A | H | E | N | D | O |
| M | D | I | S | T | R | I | B | U | T | I | V | E | L | A | W |

Circle the 20 math terms hidden in the puzzle. Be ready to explain what each term means.

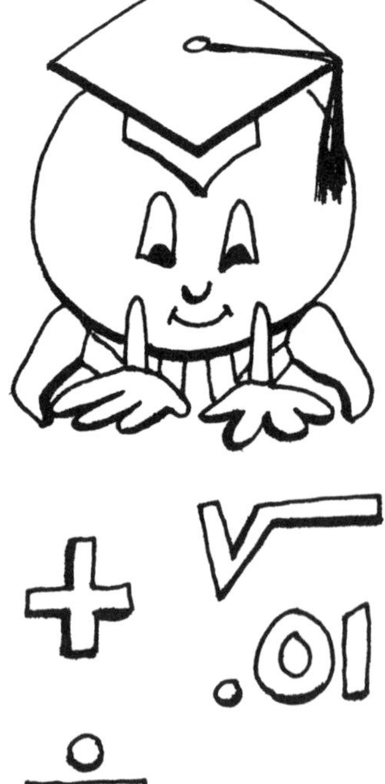

**Word Bank**

| | | | |
|---|---|---|---|
| addend | sum | multiplicand | multiplier |
| product | minuend | subtrahend | difference |
| divisor | dividend | quotient | remainder |
| Commutative law | Associative law | Distributive law | numerator |
| denominator | fraction | geometry | decimals |

 

# Preppy Prepositions

Name ________________________

Perfectly Preppy Peter prefers to prepare proper prepositions rather than practicing piano. Pacify him promptly by picking out the prepositions in this puzzle.

| J | K | L | A | B | A | L | B | K | U | P | O | N | J | O | P | O | V | E | R | G | G |
|---|---|---|---|---|---|---|---|---|---|---|---|---|---|---|---|---|---|---|---|---|---|
| I | A | F | T | E | R | C | D | T | E | F | S | E | Z | N | A | R | H | N | O | B | N |
| H | T | G | U | K | J | C | Y | H | U | G | M | A | S | M | R | S | E | O | M | E | F |
| M | N | I | N | F | R | O | N | T | O | F | W | R | F | R | O | M | H | I | T | H | A |
| A | E | K | L | R | R | J | B | B | H | A | H | T | C | S | U | Y | T | Y | F | I | T |
| N | J | V | S | Q | A | U | O | E | O | T | A | S | M | U | N | T | I | L | N | N | R |
| B | T | V | O | T | W | Q | O | N | Y | R | Q | Z | B | T | D | M | U | M | T | D | D |
| O | D | I | M | P | I | P | G | E | T | O | P | N | O | A | C | M | M | P | S | S | F |
| C | S | N | C | O | T | V | Y | A | C | S | N | C | D | A | O | O | H | F | J | R | C |
| P | Y | P | D | E | H | W | C | T | B | Y | I | D | M | H | L | U | I | K | O | Q | S |
| D | R | C | A | B | O | V | E | H | N | X | M | Z | K | R | S | C | Y | L | Z | R | B |
| Q | U | B | F | S | U | Z | U | C | K | L | L | A | G | A | I | N | S | T | P | L | L |
| F | L | E | B | R | T | X | N | M | X | U | N | N | Y | Z | Y | Y | A | O | E | Z | A |
| E | R | B | Z | U | Q | O | D | M | O | N | T | O | P | O | F | K | E | C | D | E | H |
| S | O | Q | O | F | Y | P | E | R | O | B | E | F | O | R | E | A | J | R | I | S | H |
| A | E | R | W | M | D | U | R | I | N | G | E | S | R | Q | F | M | W | I | T | H | G |

**Word Bank**

above
near
after
past
against
of
in

beneath
under
beyond
during
behind
upon

until
in front of
on top of
with
for
to

from
before
at
over
around
without

 

# Dimensions in Space

Skill: Geometry terms

Name ______________________________

Circle the 18 geometric terms hidden in this wordsearch.

| P | A | R | A | L | L | E | L | S | I | S | C | A | T | N | B | U | L | E | G | B | V |
|---|---|---|---|---|---|---|---|---|---|---|---|---|---|---|---|---|---|---|---|---|---|
| E | H | R | I | U | J | S | P | O | L | Y | G | O | N | S | H | O | A | T | I | O | R |
| R | B | O | R | H | I | R | E | S | D | A | I | T | C | C | I | R | A | Y | S | E | P |
| P | K | E | P | N | F | Y | E | M | I | Y | S | L | E | A | S | T | R | A | O | W | S |
| E | S | I | A | E | Q | U | I | L | A | T | E | R | A | L | B | R | H | E | S | I | C |
| N | T | G | R | A | O | N | F | I | R | O | R | V | U | E | I | C | D | Z | C | A | X |
| D | N | C | A | F | O | D | T | A | J | M | G | H | E | N | Q | O | I | D | E | M | O |
| I | M | O | L | R | A | D | I | U | S | H | A | K | O | E | L | B | A | E | L | Y | T |
| C | F | B | L | K | E | H | C | C | O | N | G | R | U | E | N | T | M | Y | E | N | T |
| U | U | R | E | B | I | L | G | T | E | T | N | Q | U | N | E | U | E | F | S | B | Z |
| L | E | N | L | I | L | O | U | A | I | L | A | T | G | H | P | S | T | A | P | A | P |
| A | R | H | O | M | B | U | S | H | D | C | A | N | H | C | I | E | E | X | E | N | U |
| R | I | L | G | W | R | U | O | T | W | V | E | R | T | E | X | K | R | O | L | G | D |
| O | U | T | R | A | P | E | Z | O | I | D | S | O | I | M | N | B | E | O | A | L | O |
| O | P | O | A | C | U | T | E | D | H | O | S | D | C | Y | A | N | G | W | O | E | G |
| P | F | O | M | E | N | A | E | L | I | N | E | S | E | G | M | E | N | T | R | B | V |

**Word Bank**

angle
perpendicular
congruent
parallel
isosceles

vertex
acute
obtuse
equilateral
scalene

polygons
trapezoids
parallelogram
line segment
diameter

rhombus
rays
radius

# Study These

Name ______________________________

What do each of these sciences study? Find out, then circle your answers in the wordsearch.

| | | | | | | | | | | | | | | | | | | | | | |
|---|---|---|---|---|---|---|---|---|---|---|---|---|---|---|---|---|---|---|---|---|---|
| T | L | N | O | L | S | O | J | S | S | Y | T | E | O | F | B | E | C | D | L | S | W |
| A | H | S | W | I | V | M | B | E | T | D | H | L | A | O | P | E | Y | E | N | E | W |
| P | H | M | A | N | S | R | V | R | E | A | L | M | T | E | T | A | Q | R | K | E | I |
| A | B | I | T | I | F | K | L | P | R | O | M | E | N | M | A | C | S | U | D | T | A |
| E | N | G | E | O | J | Z | A | S | I | D | R | P | E | L | F | O | S | T | Y | H | Y |
| T | A | K | R | F | R | F | R | E | I | C | A | I | S | S | K | E | W | B | R | Y | F |
| O | A | C | S | Z | C | O | K | N | T | H | A | N | D | W | R | I | T | I | N | G | Z |
| M | R | C | E | D | O | S | E | V | O | E | S | R | U | J | Z | H | I | H | U | S | O |
| A | N | I | M | A | L | S | I | L | M | A | M | M | A | L | S | I | J | H | M | W | R |
| M | I | T | N | U | I | I | L | S | U | R | A | T | E | I | Y | O | W | V | B | N | U |
| D | A | H | T | E | C | L | A | O | R | T | A | N | A | L | B | S | K | U | E | L | Q |
| E | L | E | U | B | S | S | I | B | I | R | D | S | U | I | C | K | T | S | R | V | M |
| E | T | A | A | S | I | A | L | O | F | I | H | T | I | L | F | I | S | H | S | I | M |
| P | M | I | N | R | B | S | O | N | T | H | I | T | E | U | E | N | M | F | N | W | P |
| S | L | E | R | T | T | E | H | E | R | S | A | S | M | B | E | O | T | R | E | A | V |
| M | O | O | N | R | N | H | I | S | S | U | A | S | D | C | T | U | V | O | C | B | R |

**Clue Bank**

| | | | |
|---|---|---|---|
| Anthropology | Graphology | Numerology | Paleontology |
| Cardiology | Hydrology | Ophthalmology | Philately |
| Dermatology | Ichthyology | Ornithology | Podiatry |
| Geology | Mammalogy | Osteology | Zoology |

Concept: Frequently misspelled words

# Spelling Demons

Name ______________________________

Beware...
There are 16 frequently misspelled words hidden in this puzzle. Find and circle them. Proceed with caution.

| W | Z | A | B | M | O | L | D | N | C | L | I | E | S | I | M | I | L | A | R | M | H |
|---|---|---|---|---|---|---|---|---|---|---|---|---|---|---|---|---|---|---|---|---|---|
| E | U | M | A | N | E | U | V | E | R | T | A | B | C | T | H | S | T | K | Q | U | O |
| H | R | I | W | N | A | T | E | K | V | A | S | F | O | D | G | O | D | L | U | U | Y |
| P | A | S | T | I | M | E | T | N | A | W | B | L | O | E | A | U | O | N | E | L | T |
| D | U | S | F | A | O | A | N | E | C | T | M | E | D | I | E | V | A | L | S | T | M |
| Y | V | P | X | E | P | I | W | O | U | H | O | I | S | E | T | E | S | L | T | G | A |
| I | T | E | B | I | A | P | E | Y | U | I | Z | S | A | V | C | N | R | O | I | A | E |
| I | U | L | D | H | R | Y | U | H | M | N | K | U | A | B | S | I | Y | S | O | S | T |
| D | A | L | B | L | A | B | O | R | A | T | O | R | Y | A | D | R | V | E | N | R | R |
| T | S | E | Y | W | L | A | P | T | S | K | T | E | C | E | W | I | A | R | N | F | N |
| Y | N | D | C | C | L | R | T | N | A | U | B | O | N | H | E | R | E | G | A | M | Q |
| S | O | M | Z | Y | E | O | C | A | N | O | E | I | I | T | A | W | P | E | I | N | U |
| O | N | G | A | T | L | I | E | U | T | E | N | A | N | T | E | L | T | A | R | A | P |
| H | A | C | H | A | V | S | R | N | E | R | B | U | T | G | R | A | U | N | E | O | A |
| U | M | I | N | I | M | U | M | O | H | S | D | L | H | U | K | T | M | T | O | W | D |
| U | M | J | R | K | E | L | S | W | M | W | A | H | N | O | J | L | E | S | A | W | Y |

**Word Bank**

| | | | |
|---|---|---|---|
| laboratory | leisure | sergeant | maneuver |
| souvenir | vacuum | lieutenant | medieval |
| ninth | pursue | parallel | pastime |
| similar | minimum | misspelled | questionnaire |

# Geological Expedition

Name ______________________________

| M | U | E | R | I | M | F | E | Y | E | C | D | R | E | A | N |
|---|---|---|---|---|---|---|---|---|---|---|---|---|---|---|---|
| I | P | S | T | R | I | A | T | I | O | N | P | Q | R | E | Y |
| N | R | S | E | T | O | D | N | U | D | H | L | E | O | P | M |
| E | M | E | T | A | M | O | R | P | H | I | C | U | S | Z | G |
| R | O | R | G | I | R | O | B | U | I | N | R | L | I | P | L |
| A | U | T | L | S | C | L | O | N | R | P | U | R | O | B | A |
| L | N | A | N | U | K | R | S | D | R | A | S | A | N | E | C |
| S | T | S | G | E | O | L | O | G | I | S | T | S | N | A | I |
| V | A | L | L | E | Y | S | M | R | G | R | A | N | I | T | E |
| T | I | T | E | S | E | T | U | E | B | I | N | L | E | B | R |
| S | N | B | O | E | S | I | E | P | R | A | K | I | Y | C | I |
| C | S | E | D | I | M | E | N | T | S | N | A | O | D | O | H |
| E | T | A | L | O | M | P | D | D | A | S | E | D | M | R | H |
| R | O | C | L | O | M | P | E | S | A | H | M | E | I | A | T |
| F | S | H | A | H | N | L | R | I | G | S | W | L | N | L | G |
| E | G | E | L | V | S | E | D | I | M | E | N | T | A | R | Y |
| L | O | O | S | L | E | A | I | O | A | E | O | A | R | E | E |
| C | H | E | N | I | A | S | O | A | N | S | N | V | I | E | F |
| A | O | E | M | E | F | A | U | L | T | V | W | O | Y | F | K |
| I | E | R | A | C | S | N | M | L | L | E | F | L | E | T | D |
| T | C | M | E | H | M | I | G | N | E | O | U | S | L | C | A |

If you were a geologist, you would meet these terms in the study of the earth and its structure. Find the terms in the wordsearch and circle them.

**Word Bank**

crust
geologists
granite
valleys
coral reef
mantle
erosion
metamorphic
glacier
minerals
core
sediments
mountains
beach
sedimentary
fault
igneous
caves
delta
striation

Skill: Chemical elements and symbols

# Chemical Connections

Name ______________________________

| S | U | L | F | U | R | B | O | L | M | O | A | C | P | I | K |
|---|---|---|---|---|---|---|---|---|---|---|---|---|---|---|---|
| C | O | X | Y | G | E | N | T | W | S | C | I | A | E | E | T |
| N | M | D | O | C | H | L | O | R | I | N | E | R | W | I | T |
| L | E | V | I | S | R | I | T | R | L | Y | P | B | O | T | N |
| E | R | D | F | U | N | Q | S | O | V | A | O | O | N | L | C |
| A | K | I | E | B | M | D | L | S | E | U | E | N | H | U | T |
| O | A | B | M | P | A | S | O | O | R | N | D | I | E | O | L |
| N | I | T | R | O | G | E | N | B | U | O | Y | P | V | O | E |
| E | J | N | G | E | N | E | T | H | Y | D | R | O | G | E | N |
| G | O | L | D | I | E | S | B | E | U | P | F | T | F | A | M |
| F | V | E | S | L | S | F | U | L | L | H | I | A | B | O | L |
| E | N | F | B | H | I | R | O | I | W | O | N | S | B | R | O |
| C | A | L | C | I | U | M | V | U | R | S | Z | S | E | T | S |
| M | O | U | G | Y | M | M | V | M | E | P | H | I | A | R | I |
| L | M | O | C | T | F | W | E | A | D | H | R | U | N | S | A |
| I | Y | R | E | X | H | O | R | R | I | O | C | M | I | C | E |
| T | S | I | L | I | C | O | N | E | C | R | Y | R | M | O | T |
| H | C | N | R | D | A | M | M | B | Y | U | A | O | S | P | I |
| I | Z | E | N | B | O | R | O | N | E | S | R | I | I | P | L |
| U | T | O | P | S | I | O | C | R | T | O | S | Y | O | E | L |
| M | H | A | L | U | M | I | N | U | M | B | H | Y | B | R | F |

The Clue Bank has the chemical symbols. You find the elements and circle them in the wordsearch.

**Clue Bank**

H
He
B
Zn

Li
Ne
Al
Cu

Na
F
Si
Ag

K
O
P
Au

Ca
N
S
Hg

Mg
C
Cl

# Sentence Sense

Name ______________________________

| L | H | L | I | N | K | I | N | G | V | E | R | B | P | E | R |
|---|---|---|---|---|---|---|---|---|---|---|---|---|---|---|---|
| W | A | D | J | E | C | T | I | V | E | U | I | E | R | W | C |
| A | D | H | E | H | E | P | N | E | S | U | B | J | E | C | T |
| E | V | U | T | A | T | N | T | O | E | I | L | E | P | V | A |
| S | E | T | C | E | L | A | E | R | H | D | A | V | O | E | P |
| A | R | T | I | C | L | E | R | V | H | S | E | L | S | E | O |
| T | B | H | A | M | E | L | J | H | E | P | M | E | I | V | S |
| G | O | P | O | I | E | C | E | A | U | R | B | O | T | F | S |
| W | C | I | N | W | E | S | C | S | E | O | B | T | I | L | E |
| C | O | N | J | U | N | C | T | I | O | N | Y | E | O | G | S |
| E | M | R | U | F | I | N | I | N | V | O | D | H | N | R | S |
| T | P | S | A | H | P | O | O | T | N | U | L | L | A | N | I |
| E | L | E | P | F | I | N | N | U | E | N | I | W | L | Y | V |
| K | E | D | P | A | E | S | T | Y | N | I | L | O | P | I | E |
| K | M | W | P | R | E | D | I | C | A | T | E | E | H | B | P |
| S | E | R | L | E | K | T | R | O | D | O | E | W | R | T | R |
| O | N | P | R | E | D | A | D | E | I | D | A | I | A | I | O |
| N | T | H | E | L | P | I | N | G | V | E | R | B | S | E | N |
| V | W | O | D | R | T | A | E | U | L | N | T | G | E | N | O |
| P | R | E | P | O | S | I | T | I | O | N | E | H | G | I | U |
| O | E | U | N | U | N | O | T | R | E | T | H | E | D | E | N |

Circle the parts of speech and words related to sentence structure!

**Word Bank**

noun
preposition
possessive pronoun
subject
verb
interjection
article
predicate
adjective
conjunction
linking verb
complement
adverb
pronoun
helping verb
prepositional phrase

# Clean It Up!

Name ______________________________

| M | E | P | D | S | A | P | Y | E | S | M | N | D | C | H | T |
|---|---|---|---|---|---|---|---|---|---|---|---|---|---|---|---|
| B | I | O | D | E | G | R | A | D | A | B | L | E | T | A | F |
| E | O | L | U | W | Y | P | R | S | T | S | A | C | E | Z | Y |
| O | N | L | B | A | O | U | D | I | N | O | R | O | Y | A | I |
| N | O | U | C | G | S | A | K | A | E | B | R | M | A | R | S |
| N | H | T | D | E | R | I | A | U | D | I | L | P | R | D | V |
| C | G | I | E | R | A | H | T | R | A | O | U | O | T | O | E |
| E | W | O | Y | I | E | R | Y | O | R | C | U | S | E | U | E |
| C | O | N | S | E | R | V | A | T | I | O | N | E | G | S | E |
| O | H | I | S | M | O | K | E | H | M | N | T | O | S | W | N |
| L | V | Y | S | T | S | R | I | A | E | T | N | P | A | A | V |
| O | S | T | P | M | I | G | S | E | T | R | C | I | F | S | I |
| G | C | W | Y | Y | O | U | T | P | D | O | I | R | H | T | R |
| Y | A | L | P | C | N | G | S | E | E | L | A | H | O | E | O |
| T | H | E | R | M | A | L | P | O | L | L | U | T | I | O | N |
| A | M | R | A | T | R | O | E | N | L | R | E | I | Y | X | M |
| R | T | O | H | L | O | Y | N | T | P | E | S | T | R | C | E |
| I | M | P | U | R | I | T | I | E | S | U | F | Z | O | L | N |
| O | N | N | S | R | E | C | Y | C | L | I | N | G | T | L | T |
| N | R | F | G | L | E | O | N | A | E | L | H | S | L | S | V |
| F | E | R | T | I | L | I | Z | E | R | R | I | E | Y | I | E |

Help America clean up. Circle all the words that have to do with ecology.

**Word Bank**

| | | | |
|---|---|---|---|
| decompose | fertilizer | biocontrol | recycling |
| conservation | pollution | sewage | biodegradable |
| erosion | hazardous waste | smoke | environment |
| ecology | thermal pollution | impurities | smog |

 

# Homonym Hullabaloo!

Name ______________________________

| R | D | E | E | C | L | C | N | V | A | H | I | D | U | D | S |
|---|---|---|---|---|---|---|---|---|---|---|---|---|---|---|---|
| E | Y | L | P | N | E | L | C | O | L | O | N | E | L | A | E |
| U | T | A | A | E | A | S | A | U | M | N | A | S | H | T | B |
| C | O | U | R | S | E | W | E | B | I | T | O | K | L | O | D |
| A | F | L | D | A | L | L | G | L | A | H | N | I | A | T | G |
| P | N | O | I | T | X | I | P | C | E | L | G | I | L | L | U |
| I | M | A | F | Y | N | E | T | K | O | A | D | A | G | N | E |
| T | B | I | R | T | H | L | I | L | S | E | R | I | A | L | S |
| A | R | S | N | Y | E | E | S | C | N | D | T | Y | I | O | T |
| L | E | A | N | O | N | C | P | L | E | T | I | O | F | R | K |
| R | W | S | E | L | R | O | T | A | C | K | Y | O | J | U | S |
| E | S | V | S | A | O | W | O | M | H | U | C | I | P | L | S |
| A | N | O | I | L | T | E | G | R | O | W | N | F | E | E | S |
| R | D | S | E | L | L | E | R | O | O | U | T | E | D | M | P |
| E | J | U | S | O | F | C | E | V | S | D | P | R | D | I | R |
| R | U | I | B | W | J | U | I | H | E | U | S | T | L | S | I |
| C | U | T | R | E | P | Q | R | W | I | H | B | U | E | R | S |
| O | N | E | I | D | H | C | M | A | N | N | E | R | D | N | L |
| N | T | F | L | O | U | R | H | R | O | H | R | O | M | O | E |
| U | Q | U | A | R | T | Z | C | V | I | F | R | B | O | F | P |
| S | A | T | W | H | U | S | J | T | B | P | Y | L | E | L | G |

Confused by homonyms? Don't be! Find the homonyms for the words in the Clue Bank and circle them in the puzzle.

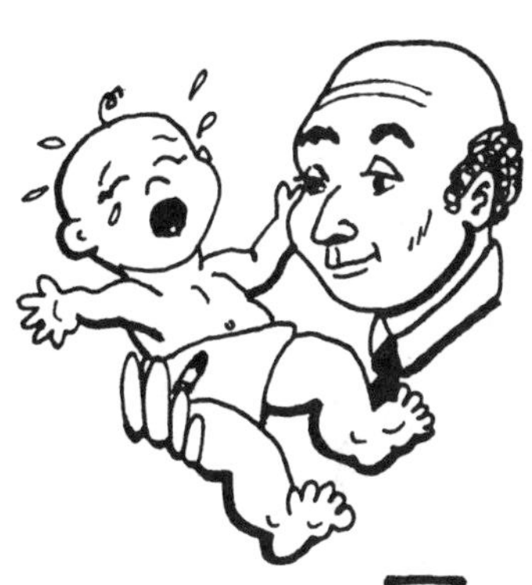

**Clue Bank**

aisle
sweet
flower
cellar
kernal

guessed
miner
bury
pedal
quarts

chews
peal
bawled
coarse
manor

groan
cereal
aloud
capitol
bruise
berth

 

# Blast Off!

Name ______________________

| P | T | A | O | P | O | E | S | R | T | B | M | A | E | C | K |
|---|---|---|---|---|---|---|---|---|---|---|---|---|---|---|---|
| F | P | H | I | U | N | E | U | T | R | O | N | S | T | A | R |
| R | U | J | Y | H | A | G | R | E | N | D | F | P | C | S | F |
| K | O | E | E | T | O | H | A | L | M | E | L | A | V | T | M |
| S | A | T | E | L | L | I | T | E | C | E | R | C | O | R | I |
| I | S | H | S | S | E | U | F | S | Y | I | U | E | R | O | E |
| L | T | O | M | T | Q | U | N | C | O | O | P | S | E | N | U |
| R | R | S | U | P | E | R | N | O | V | A | S | H | E | O | R |
| N | O | O | K | P | R | A | S | P | E | D | K | U | M | M | C |
| E | N | T | A | T | R | A | N | E | O | T | H | T | I | E | E |
| G | A | L | A | X | I | E | S | T | H | Y | E | T | A | R | O |
| U | U | N | I | V | E | R | S | E | W | I | D | L | A | N | W |
| P | T | N | C | H | I | S | B | L | E | R | H | E | H | O | H |
| S | P | A | C | E | P | R | O | B | E | W | B | T | N | E | I |
| N | T | R | U | A | E | Y | O | R | E | D | G | I | A | N | T |
| E | I | L | V | I | N | N | U | I | O | R | K | U | O | T | E |
| B | L | A | C | K | H | O | L | E | W | O | E | O | M | H | D |
| U | W | O | I | Y | E | V | T | R | A | C | T | D | E | T | W |
| L | M | O | X | Y | N | A | N | O | S | K | U | I | R | O | A |
| A | B | I | G | B | A | N | G | T | H | E | O | R | Y | N | R |
| S | L | E | C | Z | K | L | S | A | E | T | R | U | N | T | F |

Okay, all you future astronauts–blast through all of these letters and circle the 17 space words.

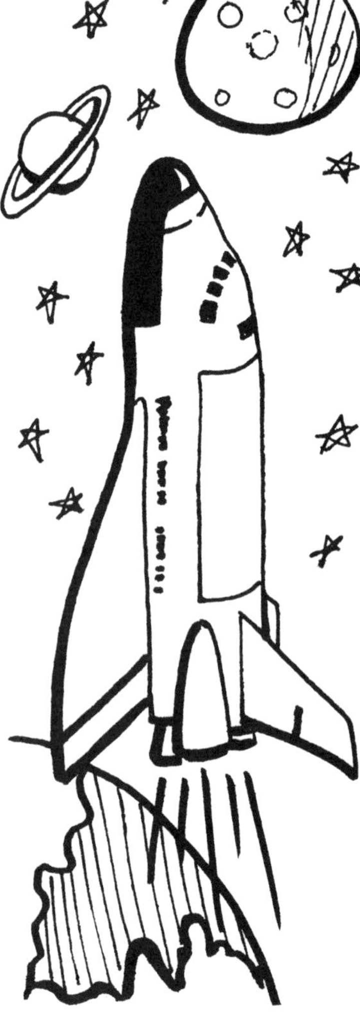

**Word Bank**

rocket
astronomer
satellite
space probe
astronaut
space shuttle
universe
galaxies
telescope
nebula
red giant
white dwarf
nova
supernova
neutron star
black hole
Big Bang Theory

Concept: Frequently misspelled words

# Spelling Gremlins

Name ___________________________

Don't let these spelling gremlins scare you. Learn how to spell them correctly. Then circle them in the puzzle.

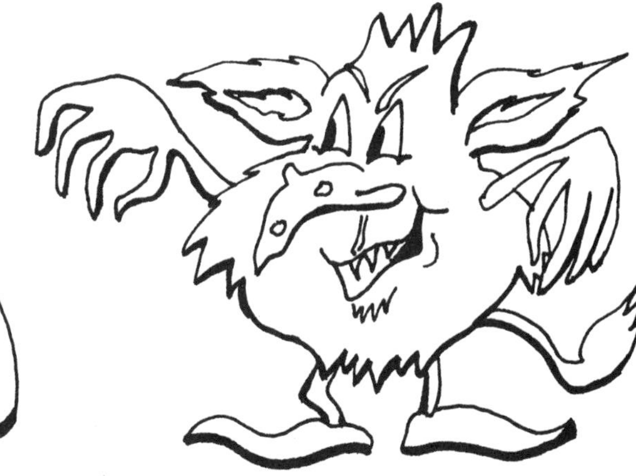

| A | R | T | N | A | T | L | E | U | H | S | A | S | W | R | T | C | I | B | R | E | K |
|---|---|---|---|---|---|---|---|---|---|---|---|---|---|---|---|---|---|---|---|---|---|
| W | B | O | O | K | K | E | E | P | E | R | N | G | E | T | F | O | R | E | I | G | N |
| B | T | A | N | A | X | Z | I | E | R | O | N | N | A | I | O | M | H | E | A | I | O |
| E | M | R | O | E | S | B | H | T | O | R | A | E | V | T | R | G | O | N | C | I | W |
| C | O | N | S | C | I | E | N | C | E | N | E | I | G | H | T | H | L | R | H | T | L |
| C | K | O | E | G | Y | E | T | A | S | B | R | M | E | A | Y | R | O | H | I | S | E |
| O | F | N | P | V | L | J | M | E | S | T | R | M | O | S | O | T | I | E | E | M | D |
| C | A | L | E | N | D | A | R | K | U | B | E | E | H | M | U | L | W | B | V | A | G |
| L | M | I | S | E | U | L | N | A | A | C | K | D | A | C | N | A | B | C | E | R | E |
| A | I | A | M | A | T | E | U | R | H | I | R | I | O | T | L | O | X | R | M | N | Y |
| D | L | J | R | V | E | B | L | T | U | C | J | A | L | T | H | V | I | N | E | G | R |
| A | I | O | H | C | T | K | R | U | T | L | O | T | T | H | E | E | S | A | N | D | E |
| E | A | L | Q | S | T | C | Y | M | E | C | E | E | Y | H | A | V | Y | A | T | V | R |
| T | R | G | A | T | S | I | E | L | R | C | O | L | O | N | E | L | R | S | H | B | U |
| M | R | E | R | O | S | A | C | W | A | L | B | Y | M | E | O | E | O | L | T | M | A |
| R | H | M | R | O | T | F | H | D | Y | A | I | T | W | H | U | M | O | R | O | U | S |

**Word Bank**

| | | | |
|---|---|---|---|
| achievement | immediately | colonel | breathe |
| forty | Arctic | amateur | conscience |
| bookkeeper | calendar | humorous | familiar |
| knowledge | eighth | foreign | heroes |

 

Skill: Irregular plurals

# Perplexing Plurals

Name ______________________

Listed in the Clue Bank are 18 simple singular nouns. Form them into plurals and find the plurals in the puzzle. Perplexed? Don't be!

| E | T | R | O | N | L | I | C | R | S | A | E | O | T | R | I |
|---|---|---|---|---|---|---|---|---|---|---|---|---|---|---|---|
| F | G | R | A | F | F | I | T | I | D | R | O | C | A | D | R |
| O | F | W | T | E | K | M | H | D | E | B | N | D | O | C | A |
| T | S | C | R | I | S | E | S | V | O | F | R | O | B | M | V |
| S | U | N | D | R | A | D | O | O | Z | M | N | R | Q | B | I |
| C | H | F | U | N | G | I | E | O | R | E | C | M | K | I | O |
| A | S | P | T | L | A | A | L | U | M | N | I | I | J | C | L |
| E | S | M | O | E | T | E | R | E | D | H | D | C | Y | X | I |
| A | R | O | I | N | M | H | Z | D | A | L | F | E | B | L | Z |
| C | T | N | R | C | U | I | O | S | I | I | E | V | N | W | B |
| A | L | G | A | E | S | Q | L | U | G | C | A | M | F | O | H |
| C | R | O | P | R | E | L | T | U | I | E | E | T | S | Q | R |
| T | L | O | N | I | C | A | R | C | M | X | Z | B | P | U | G |
| I | V | S | I | D | R | T | I | I | H | Y | O | A | S | E | S |
| E | B | E | C | L | A | R | V | A | E | Q | W | C | H | R | T |
| V | T | S | L | E | H | S | I | S | T | I | G | T | P | V | A |
| H | O | A | M | O | L | O | A | R | H | G | S | E | J | I | S |
| P | A | R | E | N | T | H | E | S | E | S | N | R | O | K | L |
| I | C | L | E | T | M | O | N | O | S | N | T | I | B | U | M |
| T | I | P | O | U | N | S | M | U | W | V | A | A | C | Q | A |
| S | R | W | Q | X | R | Y | T | Z | V | P | B | D | A | T | A |

**Clue Bank**

| | | | | |
|---|---|---|---|---|
| datum | alga | raviolo | mongoose | bacterium |
| fungus | die | alumnus | oasis | crisis |
| cactus | larva | louse | dormouse | |
| medium | trivium | parenthesis | graffito | |

 

Skill: Map terminology

# Mapping It Out

Name ____________________

| | | | | | | | | | | | | | | | |
|---|---|---|---|---|---|---|---|---|---|---|---|---|---|---|---|
| N | C | O | N | T | O | U | R | L | I | N | E | S | P | N | T |
| H | A | I | O | P | R | E | H | I | S | E | O | T | R | S | H |
| O | L | O | N | G | I | T | U | D | E | T | E | S | I | A | G |
| T | W | R | S | H | E | L | T | G | H | I | N | H | M | A | R |
| O | H | I | S | T | N | A | H | L | O | L | E | G | E | N | D |
| P | I | C | E | M | O | R | I | O | W | Y | K | T | M | D | E |
| O | D | C | R | P | H | E | O | B | A | T | R | S | E | W | F |
| G | E | O | G | R | A | P | H | E | R | O | I | A | R | O | O |
| R | O | N | A | N | I | A | Y | S | N | H | O | T | I | I | R |
| A | I | T | H | A | T | R | Y | C | U | O | M | O | D | E | L |
| P | O | I | B | O | L | A | T | I | T | U | D | E | I | Y | R |
| H | D | N | O | L | O | L | R | B | U | A | K | L | A | O | U |
| I | G | E | E | R | A | L | A | P | E | A | N | G | N | Y | G |
| C | T | N | T | O | M | E | R | I | D | I | A | N | O | N | E |
| M | L | T | E | C | A | L | T | I | T | U | D | E | I | S | E |
| A | H | U | A | R | N | S | D | L | C | N | O | Q | I | D | I |
| P | A | O | S | I | C | U | O | L | I | T | H | U | A | T | B |
| S | E | T | L | E | R | N | M | A | P | S | C | A | L | E | W |
| A | R | H | O | M | O | S | T | E | O | K | U | T | A | E | U |
| H | E | M | I | S | P | H | E | R | E | R | L | O | M | A | R |
| T | U | J | E | N | L | I | N | T | V | Y | O | R | T | R | A |

Give this one a spin. Circle 16 terms related to the study of maps.

**Word Bank**

latitude
longitude
meridian
hemisphere
globes
legend
map scale
equator
altitude
model
continent
parallels
topographic maps
contour lines
prime meridian
geographer

Skill: Greek alphabet

# It's Greek to Me!

Name ______________________

| I | N | G | E | X | D | S | O | I | A | T | I | S | V | A | Y |
|---|---|---|---|---|---|---|---|---|---|---|---|---|---|---|---|
| H | A | L | P | H | A | O | E | T | H | C | O | V | U | H | S |
| H | I | T | S | A | E | T | N | S | L | A | M | B | D | A | U |
| S | I | L | I | N | Y | H | I | V | U | N | E | Q | R | J | P |
| F | O | U | L | G | R | E | E | V | O | H | G | Z | E | V | S |
| Y | R | I | O | T | A | E | R | P | I | Y | A | T | M | I | I |
| M | O | T | N | A | M | I | L | U | M | D | R | O | Z | R | L |
| E | M | E | V | L | Z | A | T | A | U | X | B | R | O | Q | O |
| R | H | O | R | M | T | O | L | S | I | Z | E | T | A | V | N |
| T | C | H | I | L | E | W | M | J | T | C | T | N | P | O | I |
| O | R | Z | M | R | E | V | K | I | A | S | A | Q | U | R | N |
| S | F | K | J | O | T | U | Q | K | C | P | O | W | M | S | O |
| K | G | A | M | M | A | R | O | P | R | R | N | R | I | E | I |
| A | N | P | R | E | S | M | V | U | L | O | O | U | L | M | V |
| T | H | P | U | M | X | I | R | P | S | I | R | N | A | U | B |
| S | T | A | R | W | H | O | D | Z | E | I | L | T | B | L | E |
| K | L | M | O | Y | Z | T | H | E | T | A | J | L | I | A | X |
| J | I | H | M | Z | H | E | Z | T | L | M | E | P | H | I | W |
| F | N | G | K | V | Z | O | T | O | L | T | V | E | N | O | T |
| E | P | D | S | I | G | M | A | O | M | N | A | U | Q | N | H |
| A | L | C | R | J | E | G | K | L | U | B | R | E | A | V | A |

The Greeks had their own alphabet. Circle the 24 Greek letters in the puzzle.

**Word Bank**

| | | | | | |
|---|---|---|---|---|---|
| Alpha | Eta | Nu | Tau | Epsilon | Zeta |
| Beta | Theta | Xi | Upsilon | Lambda | Mu |
| Gamma | Iota | Omicron | Phi | Rho | Sigma |
| Delta | Kappa | Pi | Chi | Psi | Omega |

# Answer Key

**SINK YOUR TEETH INTO THESE!**

Name ______________

Use words from the Word Bank to finish the riddle. Then use the same words to complete the puzzle.

**Question**

Why are 1→ VAMPIRES not very 4→ POPULAR?

**Answer**

2→ BECAUSE they are a 3→ PAIN in the 5→ NECK.

Page 1

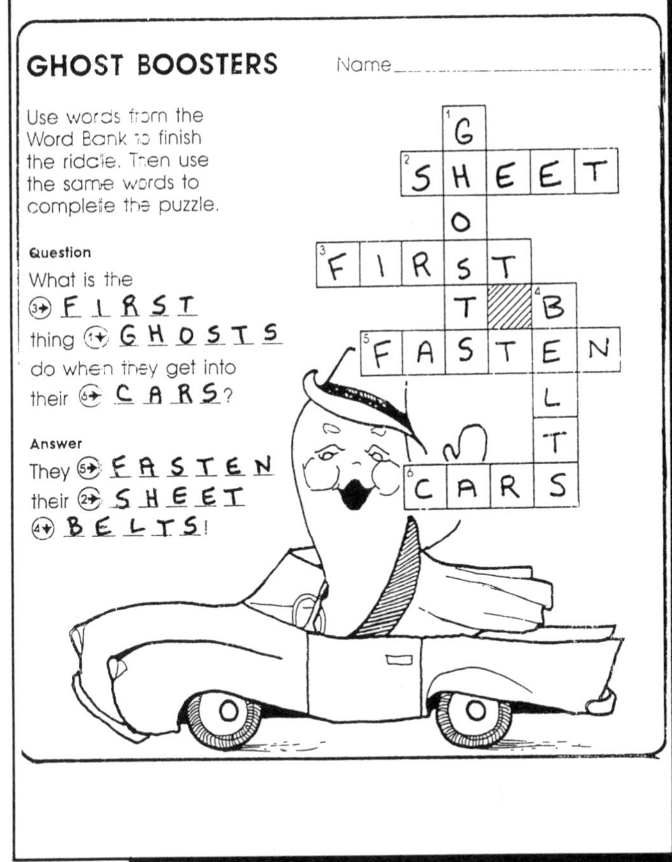

**GHOST BOOSTERS**

Name ______________

Use words from the Word Bank to finish the riddle. Then use the same words to complete the puzzle.

**Question**

What is the 3→ FIRST thing 1→ GHOSTS do when they get into their 6→ CARS?

**Answer**

They 5→ FASTEN their 2→ SHEET 4→ BELTS!

Page 2

**PILGRIM'S PRIDE**

Name ______________

Use words from the Word Bank to finish the riddle. Then use the same words to complete the puzzle.

**Question**

What 1→ DANCE did the 4→ PILGRIMS do when they came to 2→ AMERICA?

**Answer**

The 3→ PLYMOUTH 5→ ROCK!

Page 3

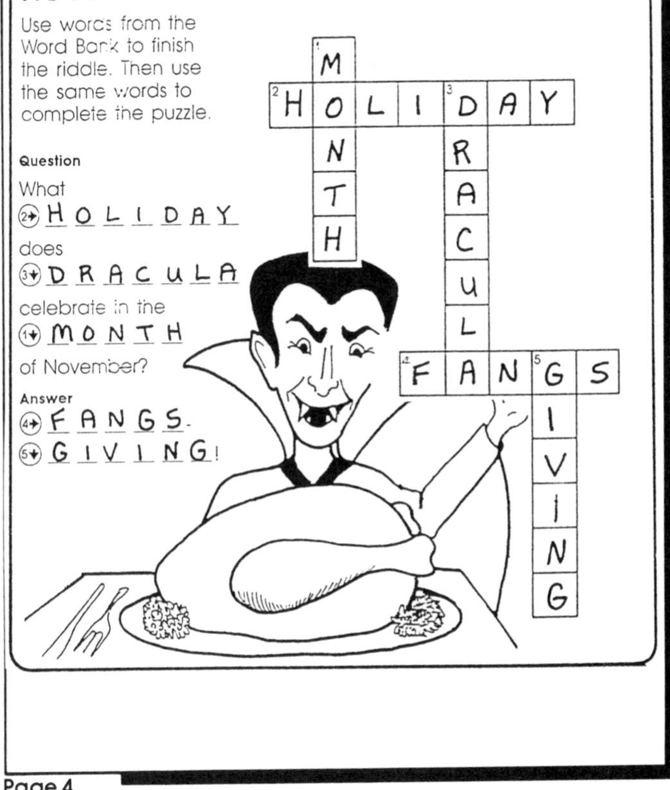

**REMEMBER NOVEMBER**

Name ______________

Use words from the Word Bank to finish the riddle. Then use the same words to complete the puzzle.

**Question**

What 2→ HOLIDAY does 3→ DRACULA celebrate in the 1→ MONTH of November?

**Answer**

4→ FANGS. 5→ GIVING!

Page 4

# Answer Key

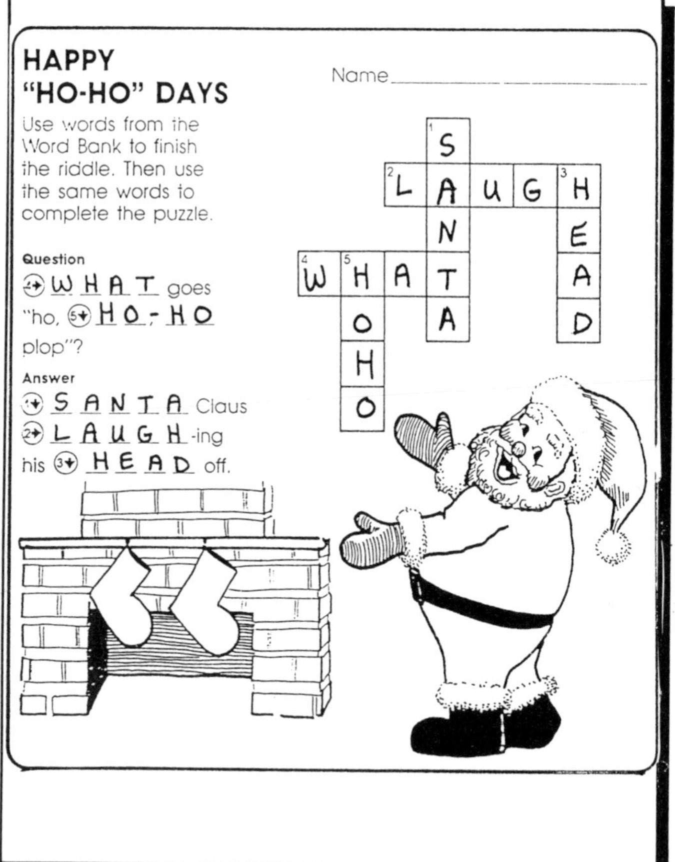

**HAPPY "HO-HO" DAYS**

Name________________________

Use words from the Word Bank to finish the riddle. Then use the same words to complete the puzzle.

**Question**

(4→) WHAT goes "ho, (5→) HO-HO plop"?

**Answer**

(1→) SANTA Claus (2→) LAUGH-ing his (3→) HEAD off.

Page 5

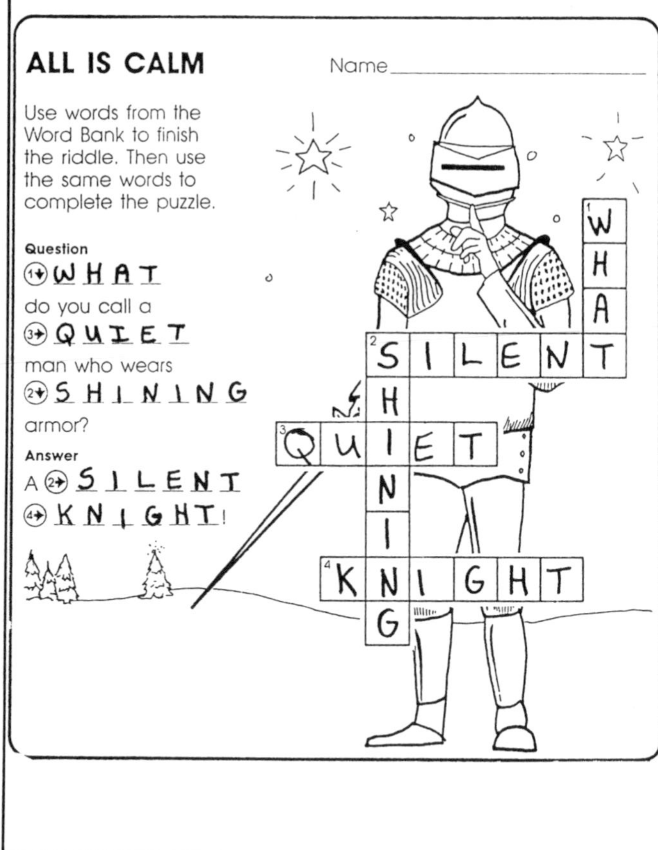

**ALL IS CALM**

Name________________________

Use words from the Word Bank to finish the riddle. Then use the same words to complete the puzzle.

**Question**

(1→) WHAT do you call a (3→) QUIET man who wears (2→) SHINING armor?

**Answer**

A (2→) SILENT (4→) KNIGHT!

Page 6

**HEART THROBS**

Name________________________

Use words from the Word Bank to finish the riddle. Then use the same words to complete the puzzle.

**Question**

What kind of (1→) DOCTORS are (5→) BORN in the (3→) MONTH of February?

**Answer**

(4→) HEART (2→) SPECIAL-ists!

Page 7

**"EGGS"-PERTS**

Name________________________

Use words from the Word Bank to finish the riddle. Then use the same words to complete the puzzle.

**Question**

Why did the (3→) RABBIT keeper's (5→) WIFE wear a (1→) WIG?

**Answer**

She had too (4→) MANY (2→) GRAY hares!

Page 8

# Answer Key

## "TREE"-MENDOUS ARBOR DAY

Name ____________

Use words from the Word Bank to finish the riddle. Then use the same words to complete the puzzle.

**Question**

What is (4→) GREEN and (2→) PECKS on (1↓) TREES on (3↓) ARBOR Day?

**Answer**

Woody Wood (2↓) PICKLE.



Page 9

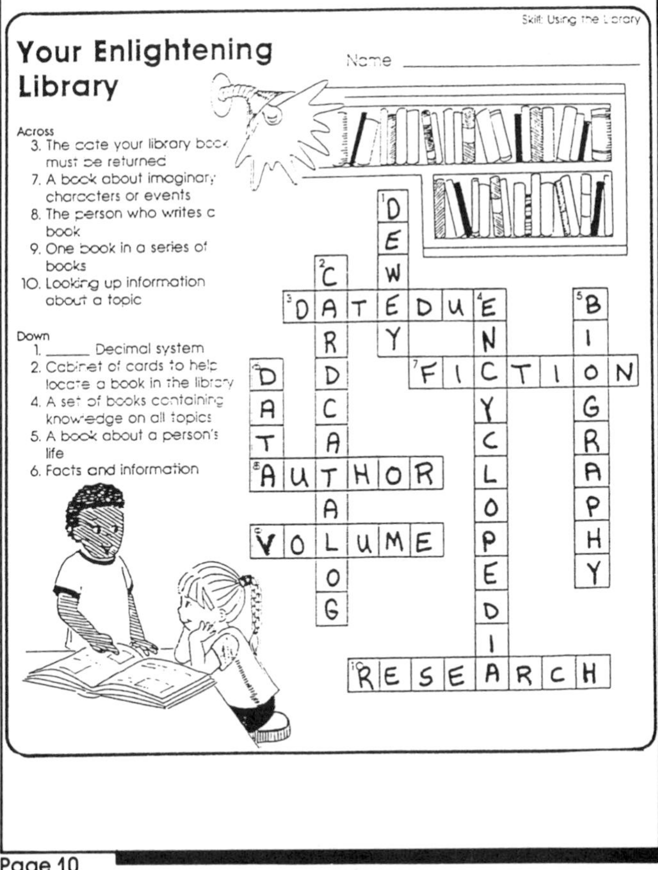

## Your Enlightening Library

Skill: Using the Library

Name ____________

Across
3. The date your library book must be returned
7. A book about imaginary characters or events
8. The person who writes a book
9. One book in a series of books
10. Looking up information about a topic

Down
1. ______ Decimal system
2. Cabinet of cards to help locate a book in the library
4. A set of books containing knowledge on all topics
5. A book about a person's life
6. Facts and information



Page 10

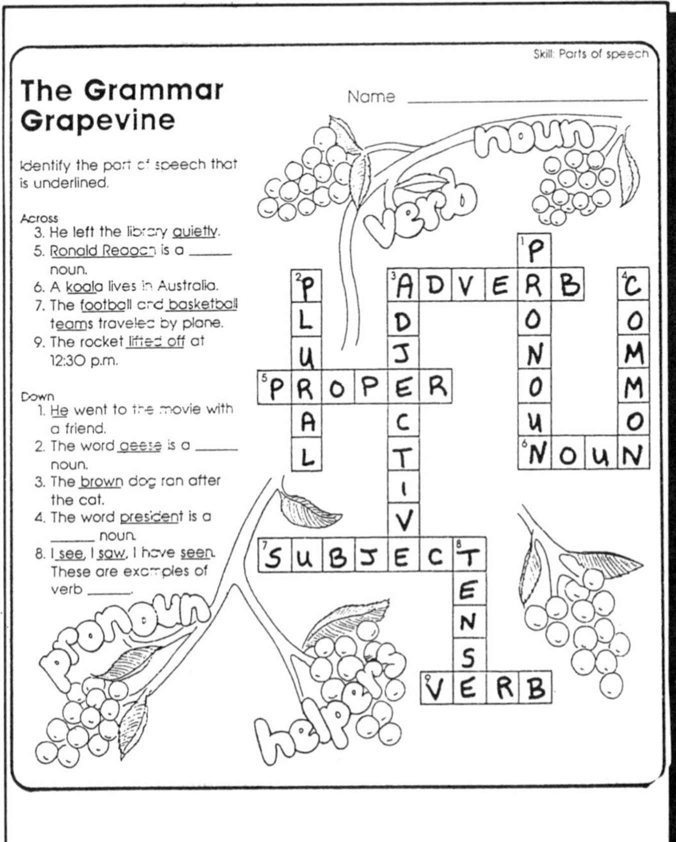

## The Grammar Grapevine

Skill: Parts of speech

Name ____________

Identify the part of speech that is underlined.

Across
3. He left the library quietly.
5. Ronald Reagan is a ______ noun.
6. A koala lives in Australia.
7. The football and basketball teams traveled by plane.
9. The rocket lifted off at 12:30 p.m.

Down
1. He went to the movie with a friend.
2. The word geese is a ______ noun.
3. The brown dog ran after the cat.
4. The word president is a ______ noun.
8. I see, I saw, I have seen. These are examples of verb ______.



Page 11

## Fighting Disease

Concept: Communicable diseases

Name ____________

Across
1. Washing your hands with ______ and water helps prevent the spread of diseases.
4. Microscopic organisms that can cause disease
7. Microscopic organisms that can cause disease – includes bacteria
8. A liquid used to prevent or cure a disease
9. A disease that many of us catch – it causes headache, vomiting, and diarrhea.
11. A follow-up dose of a vaccine

Down
2. ______ is the key to good health.
3. Substance that is given to the body to produce immunity to a disease
5. When a disease is spread by contact between two people
6. When your body cannot catch a certain disease, you are ______.
10. A viral disease which causes a stuffed-up nose is the common ______.

SOAP
PREVENTION
VACCINE
BACTERIA
CONTAGIOUS
IMMUNE
GERMS
SERUM
FLU
COLD
BOOSTER

germs virus disease

Page 12

# Answer Key

Skill: Understanding maps

## Map Mania

Name ______________________

Across
3. North America, Asia, and Australia are examples of this land form.
5. The distance north and south of the Equator
7. The earth's shape
9. An imaginary line that divides the earth's surface into the Northern and Southern Hemispheres

Down
1. Lines east and west of the Prime Meridian
2. An imaginary, straight line on which the earth rotates
4. Half of the earth
5. A key (or description) accompanying a map
6. The distance above sea level
8. The most accurate model of the earth



Page 13

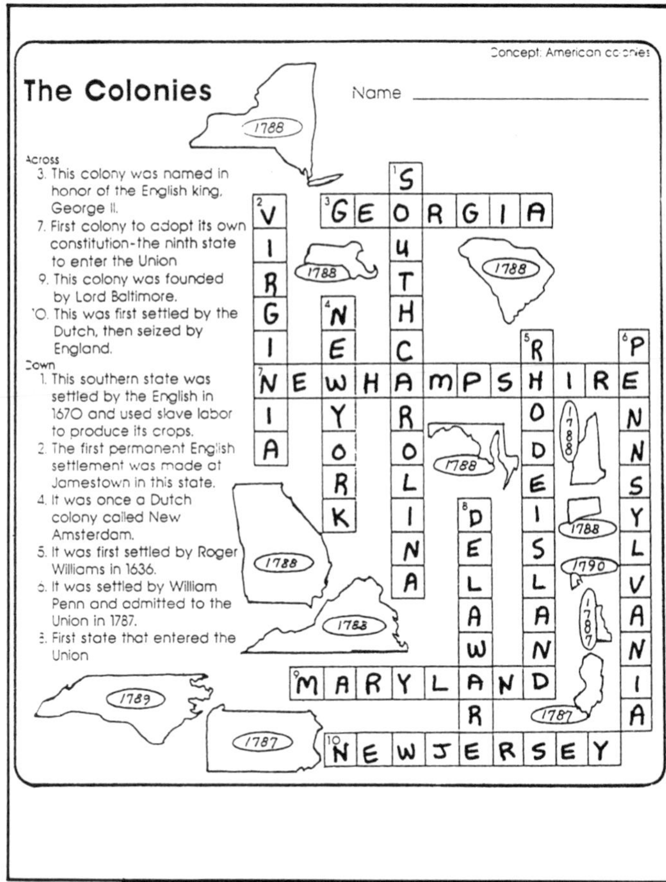

Concept: American colonies

## The Colonies

Name ______________________

Across
3. This colony was named in honor of the English king, George II.
7. First colony to adopt its own constitution-the ninth state to enter the Union
9. This colony was founded by Lord Baltimore.
10. This was first settled by the Dutch, then seized by England.

Down
1. This southern state was settled by the English in 1670 and used slave labor to produce its crops.
2. The first permanent English settlement was made at Jamestown in this state.
4. It was once a Dutch colony called New Amsterdam.
5. It was first settled by Roger Williams in 1636.
6. It was settled by William Penn and admitted to the Union in 1787.
8. First state that entered the Union



Page 14

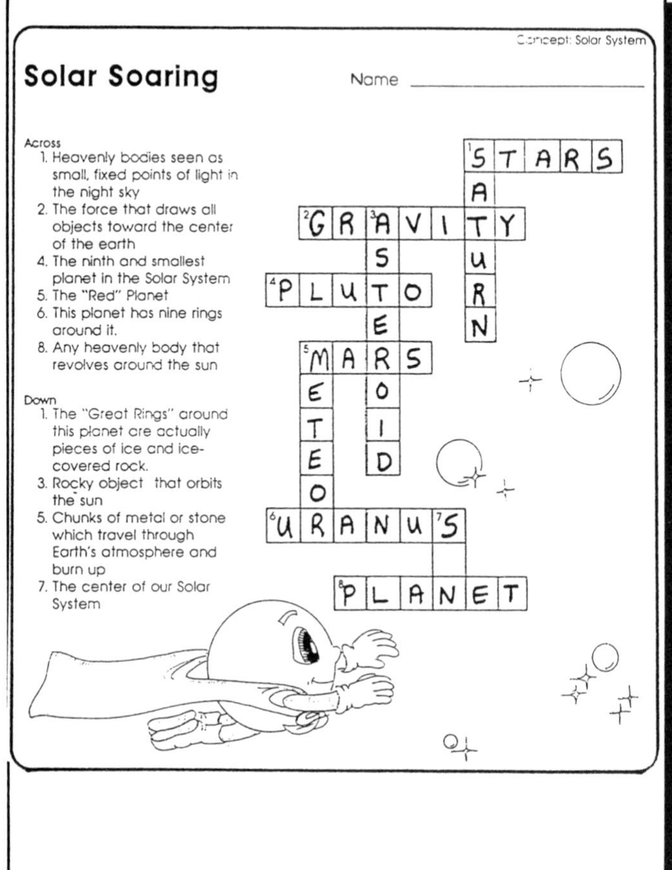

Concept: Solar System

## Solar Soaring

Name ______________________

Across
1. Heavenly bodies seen as small, fixed points of light in the night sky
2. The force that draws all objects toward the center of the earth
4. The ninth and smallest planet in the Solar System
5. The "Red" Planet
6. This planet has nine rings around it.
8. Any heavenly body that revolves around the sun

Down
1. The "Great Rings" around this planet are actually pieces of ice and ice-covered rock.
3. Rocky object that orbits the sun
5. Chunks of metal or stone which travel through Earth's atmosphere and burn up
7. The center of our Solar System



Page 15

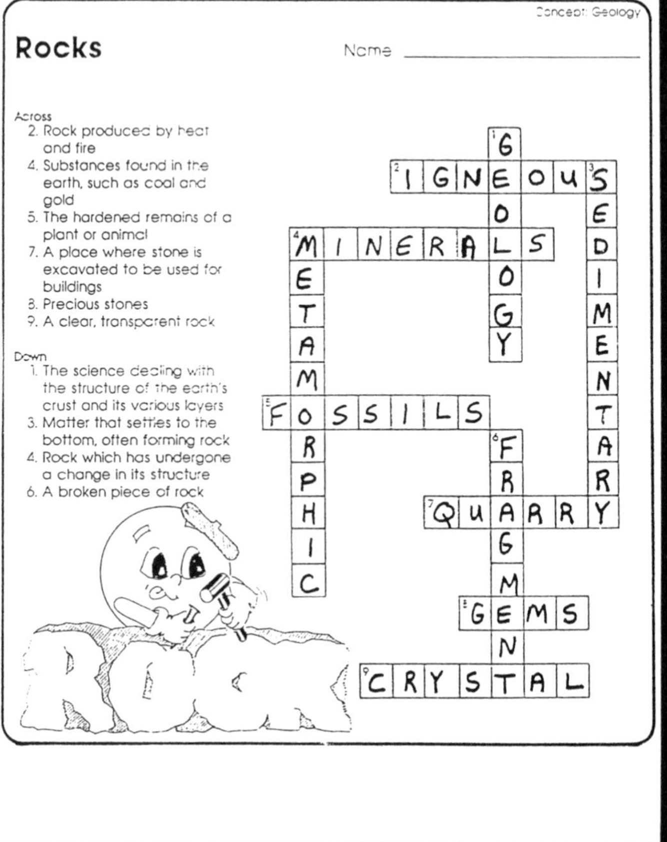

Concept: Geology

## Rocks

Name ______________________

Across
2. Rock produced by heat and fire
4. Substances found in the earth, such as coal and gold
5. The hardened remains of a plant or animal
7. A place where stone is excavated to be used for buildings
8. Precious stones
9. A clear, transparent rock

Down
1. The science dealing with the structure of the earth's crust and its various layers
3. Matter that settles to the bottom, often forming rock
4. Rock which has undergone a change in its structure
6. A broken piece of rock



Page 16

 

# Answer Key

Skill: Geometry terms

## Circles and Squares

Name ____________________

Across
2. When 2 halves of a shape are exactly the same, they are said to have ________.
6. The shape made by two straight lines meeting in a point
7. A shape having four equal sides and four right angles
9. Something which has a definite position in space, but no size or shape
10. The outside surface of a figure

Down
1. Part of a line with one end point
3. A three-sided figure
4. A part of a line with two end points
5. The sum of the length of all the sides of a figure
8. A straight line passing through the center of a circle

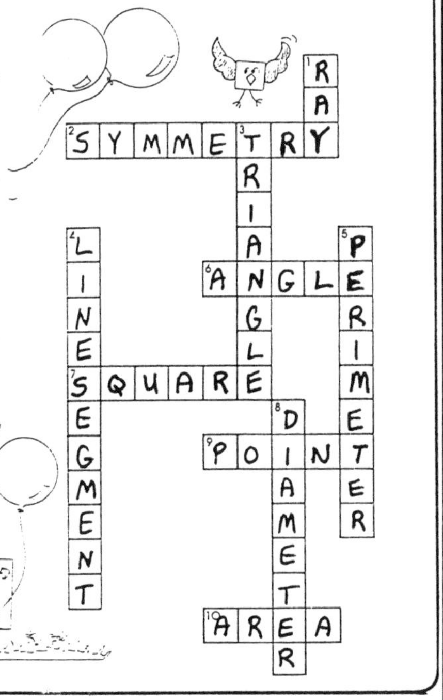

Page 17

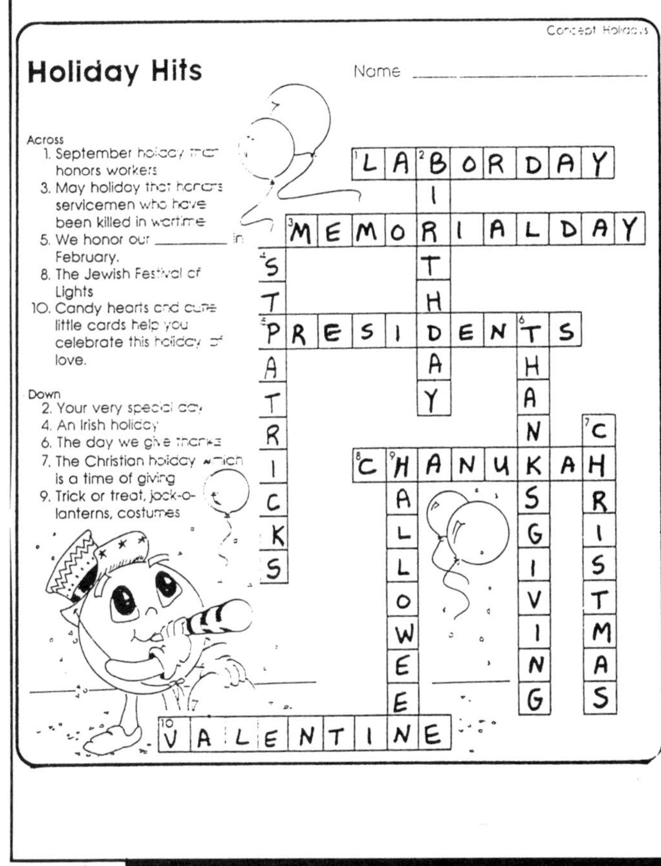

Concept: Holidays

## Holiday Hits

Name ____________________

Across
1. September holiday that honors workers
3. May holiday that honors servicemen who have been killed in wartime
5. We honor our ________ in February.
8. The Jewish Festival of Lights
10. Candy hearts and cute little cards help you celebrate this holiday of love.

Down
2. Your very special day
4. An Irish holiday
6. The day we give thanks
7. The Christian holiday which is a time of giving
9. Trick or treat, jack-o-lanterns, costumes

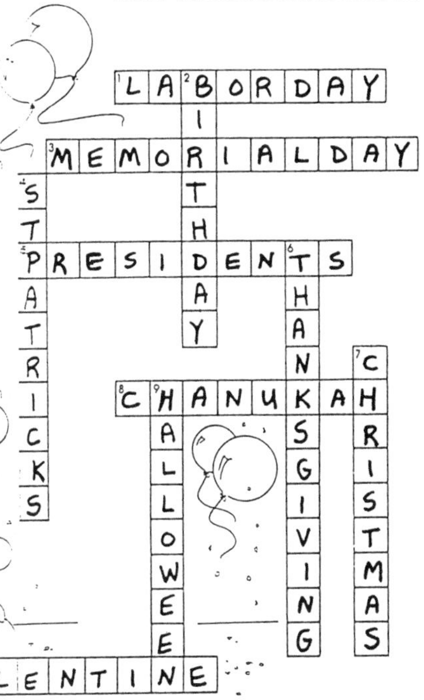

Page 18

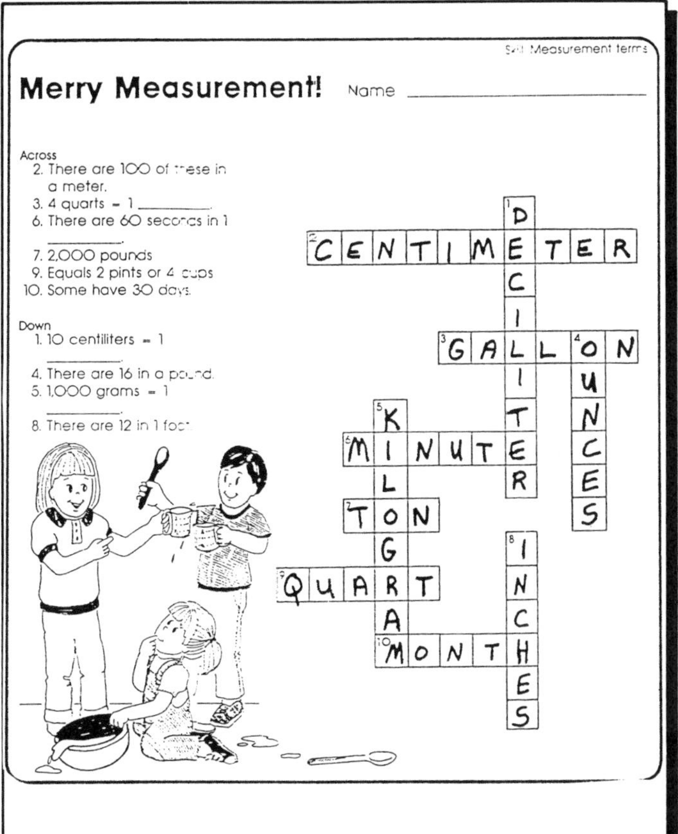

Skill: Measurement terms

## Merry Measurement!

Name ____________________

Across
2. There are 100 of these in a meter.
3. 4 quarts = 1 ________
6. There are 60 seconds in 1 ________.
7. 2,000 pounds
9. Equals 2 pints or 4 cups
10. Some have 30 days.

Down
1. 10 centiliters = 1 ________
4. There are 16 in a pound.
5. 1,000 grams = 1 ________
8. There are 12 in 1 foot

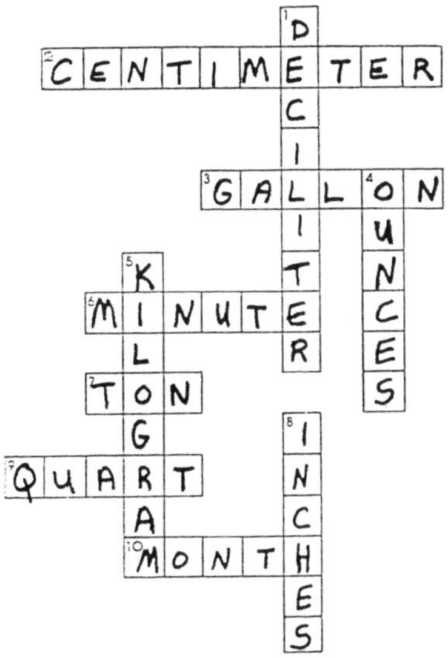

Page 19

Skill: Library terms

## Librarians Go By the Book!

Name ____________________

| | | | | | | | | | | | | | | | |
|---|---|---|---|---|---|---|---|---|---|---|---|---|---|---|---|
| K | L | O | I | S | B | O | A | L | R | E | M | E | D | I | A |
| A | D | R | A | N | W | I | K | S | R | L | B | B | O | E | U |
| P | E | N | C | Y | C | L | O | P | E | D | I | A | L | S | T |
| E | W | O | L | I | F | G | N | A | F | M | O | E | F | R | H |
| R | E | S | E | A | R | C | H | K | E | S | G | W | I | B | O |
| I | Y | D | K | C | A | L | I | N | R | W | R | E | C | N | R |
| O | D | L | P | O | S | I | H | A | E | Z | A | U | T | I | M |
| D | E | T | A | M | G | E | O | Y | N | L | P | B | I | L | O |
| I | C | F | U | R | E | T | N | I | C | L | H | M | O | L | I |
| C | I | Z | C | O | N | W | A | B | E | Z | Y | X | N | U | A |
| A | M | R | O | A | M | R | K | L | D | N | S | T | E | S | R |
| L | A | U | T | O | B | I | O | G | R | A | P | H | Y | T | M |
| S | L | O | Y | N | U | S | L | T | E | K | A | C | O | R | I |
| N | O | N | F | I | C | T | I | O | N | Y | F | W | B | A | L |
| I | L | Y | A | S | O | R | H | L | M | A | O | G | R | T | B |
| D | A | T | E | D | U | E | W | E | T | D | R | S | E | O | N |
| M | H | I | C | A | E | B | F | O | L | G | Y | A | F | R | W |
| S | T | U | V | O | L | U | M | E | S | O | I | G | L | E | C |
| R | S | Y | E | L | W | O | D | O | R | E | S | D | T | A | S |
| D | C | A | R | D | C | A | T | A | L | O | G | U | E | O | T |

Sh...You won't need the card catalogue to find these library words. Identify each word.

Page 20

# Answer Key

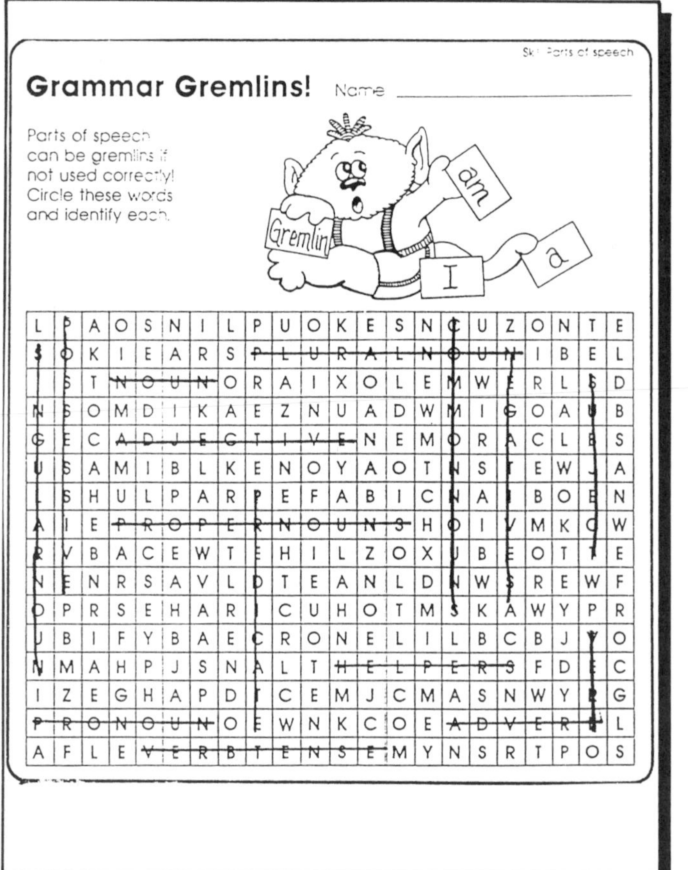

Skill: Parts of speech

## Grammar Gremlins!

Name ____________________

Parts of speech can be gremlins if not used correctly! Circle these words and identify each.



| L | P | A | O | S | N | I | L | P | U | O | K | E | S | N | C | U | Z | O | N | T | E |
|---|---|---|---|---|---|---|---|---|---|---|---|---|---|---|---|---|---|---|---|---|---|
| S | O | K | I | E | A | R | S | P | L | U | R | A | L | N | O | U | N | I | B | E | L |
| I | S | T | N | O | U | N | O | R | A | I | X | O | L | E | M | W | E | R | L | S | D |
| N | S | O | M | D | I | K | A | E | Z | N | U | A | D | W | M | I | G | O | A | U | B |
| G | E | C | A | D | J | E | C | T | I | V | E | N | E | M | O | R | A | C | L | B | S |
| U | S | A | M | I | B | L | K | E | N | O | Y | A | O | T | N | S | T | E | W | J | A |
| L | S | H | U | L | P | A | R | P | E | F | A | B | I | C | N | A | I | B | O | E | N |
| A | I | E | P | R | O | P | E | R | N | O | U | N | S | H | O | I | V | M | K | C | W |
| R | V | B | A | C | E | W | T | E | H | I | L | Z | O | X | U | B | E | O | T | T | E |
| N | E | N | R | S | A | V | L | D | T | E | A | N | L | D | N | W | S | R | E | W | F |
| O | P | R | S | E | H | A | R | I | C | U | H | O | T | M | S | K | A | W | Y | P | R |
| U | B | I | F | Y | B | A | E | C | R | O | N | E | L | I | L | B | C | B | J | Y | O |
| N | M | A | H | P | J | S | N | A | L | T | H | E | L | P | E | R | S | F | D | E | C |
| I | Z | E | G | H | A | P | D | T | C | E | M | J | C | M | A | S | N | W | Y | R | G |
| P | R | O | N | O | U | N | O | E | W | N | K | C | O | E | A | D | V | E | R | B | L |
| A | F | L | E | V | E | R | B | T | E | N | S | E | M | Y | N | S | R | T | P | O | S |

Page 21

Concept: Communicable diseases

## It's Catching!

Name ____________________

"Catch" these communicable disease words and look up their meanings.

| L | D | S | E | V | I | A | D | V | U | C | M | U | N | I | M |
|---|---|---|---|---|---|---|---|---|---|---|---|---|---|---|---|
| A | B | T | E | H | C | N | O | I | P | K | P | E | L | M | O |
| V | A | C | C | I | N | E | K | R | S | I | R | N | F | I | F |
| O | C | H | O | V | B | I | S | U | E | A | E | L | N | C | K |
| S | T | R | M | T | A | L | O | S | L | E | V | H | S | R | E |
| B | E | U | M | R | X | E | N | F | I | Y | E | T | I | O | F |
| N | R | S | U | O | G | E | R | M | S | T | N | E | L | B | N |
| I | I | G | N | H | B | A | S | I | R | O | T | A | S | E | A |
| P | A | O | I | D | I | N | F | L | U | R | I | G | L | S | V |
| R | S | A | C | O | C | C | E | D | B | O | O | S | T | E | R |
| O | A | P | A | E | L | H | K | W | I | L | N | E | M | O | H |
| T | I | N | B | L | E | I | I | S | G | I | B | R | I | A | E |
| O | Y | S | L | O | M | C | C | E | B | D | O | N | M | G | B |
| Z | A | O | E | H | S | K | U | G | R | I | Y | K | M | S | O |
| O | B | E | O | L | I | E | N | T | O | S | V | A | U | L | L |
| A | I | V | S | Y | C | N | D | E | R | E | Y | O | N | G | Y |
| N | S | R | A | L | B | P | C | L | T | A | S | E | I | R | M |
| S | A | N | T | I | B | O | D | Y | O | S | L | M | T | O | L |
| P | I | L | O | H | N | K | E | K | L | E | N | I | Y | V | S |
| C | O | M | M | O | N | C | O | L | D | S | D | A | V | S | I |

Page 22

Skill: Map skills

## Map Maze

Name ____________________

| W | H | R | O | T | A | T | I | O | N | I | H | T | D | Y | R |
|---|---|---|---|---|---|---|---|---|---|---|---|---|---|---|---|
| N | A | D | L | O | E | Y | W | H | A | R | M | N | E | O | L |
| H | L | A | D | O | N | A | U | E | Q | U | A | T | O | R | K |
| Y | H | O | E | M | T | R | U | M | Y | E | E | A | T | W | T |
| A | R | E | V | O | L | U | T | I | O | N | A | L | S | R | O |
| T | W | Y | I | C | C | D | E | S | T | A | L | L | E | N | P |
| T | L | Y | O | E | G | A | S | P | H | E | R | E | F | O | O |
| C | O | M | P | A | S | S | R | H | T | C | B | E | V | R | G |
| H | S | O | N | N | L | T | B | E | S | O | R | H | I | T | R |
| Y | A | O | T | V | L | A | U | R | S | N | N | G | I | H | A |
| I | L | A | T | I | T | U | D | E | I | T | O | E | M | P | P |
| P | O | L | E | O | A | O | R | H | N | I | F | R | L | O | H |
| O | N | U | R | E | I | L | E | G | E | N | D | N | E | L | Y |
| N | G | L | O | B | E | M | Y | A | O | E | A | S | L | E | N |
| U | I | U | N | R | L | O | A | C | R | N | P | C | R | T | H |
| G | T | G | V | A | W | D | Y | T | S | T | M | A | E | T | A |
| S | U | S | O | U | T | H | P | O | L | E | N | L | X | A | B |
| A | D | H | A | R | D | R | W | S | I | T | I | E | G | I | N |
| F | E | L | E | V | A | T | I | O | N | C | O | L | T | E | S |
| T | I | G | R | E | A | T | C | I | R | C | L | E | I | R | H |

Work your way through this maze of map study words.

X = treasure directions:

1.
2.
3.
4.

Page 23

Concept: American colonies

## 13 Strong

Name ____________________

| P | I | E | T | T | L | S | L | I | E | L | N | O | I | P | S |
|---|---|---|---|---|---|---|---|---|---|---|---|---|---|---|---|
| I | L | I | N | E | W | H | A | M | P | S | H | I | R | E | R |
| S | J | M | S | P | S | Y | E | E | O | D | A | T | N | N | T |
| O | O | A | A | N | I | G | T | T | R | L | E | T | R | N | E |
| U | I | R | I | S | D | I | S | A | D | P | N | S | A | S | M |
| T | S | Y | T | E | E | N | A | N | G | S | D | S | H | Y | C |
| H | N | L | N | C | L | N | O | S | D | N | R | F | M | L | A |
| C | M | A | S | S | A | C | H | U | S | E | T | T | S | V | O |
| A | T | N | R | K | W | I | Y | T | N | W | H | E | C | A | S |
| R | G | D | G | R | A | J | N | Y | N | J | C | O | E | N | R |
| O | R | L | A | W | R | D | R | V | I | E | A | H | R | I | H |
| L | H | O | A | R | E | U | G | I | U | R | R | E | F | A | D |
| I | E | S | M | P | N | L | O | R | H | S | O | T | A | S | O |
| N | E | W | Y | O | R | K | A | G | H | E | L | T | W | A | F |
| A | F | B | G | E | O | R | G | I | A | Y | I | O | E | R | U |
| C | B | S | S | Y | C | L | T | N | T | R | N | H | N | L | O |
| Y | L | M | R | H | O | D | E | I | S | L | A | N | D | M | S |
| W | O | E | S | E | M | L | M | A | E | B | R | L | Y | E | W |
| C | O | N | N | E | C | T | I | C | U | T | S | I | A | H | E |
| C | A | O | Y | F | A | Y | S | O | N | E | Y | C | S | S | E |

You've got to start somewhere and that's what the United States did. Locate the thirteen original colonies in this puzzle.

Page 24

 

# Answer Key

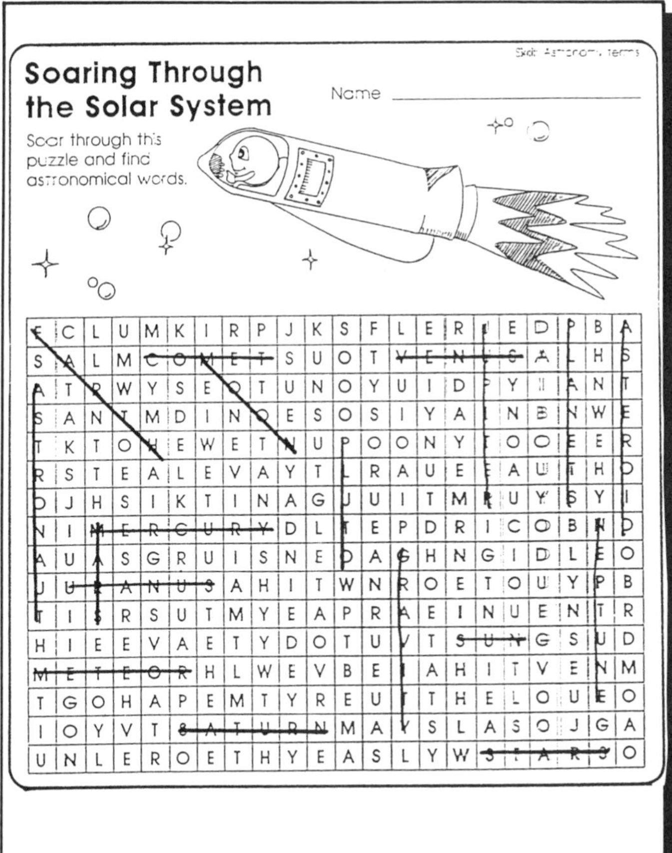

Skill: Astronomy terms

## Soaring Through the Solar System

Name ____________________

Soar through this puzzle and find astronomical words.

| F | C | L | U | M | K | I | R | P | J | K | S | F | L | E | R | J | E | D | P | B | A |
|---|---|---|---|---|---|---|---|---|---|---|---|---|---|---|---|---|---|---|---|---|---|
| S | A | L | M | C | O | M | E | T | S | U | O | T | V | E | N | U | S | A | L | H | S |
| A | T | R | W | Y | S | E | O | T | U | N | O | Y | U | I | D | P | Y | I | A | N | T |
| S | A | N | T | M | D | I | N | O | E | S | O | S | I | Y | A | I | N | B | N | W | E |
| T | K | T | O | H | E | W | E | T | N | U | P | O | O | N | Y | T | O | O | E | E | R |
| R | S | T | E | A | L | E | V | A | Y | T | L | R | A | U | E | E | A | U | T | H | O |
| O | J | H | S | I | K | T | I | N | A | G | U | U | I | T | M | R | U | Y | S | Y | I |
| N | I | M | E | R | C | U | R | Y | D | L | T | E | P | D | R | I | C | O | B | N | D |
| A | U | A | S | G | R | U | I | S | N | E | O | A | G | H | N | G | I | D | L | E | O |
| U | U | R | A | N | U | S | A | H | I | T | W | N | R | O | E | T | O | U | Y | P | B |
| T | I | S | R | S | U | T | M | Y | E | A | P | R | A | E | I | N | U | E | N | T | R |
| H | I | E | E | V | A | E | T | Y | D | O | T | U | V | T | S | U | N | G | S | U | D |
| M | E | T | E | O | R | H | L | W | E | V | B | E | I | A | H | I | T | V | E | N | M |
| T | G | O | H | A | P | E | M | T | Y | R | E | U | T | T | H | E | L | O | U | E | O |
| I | O | Y | V | T | S | A | T | U | R | N | M | A | Y | S | L | A | S | O | J | G | A |
| U | N | L | E | R | O | E | T | H | Y | E | A | S | L | Y | W | S | T | A | R | S | O |

Page 25

Skill: Geology terms

## Rock Hounds!

Name ____________________

This rock and mineral word search is a "gem." Dig out the words and be ready to define them. Look up the names of some rocks and minerals.

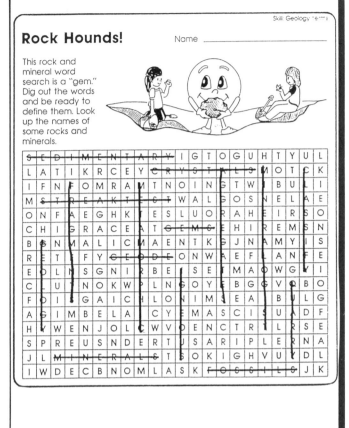

| S | E | D | I | M | E | N | T | A | R | Y | I | G | T | O | G | U | H | T | Y | U | L |
|---|---|---|---|---|---|---|---|---|---|---|---|---|---|---|---|---|---|---|---|---|---|
| L | A | T | I | K | R | C | E | Y | C | R | Y | S | T | A | L | S | M | O | T | C | K |
| I | F | N | F | O | M | R | A | M | T | N | O | I | N | G | T | W | I | B | U | L | I |
| M | S | T | R | E | A | K | T | E | S | T | W | A | L | G | O | S | N | E | L | A | E |
| O | N | F | A | E | G | H | K | T | E | S | L | U | O | R | A | H | E | I | R | S | O |
| C | H | I | G | R | A | C | E | A | T | G | E | M | S | E | H | I | R | E | M | S | N |
| B | G | N | M | A | L | I | C | M | A | E | N | T | K | G | J | N | A | M | Y | I | S |
| R | E | T | E | F | Y | G | E | O | D | E | O | N | W | A | E | F | L | A | N | F | E |
| E | O | L | N | S | G | N | I | R | B | E | I | S | E | T | M | A | O | W | G | Y | I |
| C | L | U | T | N | O | K | W | P | L | N | G | O | Y | E | B | G | G | V | Q | B | O |
| F | O | I | S | G | A | I | C | H | L | O | N | I | M | S | E | A | I | B | U | L | G |
| A | G | I | M | B | E | L | A | I | C | Y | E | M | A | S | C | I | S | U | A | D | F |
| H | Y | W | E | N | J | O | L | C | W | V | O | E | N | C | T | R | T | L | R | S | E |
| S | P | R | E | U | S | N | D | E | R | T | U | S | A | R | I | P | L | E | R | N | A |
| J | L | M | I | N | E | R | A | L | S | T | S | O | K | I | G | H | V | U | Y | D | L |
| I | W | D | E | C | B | N | O | M | L | A | S | K | F | O | S | S | I | L | S | J | K |

Page 26

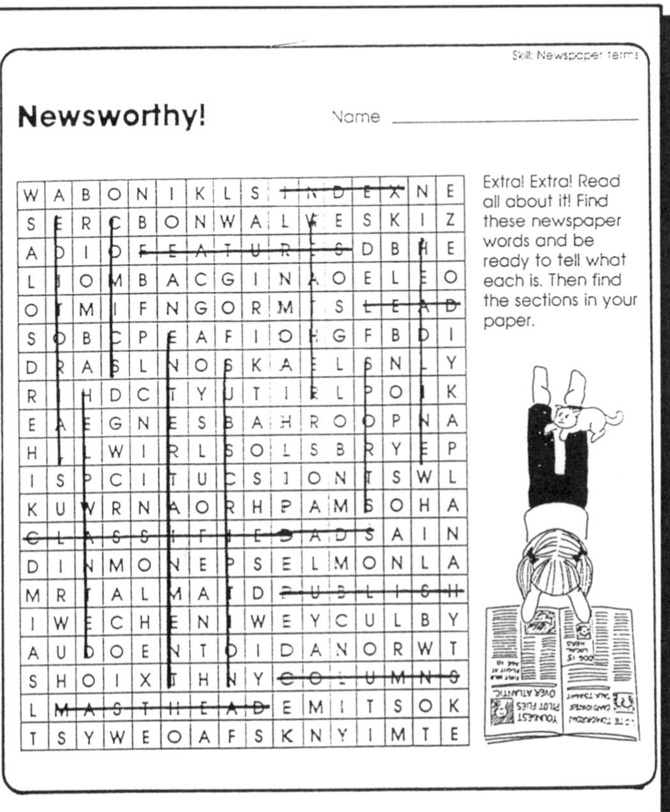

Skill: Newspaper terms

## Newsworthy!

Name ____________________

Extra! Extra! Read all about it! Find these newspaper words and be ready to tell what each is. Then find the sections in your paper.

| W | A | B | O | N | I | K | L | S | I | N | D | E | X | N | E |
|---|---|---|---|---|---|---|---|---|---|---|---|---|---|---|---|
| S | E | R | C | B | O | N | W | A | L | W | E | S | K | I | Z |
| A | D | I | O | F | E | A | T | U | R | E | S | D | B | H | E |
| L | I | O | M | B | A | C | G | I | N | A | O | E | L | E | O |
| O | T | M | I | F | N | G | O | R | M | T | S | L | E | A | D |
| S | O | B | C | P | E | A | F | I | O | H | G | F | B | D | I |
| D | R | A | S | L | N | O | S | K | A | E | L | S | N | L | Y |
| R | I | H | D | C | T | Y | U | T | I | R | L | P | O | I | K |
| E | A | E | G | N | E | S | B | A | H | R | O | O | P | N | A |
| H | L | L | W | I | R | L | S | O | L | S | B | R | Y | E | P |
| I | S | P | C | I | T | U | C | S | I | O | N | T | S | W | L |
| K | U | W | R | N | A | O | R | H | P | A | M | S | O | H | A |
| C | L | A | S | S | I | F | I | E | D | A | D | S | A | I | N |
| D | I | N | M | O | N | E | P | S | E | L | M | O | N | L | A |
| M | R | T | A | L | M | A | T | D | P | U | B | L | I | S | H |
| I | W | E | C | H | E | N | I | W | E | Y | C | U | L | B | Y |
| A | U | D | O | E | N | T | O | I | D | A | N | O | R | W | T |
| S | H | O | I | X | T | H | N | Y | C | O | L | U | M | N | S |
| L | M | A | S | T | H | E | A | D | E | M | I | T | S | O | K |
| T | S | Y | W | E | O | A | F | S | K | N | Y | I | M | T | E |

Page 27

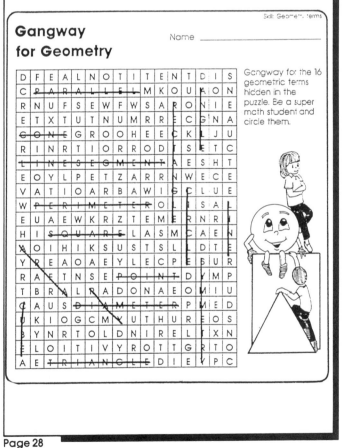

Skill: Geometry terms

## Gangway for Geometry

Name ____________________

Gangway for the 16 geometric terms hidden in the puzzle. Be a super math student and circle them.

| D | F | E | A | L | N | O | T | I | T | E | N | T | D | I | S |
|---|---|---|---|---|---|---|---|---|---|---|---|---|---|---|---|
| C | P | A | R | A | L | L | E | L | M | K | O | U | A | O | N |
| R | N | U | F | S | E | W | F | W | S | A | R | O | N | I | E |
| E | T | X | T | U | T | N | U | M | R | R | E | C | G | N | A |
| C | O | N | E | G | R | O | O | H | E | E | C | K | L | J | U |
| R | I | N | R | T | I | O | R | R | O | D | T | S | E | T | C |
| L | I | N | E | S | E | G | M | E | N | T | A | E | S | H | T |
| E | O | Y | L | P | E | T | Z | A | R | R | N | W | E | C | E |
| V | A | T | I | O | A | R | B | A | W | I | G | C | L | U | E |
| W | P | E | R | I | M | E | T | E | R | O | L | I | S | A | L |
| E | U | A | E | W | K | R | Z | T | E | M | E | R | N | R | I |
| H | I | S | Q | U | A | R | E | L | A | S | M | C | A | E | N |
| A | O | I | H | I | K | S | U | S | T | S | L | L | D | T | E |
| Y | R | E | A | O | A | E | Y | L | E | C | P | E | S | U | R |
| R | A | E | T | N | S | E | P | O | I | N | T | D | Y | M | P |
| T | B | R | A | L | R | A | D | O | N | A | E | O | M | I | U |
| C | A | U | S | D | I | A | M | E | T | E | R | P | M | E | D |
| U | K | I | O | G | C | M | Y | U | T | H | U | R | E | O | S |
| B | Y | N | R | T | O | L | D | N | I | R | E | L | T | X | N |
| E | L | O | I | T | I | V | Y | R | O | T | T | G | R | T | O |
| A | E | T | R | I | A | N | G | L | E | D | I | E | Y | P | C |

Page 28

# Answer Key

Concept: Holidays

## Happy Holidays!

Name ______________________

Celebrate by finding 14 holidays in the puzzle.

Page 29

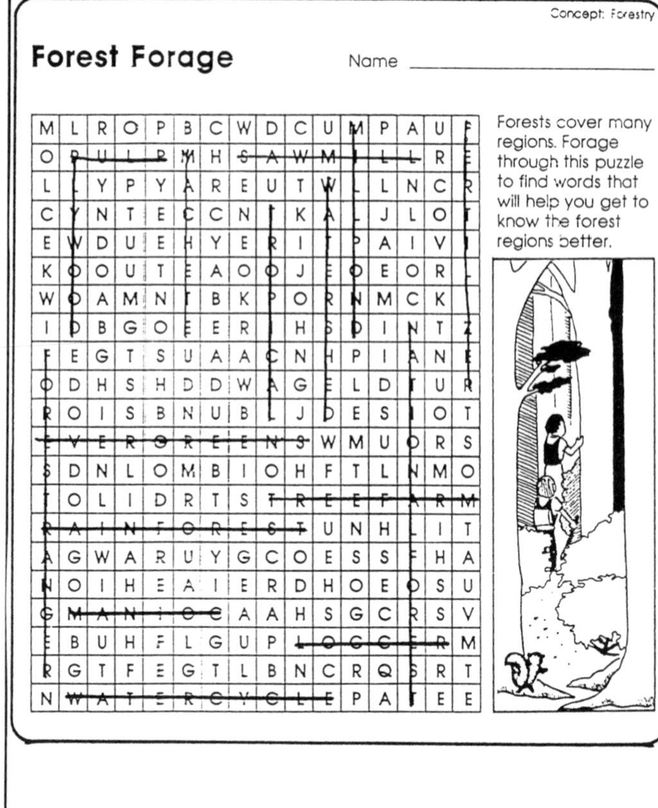

Concept: Forestry

## Forest Forage

Name ______________________

Forests cover many regions. Forage through this puzzle to find words that will help you get to know the forest regions better.

Page 30

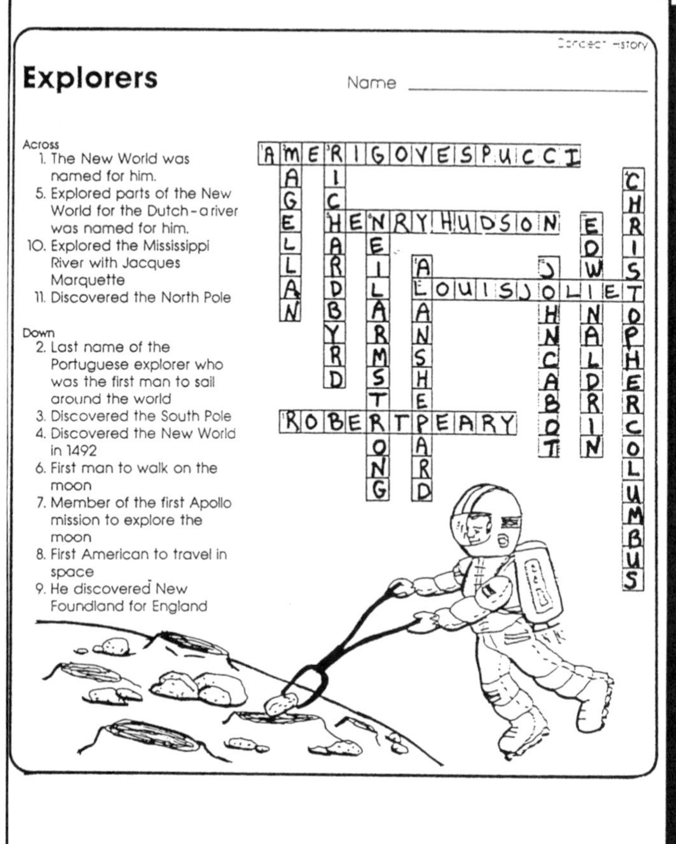

Concept: History

## Explorers

Name ______________________

Across
1. The New World was named for him.
5. Explored parts of the New World for the Dutch - a river was named for him.
10. Explored the Mississippi River with Jacques Marquette
11. Discovered the North Pole

Down
2. Last name of the Portuguese explorer who was the first man to sail around the world
3. Discovered the South Pole
4. Discovered the New World in 1492
6. First man to walk on the moon
7. Member of the first Apollo mission to explore the moon
8. First American to travel in space
9. He discovered New Foundland for England

Page 31

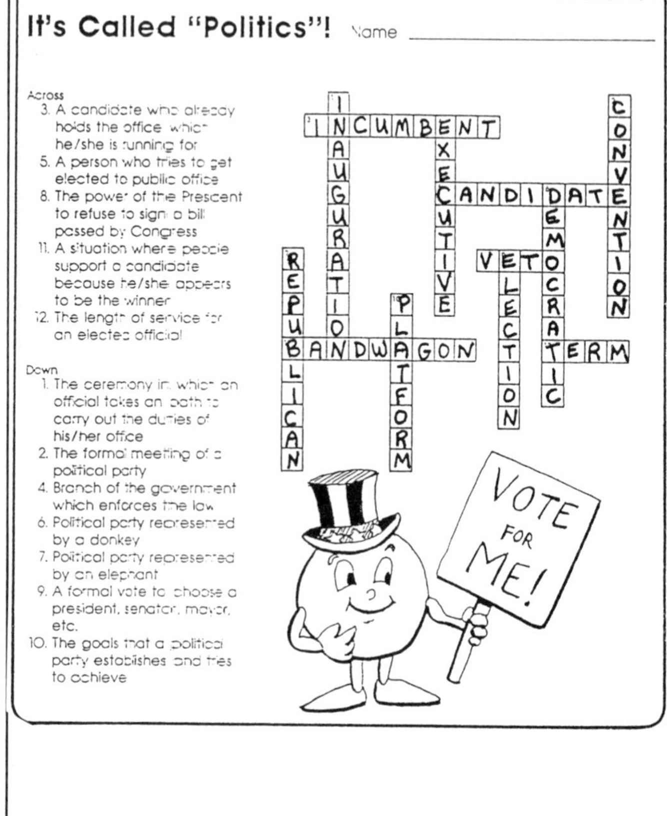


Skill: Government

## It's Called "Politics"!

Name ______________________

Across
3. A candidate who already holds the office which he/she is running for
5. A person who tries to get elected to public office
8. The power of the President to refuse to sign a bill passed by Congress
11. A situation where people support a candidate because he/she appears to be the winner
12. The length of service for an elected official

Down
1. The ceremony in which an official takes an oath to carry out the duties of his/her office
2. The formal meeting of a political party
4. Branch of the government which enforces the law
6. Political party represented by a donkey
7. Political party represented by an elephant
9. A formal vote to choose a president, senator, mayor, etc.
10. The goals that a political party establishes and tries to achieve

Page 32

# Answer Key

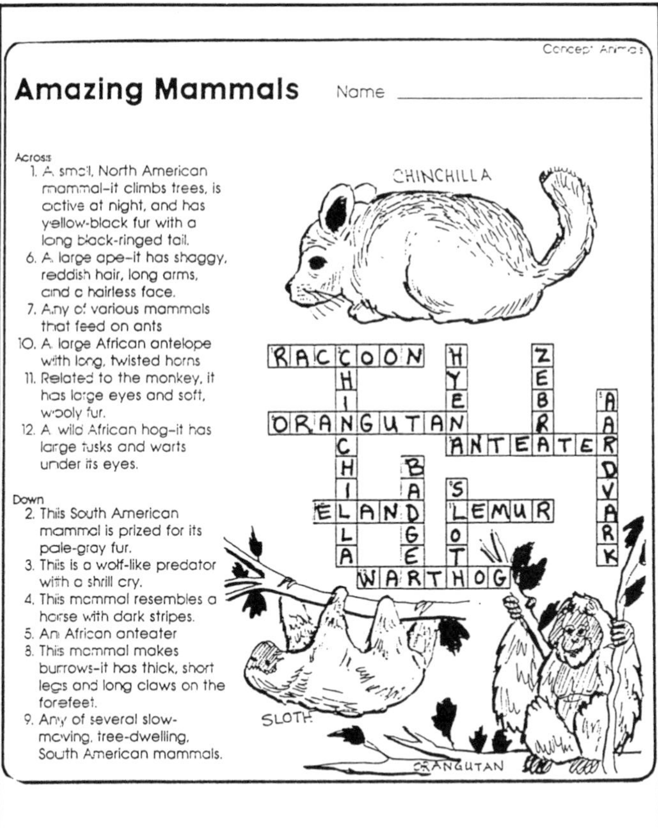

Concept: Animals

## Amazing Mammals

Name ____________________________

Across
1. A small, North American mammal–it climbs trees, is active at night, and has yellow-black fur with a long black-ringed tail.
6. A large ape–it has shaggy, reddish hair, long arms, and a hairless face.
7. Any of various mammals that feed on ants
10. A large African antelope with long, twisted horns
11. Related to the monkey, it has large eyes and soft, wooly fur.
12. A wild African hog–it has large tusks and warts under its eyes.

Down
2. This South American mammal is prized for its pale-gray fur.
3. This is a wolf-like predator with a shrill cry.
4. This mammal resembles a horse with dark stripes.
5. An African anteater
8. This mammal makes burrows–it has thick, short legs and long claws on the forefeet.
9. Any of several slow-moving, tree-dwelling, South American mammals.



Page 33

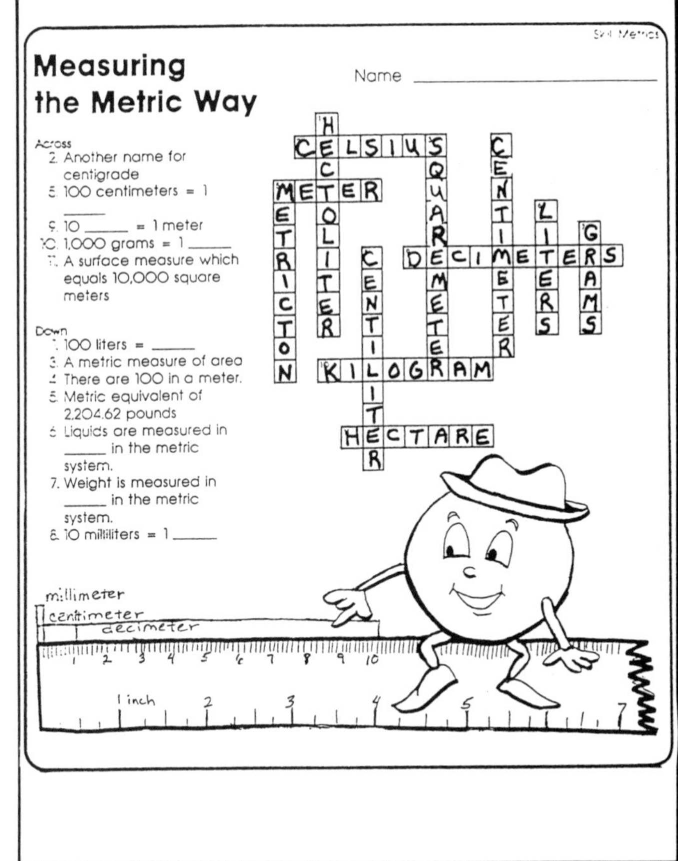

Skill: Metrics

## Measuring the Metric Way

Name ____________________________

Across
2. Another name for centigrade
5. 100 centimeters = 1 _____
9. 10 _____ = 1 meter
10. 1,000 grams = 1 _____
11. A surface measure which equals 10,000 square meters

Down
1. 100 liters = _____
3. A metric measure of area
4. There are 100 in a meter.
5. Metric equivalent of 2,204.62 pounds
6. Liquids are measured in _____ in the metric system.
7. Weight is measured in _____ in the metric system.
8. 10 milliliters = 1 _____



Page 34

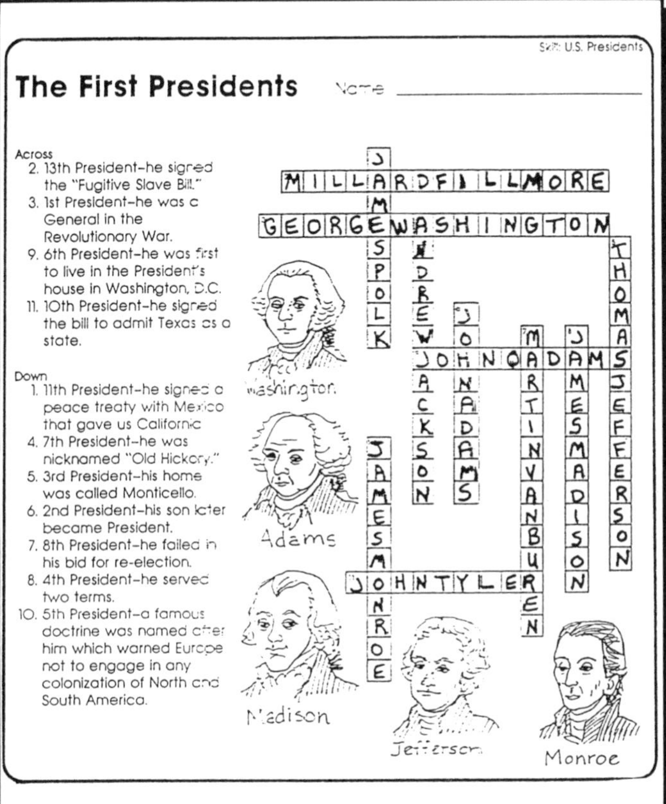

Skill: U.S. Presidents

## The First Presidents

Name ____________________________

Across
2. 13th President–he signed the "Fugitive Slave Bill."
3. 1st President–he was a General in the Revolutionary War.
9. 6th President–he was first to live in the President's house in Washington, D.C.
11. 10th President–he signed the bill to admit Texas as a state.

Down
1. 11th President–he signed a peace treaty with Mexico that gave us California.
4. 7th President–he was nicknamed "Old Hickory."
5. 3rd President–his home was called Monticello.
6. 2nd President–his son later became President.
7. 8th President–he failed in his bid for re-election.
8. 4th President–he served two terms.
10. 5th President–a famous doctrine was named after him which warned Europe not to engage in any colonization of North and South America.



Page 35

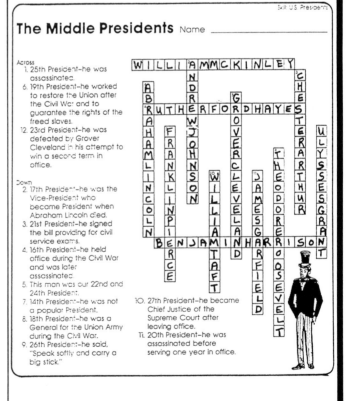

Skill: U.S. Presidents

## The Middle Presidents

Name ____________________________

Across
1. 25th President–he was assassinated.
6. 19th President–he worked to restore the Union after the Civil War and to guarantee the rights of the freed slaves.
12. 23rd President–he was defeated by Grover Cleveland in his attempt to win a second term in office.

Down
2. 17th President–he was the Vice-President who became President when Abraham Lincoln died.
3. 21st President–he signed the bill providing for civil service exams.
4. 16th President–he held office during the Civil War and was later assassinated.
5. This man was our 22nd and 24th President.
7. 14th President–he was not a popular President.
8. 18th President–he was a General for the Union Army during the Civil War.
9. 26th President–he said, "Speak softly and carry a big stick."
10. 27th President–he became Chief Justice of the Supreme Court after leaving office.
11. 20th President–he was assassinated before serving one year in office.

WILLIAMMCKINLEY
RUTHERFORDHAYES
BENJAMINHARRISON
ANDREWJOHNSON
CHESTERARTHUR
ABRAHAMLINCOLN
GROVERCLEVELAND
FRANKLINPIERCE
ULYSSESGRANT
THEODOREROOSEVELT
WILLIAMTAFT
JAMESGARFIELD

Page 36

 

# Answer Key

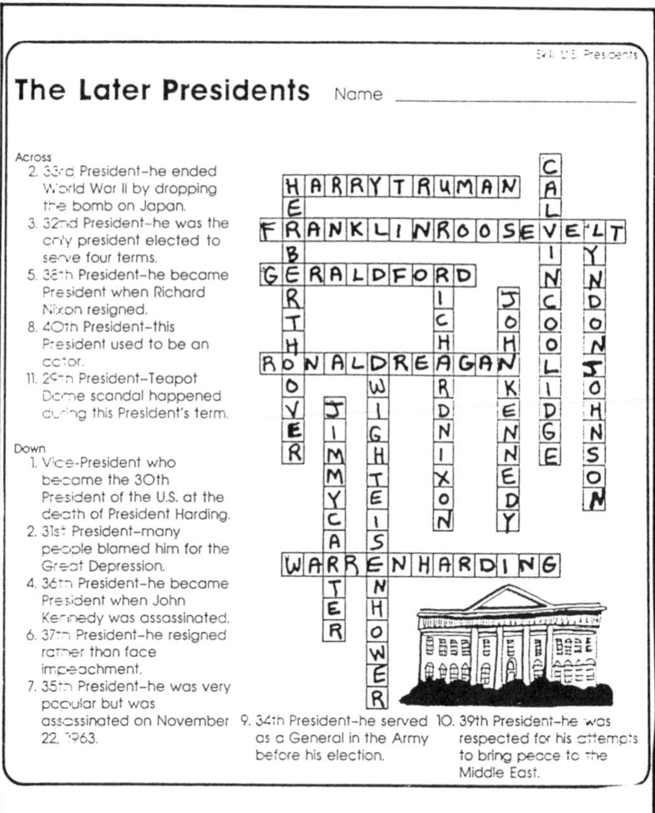

Skill: U.S. Presidents

## The Later Presidents

Name ____________

Across

2. 33rd President–he ended World War II by dropping the bomb on Japan.
3. 32nd President–he was the only president elected to serve four terms.
5. 38th President–he became President when Richard Nixon resigned.
8. 40th President–this President used to be an actor.
11. 29th President–Teapot Dome scandal happened during this President's term.

Down

1. Vice-President who became the 30th President of the U.S. at the death of President Harding.
2. 31st President–many people blamed him for the Great Depression.
4. 36th President–he became President when John Kennedy was assassinated.
6. 37th President–he resigned rather than face impeachment.
7. 35th President–he was very popular but was assassinated on November 22, 1963.
9. 34th President–he served as a General in the Army before his election.
10. 39th President–he was respected for his attempts to bring peace to the Middle East.

Page 37

Skill: Geography terms

## Land and Water

Name ____________

Across

4. High, rocky land, usually with steep sides and round or pointed top
7. A point of land sticking out into a body of water
8. A ridge of rock or sand at or near the surface of water
9. A narrow strip of land that connects two larger bodies of land
12. Low land between hills or mountains

Down

1. A long, narrow valley between high cliffs
2. One of seven large bodies of land on the Earth
3. Hills, mountains, or plateaus
5. A level area of land found in the mountains
6. A body of land almost surrounded by water
10. A river or stream that flows into a larger river
11. Land deposited at the mouth of a river

Page 38

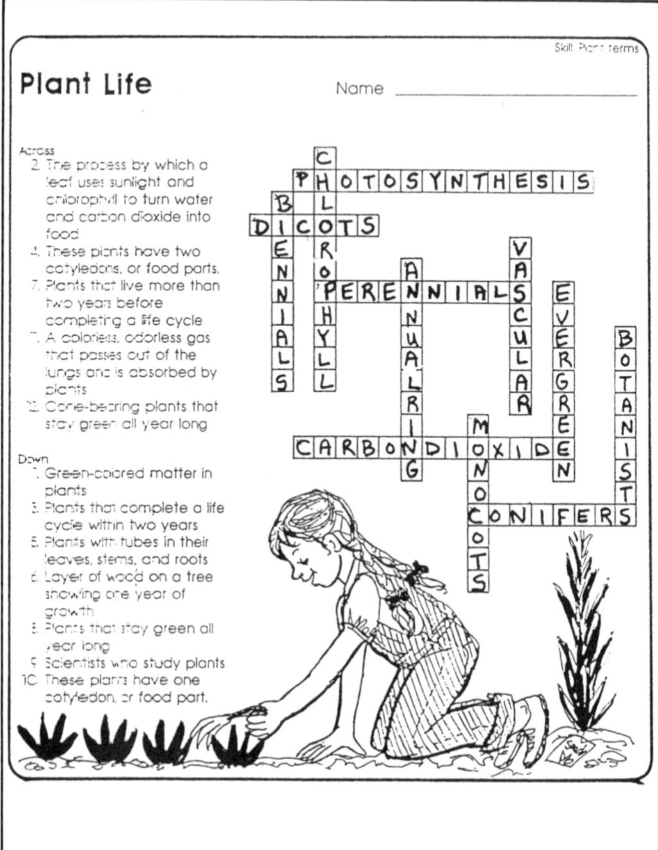

Skill: Plant terms

## Plant Life

Name ____________

Across

2. The process by which a leaf uses sunlight and chlorophyll to turn water and carbon dioxide into food
4. These plants have two cotyledons, or food parts.
7. Plants that live more than two years before completing a life cycle
11. A colorless, odorless gas that passes out of the lungs and is absorbed by plants
12. Cone-bearing plants that stay green all year long

Down

1. Green-colored matter in plants
3. Plants that complete a life cycle within two years
5. Plants with tubes in their leaves, stems, and roots
6. Layer of wood on a tree showing one year of growth
8. Plants that stay green all year long
9. Scientists who study plants
10. These plants have one cotyledon, or food part.

Page 39

Skill: Classifying animals

## The Animal World

Name ____________

Across

5. Animals without backbones
7. Warm-blooded vertebrates with feathers
8. Animals that maintain a constant body temperature with the help of hair or feathers as insulation
11. Cold-blooded vertebrate that lives part of its life in the water and part on land
12. Animals with a body temperature that varies according to the temperature of their environment

Down

1. Soft-bodied invertebrates that are classified into three groups: flat, round, or segmented
2. Invertebrates with soft bodies–many have shells.
3. Simplest group of vertebrates having scales, fins, and gills
4. Alligators, lizards, snakes, turtles
6. Animals with backbones
9. Warm-blooded vertebrates with fur or hair–females can produce milk for their young.
10. Plant-like sea animals

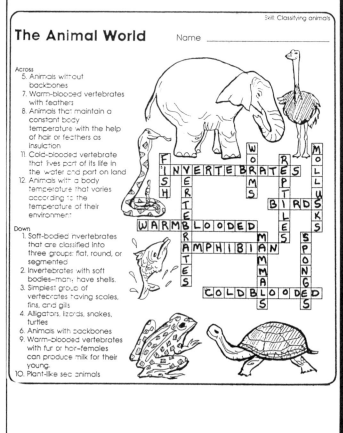

Page 40

# Answer Key

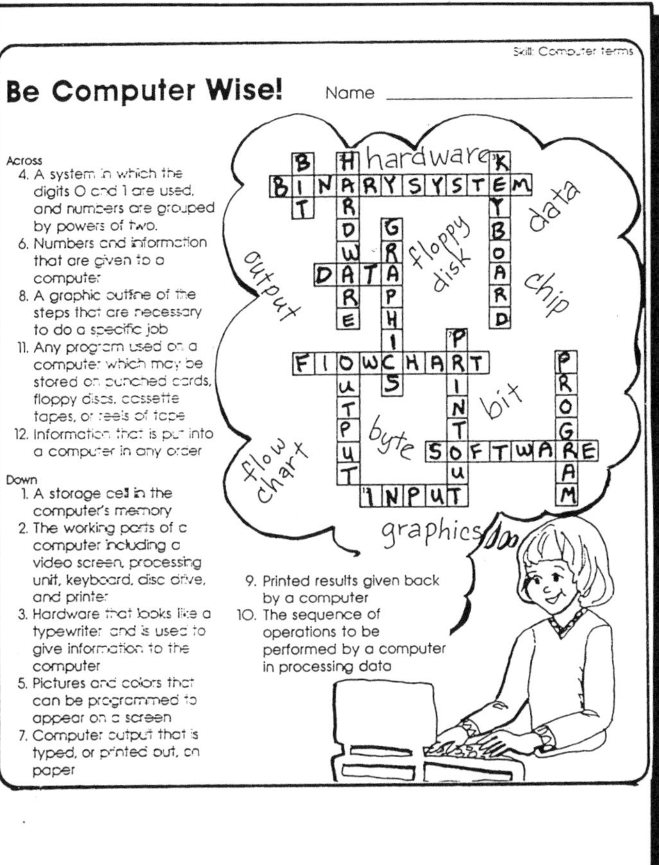

Skill: Computer terms

## Be Computer Wise!

Name ______________________

Across
4. A system in which the digits 0 and 1 are used, and numbers are grouped by powers of two.
6. Numbers and information that are given to a computer
8. A graphic outline of the steps that are necessary to do a specific job
11. Any program used on a computer which may be stored on punched cards, floppy discs, cassette tapes, or reels of tape
12. Information that is put into a computer in any order

Down
1. A storage cell in the computer's memory
2. The working parts of a computer including a video screen, processing unit, keyboard, disc drive, and printer
3. Hardware that looks like a typewriter and is used to give information to the computer
5. Pictures and colors that can be programmed to appear on a screen
7. Computer output that is typed, or printed out, on paper
9. Printed results given back by a computer
10. The sequence of operations to be performed by a computer in processing data



Page 41

Skill: Measurement terms

## Measuring – Let's Compare!

Name ______________________

Across
3. 3 teaspoons = 1 _____
5. Equals 4 pecks or 8 gallons
7. ⅛ of a mile or 220 yards
8. 2,000 pounds
11. A measure of land which equals 43,560 square feet
12. 4 cups = 1 _____

Down
1. A unit of weight for precious stones which equals .2 of a gram
2. A measure of length equal to 1/12 of a foot
4. Liquid measure in the metric system
6. 12 inches or ⅓ of a yard
9. 1/16 of a pound
10. Length measure in the metric system



Page 42

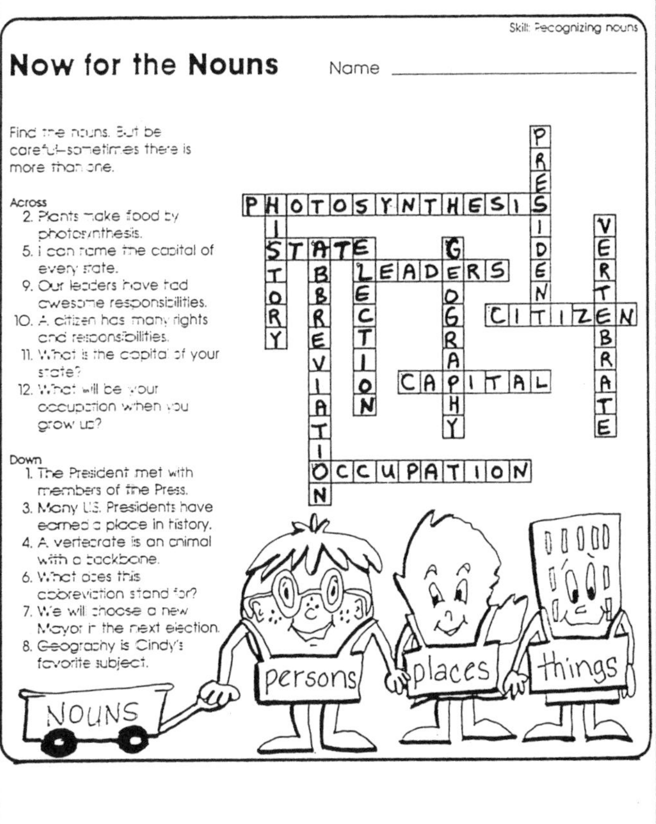

Skill: Recognizing nouns

## Now for the Nouns

Name ______________________

Find the nouns. But be careful—sometimes there is more than one.

Across
2. Plants make food by photosynthesis.
5. I can name the capital of every state.
9. Our leaders have had awesome responsibilities.
10. A citizen has many rights and responsibilities.
11. What is the capital of your state?
12. What will be your occupation when you grow up?

Down
1. The President met with members of the Press.
3. Many U.S. Presidents have earned a place in history.
4. A vertebrate is an animal with a backbone.
6. What does this abbreviation stand for?
7. We will choose a new Mayor in the next election.
8. Geography is Cindy's favorite subject.



Page 43

Skill: State capitals

## Name that State!

Name ______________________

These are all state capitals. Write the state for each one.

Across
3. Baton Rouge
5. Madison
7. Lansing
9. Montgomery
10. Topeka
12. Pierre

Down
1. Columbus
2. Jackson
4. Indianapolis
6. Des Moines
8. Springfield
11. Little Rock



Page 44

# Answer Key

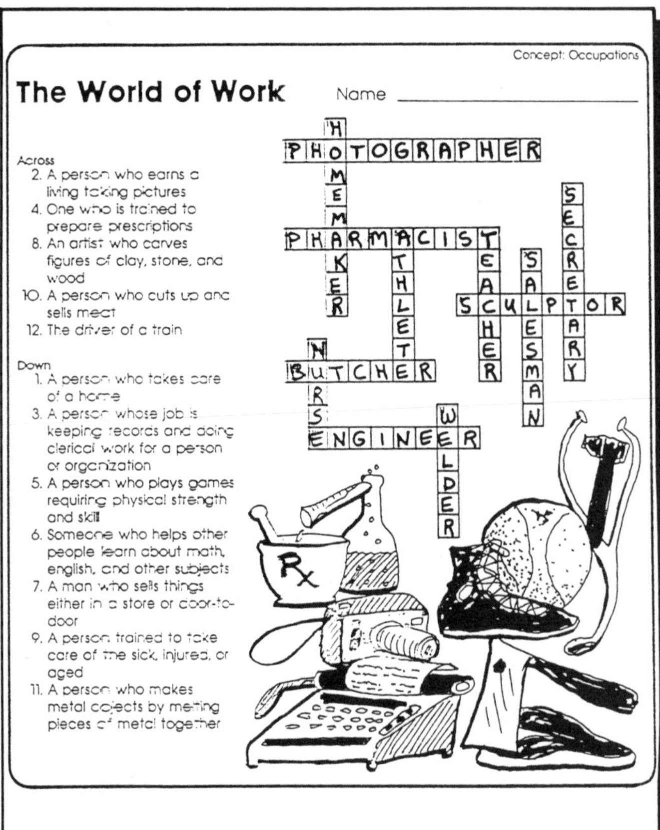
Concept: Occupations

## The World of Work

Name ____________________

Across
2. A person who earns a living taking pictures
4. One who is trained to prepare prescriptions
8. An artist who carves figures of clay, stone, and wood
10. A person who cuts up and sells meat
12. The driver of a train

Down
1. A person who takes care of a home
3. A person whose job is keeping records and doing clerical work for a person or organization
5. A person who plays games requiring physical strength and skill
6. Someone who helps other people learn about math, english, and other subjects
7. A man who sells things either in a store or door-to-door
9. A person trained to take care of the sick, injured, or aged
11. A person who makes metal objects by melting pieces of metal together



Page 45

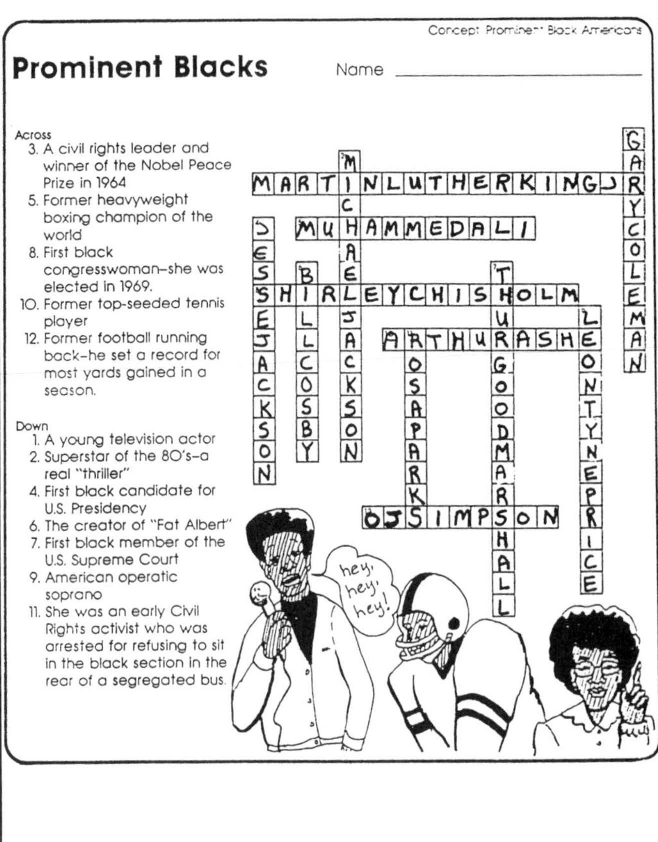
Concept: Prominent Black Americans

## Prominent Blacks

Name ____________________

Across
3. A civil rights leader and winner of the Nobel Peace Prize in 1964
5. Former heavyweight boxing champion of the world
8. First black congresswoman–she was elected in 1969.
10. Former top-seeded tennis player
12. Former football running back–he set a record for most yards gained in a season.

Down
1. A young television actor
2. Superstar of the 80's–a real "thriller"
4. First black candidate for U.S. Presidency
6. The creator of "Fat Albert"
7. First black member of the U.S. Supreme Court
9. American operatic soprano
11. She was an early Civil Rights activist who was arrested for refusing to sit in the black section in the rear of a segregated bus.



Page 46

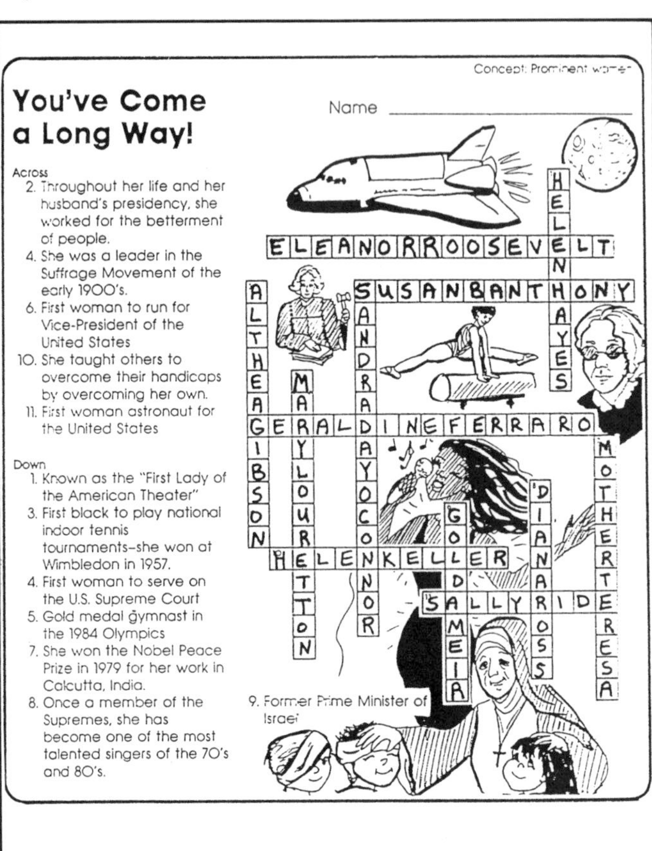
Concept: Prominent women

## You've Come a Long Way!

Name ____________________

Across
2. Throughout her life and her husband's presidency, she worked for the betterment of people.
4. She was a leader in the Suffrage Movement of the early 1900's.
6. First woman to run for Vice-President of the United States
10. She taught others to overcome their handicaps by overcoming her own.
11. First woman astronaut for the United States

Down
1. Known as the "First Lady of the American Theater"
3. First black to play national indoor tennis tournaments–she won at Wimbledon in 1957.
4. First woman to serve on the U.S. Supreme Court
5. Gold medal gymnast in the 1984 Olympics
7. She won the Nobel Peace Prize in 1979 for her work in Calcutta, India.
8. Once a member of the Supremes, she has become one of the most talented singers of the 70's and 80's.
9. Former Prime Minister of Israel



Page 47

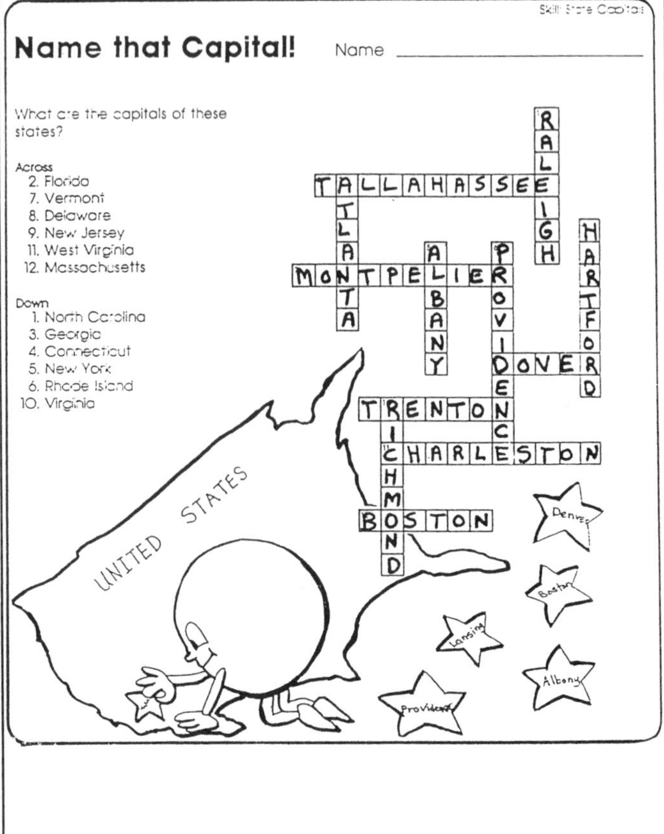
Skill: State Capitals

## Name that Capital!

Name ____________________

What are the capitals of these states?

Across
2. Florida
7. Vermont
8. Delaware
9. New Jersey
11. West Virginia
12. Massachusetts

Down
1. North Carolina
3. Georgia
4. Connecticut
5. New York
6. Rhode Island
10. Virginia



Page 48

# Answer Key

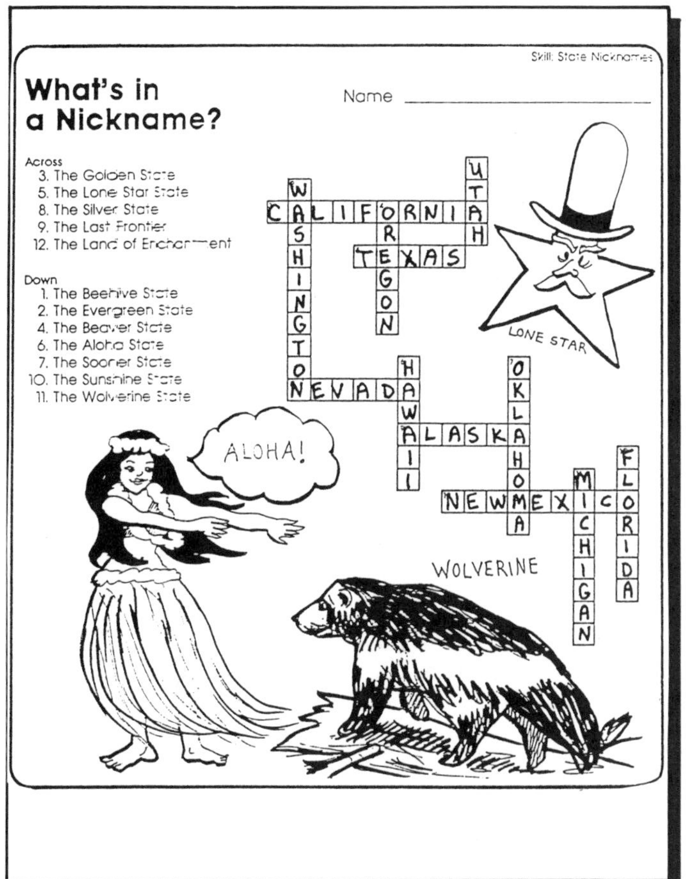

Skill: State Nicknames

## What's in a Nickname?

Name ______________________

Across
3. The Golden State
5. The Lone Star State
8. The Silver State
9. The Last Frontier
12. The Land of Enchantment

Down
1. The Beehive State
2. The Evergreen State
4. The Beaver State
6. The Aloha State
7. The Sooner State
10. The Sunshine State
11. The Wolverine State



Page 49

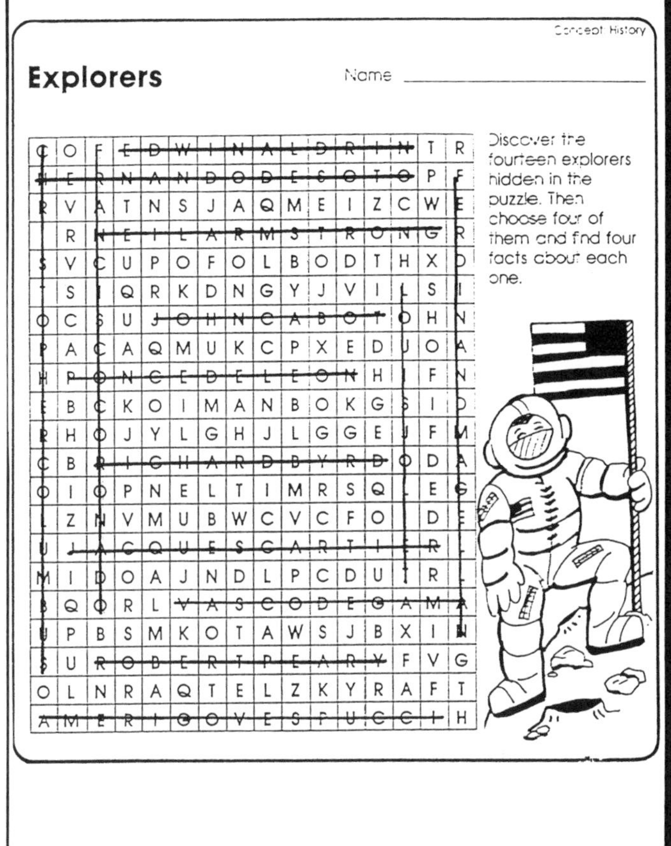

Concept: History

## Explorers

Name ______________________

Discover the fourteen explorers hidden in the puzzle. Then choose four of them and find four facts about each one.

| | | | | | | | | | | | | | | | |
|---|---|---|---|---|---|---|---|---|---|---|---|---|---|---|---|
| C | O | F | E | D | W | I | N | A | L | D | R | I | N | T | R |
| H | E | R | N | A | N | D | O | D | E | S | O | T | O | P | F |
| R | V | A | T | N | S | J | A | Q | M | E | I | Z | C | W | E |
| I | R | N | E | I | L | A | R | M | S | T | R | O | N | G | R |
| S | V | C | U | P | O | F | O | L | B | O | D | T | H | X | D |
| T | S | I | Q | R | K | D | N | G | Y | J | V | I | L | S | I |
| O | C | S | U | J | O | H | N | C | A | B | O | T | O | H | N |
| P | A | C | A | Q | M | U | K | C | P | X | E | D | U | O | A |
| H | P | O | N | C | E | D | E | L | E | O | N | H | I | F | N |
| E | B | C | K | O | I | M | A | N | B | O | K | G | S | I | D |
| R | H | O | J | Y | L | G | H | J | L | G | G | E | J | F | M |
| C | B | R | I | C | H | A | R | D | B | Y | R | D | O | D | A |
| O | I | O | P | N | E | L | T | I | M | R | S | Q | L | E | G |
| L | Z | N | V | M | U | B | W | C | V | C | F | O | I | D | E |
| U | J | A | C | Q | U | E | S | C | A | R | T | I | E | R | L |
| M | I | D | O | A | J | N | D | L | P | C | D | U | T | R | L |
| B | Q | O | R | L | V | A | S | C | O | D | E | G | A | M | A |
| U | P | B | S | M | K | O | T | A | W | S | J | B | X | I | N |
| S | U | R | O | B | E | R | T | P | E | A | R | Y | F | V | G |
| O | L | N | R | A | Q | T | E | L | Z | K | Y | R | A | F | T |
| A | M | E | R | I | G | O | V | E | S | P | U | C | C | I | H |

Page 50

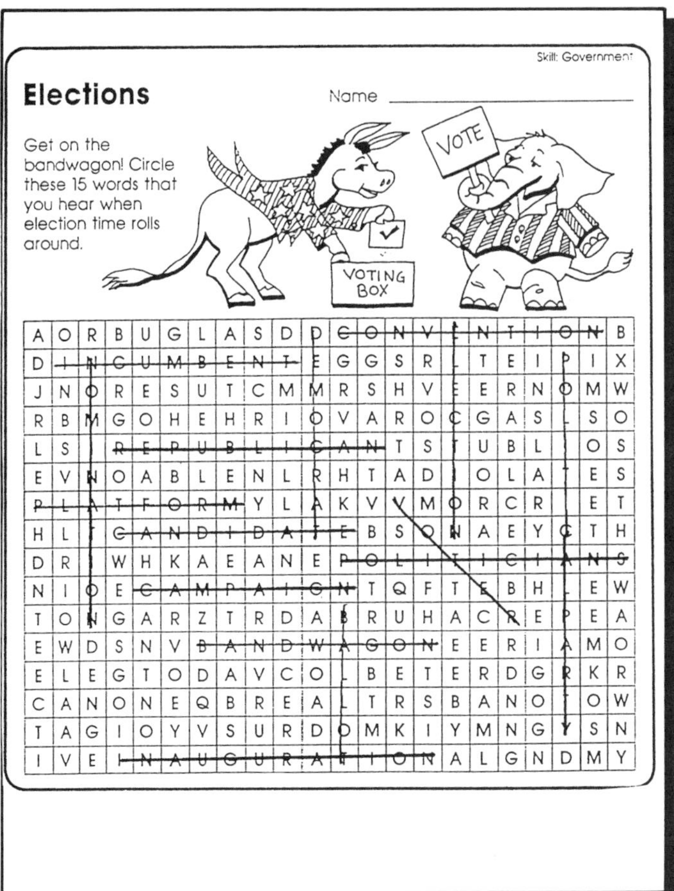

Skill: Government

## Elections

Name ______________________

Get on the bandwagon! Circle these 15 words that you hear when election time rolls around.



| | | | | | | | | | | | | | | | | | | | | | |
|---|---|---|---|---|---|---|---|---|---|---|---|---|---|---|---|---|---|---|---|---|---|
| A | O | R | B | U | G | L | A | S | D | D | C | O | N | V | E | N | T | I | O | N | B |
| D | I | N | C | U | M | B | E | N | T | E | G | G | S | R | L | T | E | I | P | I | X |
| J | N | O | R | E | S | U | T | C | M | M | R | S | H | V | E | E | R | N | O | M | W |
| R | B | M | G | O | H | E | H | R | I | O | V | A | R | O | C | G | A | S | L | S | O |
| L | S | I | R | E | P | U | B | L | I | C | A | N | T | S | T | U | B | L | I | O | S |
| E | V | N | O | A | B | L | E | N | L | R | H | T | A | D | I | O | L | A | T | E | S |
| P | L | A | T | F | O | R | M | Y | L | A | K | V | V | M | O | R | C | R | L | E | T |
| H | L | T | C | A | N | D | I | D | A | T | E | B | S | O | N | A | E | Y | C | T | H |
| D | R | I | W | H | K | A | E | A | N | E | P | O | L | I | T | I | C | I | A | N | S |
| N | I | O | E | C | A | M | P | A | I | G | N | T | Q | F | T | E | B | H | L | E | W |
| T | O | N | G | A | R | Z | T | R | D | A | B | R | U | H | A | C | R | E | P | E | A |
| E | W | D | S | N | V | B | A | N | D | W | A | G | O | N | E | E | R | I | A | M | O |
| E | L | E | G | T | O | D | A | V | C | O | L | B | E | T | E | R | D | G | R | K | R |
| C | A | N | O | N | E | Q | B | R | E | A | L | T | R | S | B | A | N | O | T | O | W |
| T | A | G | I | O | Y | V | S | U | R | D | O | M | K | I | Y | M | N | G | Y | S | N |
| I | V | E | I | N | A | U | G | U | R | A | T | I | O | N | A | L | G | N | D | M | Y |

Page 51

Skill: Metrics

## Metric Madness

Name ______________________

Find the 16 metric math terms in this puzzle.



| | | | | | | | | | | | | | | | | | | | | | |
|---|---|---|---|---|---|---|---|---|---|---|---|---|---|---|---|---|---|---|---|---|---|
| B | E | G | A | K | I | L | O | M | E | T | E | R | N | A | D | N | H | N | G | T | O |
| S | O | M | H | U | K | S | F | T | R | I | L | E | W | O | E | M | E | S | M | L | E |
| A | D | E | C | I | M | E | T | E | R | O | L | I | P | I | C | E | L | S | I | U | S |
| C | O | J | E | Y | O | Y | S | L | E | R | E | A | L | V | I | T | F | O | L | I | Q |
| Z | B | E | N | E | R | C | O | M | T | M | C | G | A | Z | G | R | E | P | L | R | U |
| E | V | A | T | K | T | D | A | E | E | N | L | S | R | A | R | I | O | F | I | C | A |
| Z | O | K | I | L | O | G | R | A | M | T | A | R | N | A | A | C | R | A | M | I | R |
| N | E | S | L | T | E | O | H | S | E | N | E | O | B | E | M | T | R | L | E | K | E |
| A | R | L | I | T | E | R | S | G | H | A | O | R | T | L | I | O | W | L | T | W | M |
| E | O | T | T | E | M | C | L | O | D | T | R | I | T | M | O | N | T | S | E | L | E |
| A | P | S | E | T | L | M | J | E | R | M | E | T | U | E | V | M | N | S | R | U | T |
| W | I | N | R | R | N | D | A | B | E | N | H | E | C | T | A | R | E | O | L | M | E |
| R | H | W | R | D | O | E | A | B | O | L | A | F | M | R | L | G | F | N | O | L | R |
| H | E | C | T | O | L | I | T | E | R | G | S | O | M | I | Y | I | W | M | I | T | S |
| I | L | L | A | H | S | A | L | F | N | E | H | D | E | C | A | M | E | T | E | R | O |
| W | T | U | G | A | C | L | H | A | M | C | R | Y | W | L | E | Z | L | N | A | E | M |

Page 52

 

# Answer Key

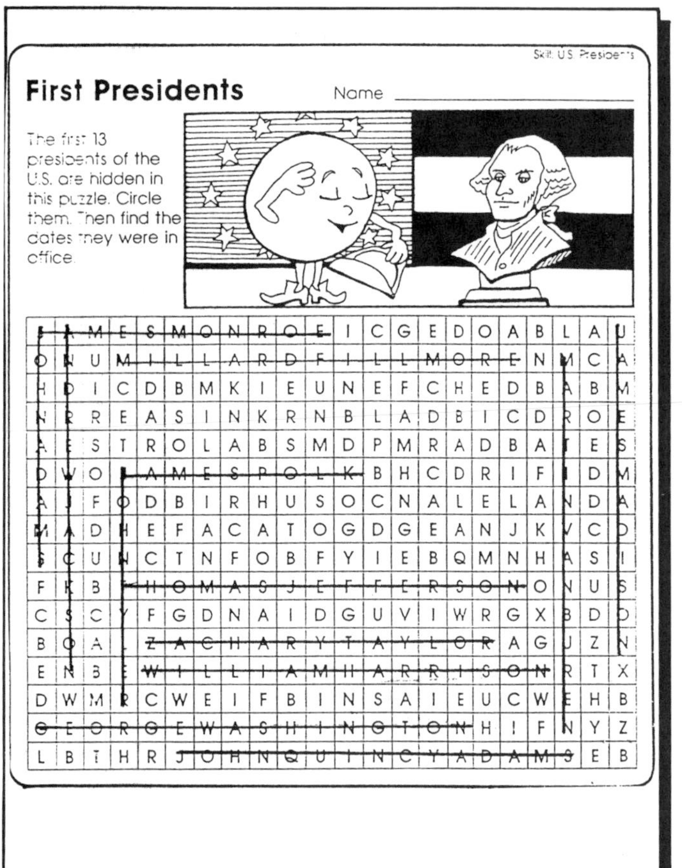

Skill: U.S. Presidents

## First Presidents

Name ____________________

The first 13 presidents of the U.S. are hidden in this puzzle. Circle them. Then find the dates they were in office.

| | | | | | | | | | | | | | | | | | | | | | |
|---|---|---|---|---|---|---|---|---|---|---|---|---|---|---|---|---|---|---|---|---|---|
| J | A | M | E | S | M | O | N | R | O | E | I | C | G | E | D | O | A | B | L | A | J |
| O | N | U | M | I | L | L | A | R | D | F | I | L | L | M | O | R | E | N | M | C | A |
| H | D | I | C | D | B | M | K | I | E | U | N | E | F | C | H | E | D | B | A | B | M |
| N | R | R | E | A | S | I | N | K | R | N | B | L | A | D | B | I | C | D | R | O | E |
| A | E | S | T | R | O | L | A | B | S | M | D | P | M | R | A | D | B | A | T | E | S |
| D | W | O | J | A | M | E | S | P | O | L | K | B | H | C | D | R | I | F | I | D | M |
| A | J | F | O | D | B | I | R | H | U | S | O | C | N | A | L | E | L | A | N | D | A |
| M | A | D | H | E | F | A | C | A | T | O | G | D | G | E | A | N | J | K | V | C | D |
| S | C | U | N | C | T | N | F | O | B | F | Y | I | E | B | Q | M | N | H | A | S | I |
| F | K | B | T | H | O | M | A | S | J | E | F | F | E | R | S | O | N | O | N | U | S |
| C | S | C | Y | F | G | D | N | A | I | D | G | U | V | I | W | R | G | X | B | D | O |
| B | O | A | L | Z | A | C | H | A | R | Y | T | A | Y | L | O | R | A | G | U | Z | N |
| E | N | B | E | W | I | L | L | I | A | M | H | A | R | R | I | S | O | N | R | T | X |
| D | W | M | R | C | W | E | I | F | B | I | N | S | A | I | E | U | C | W | E | H | B |
| G | E | O | R | G | E | W | A | S | H | I | N | G | T | O | N | H | I | F | N | Y | Z |
| L | B | T | H | R | J | O | H | N | Q | U | I | N | C | Y | A | D | A | M | S | E | B |

Page 53

Skill: U.S. Presidents

## America's Best

Name ____________________

We've been lucky to have so many outstanding presidents. Show your patriotism by circling 13 presidents in red crayon or red pen.

| | | | | | | | | | | | | | | | | | | | | | |
|---|---|---|---|---|---|---|---|---|---|---|---|---|---|---|---|---|---|---|---|---|---|
| B | W | B | E | L | D | R | U | T | H | E | R | F | O | R | D | H | A | Y | E | S | G |
| A | F | A | K | C | W | I | L | L | I | A | M | T | A | F | T | S | Z | C | W | A | R |
| F | E | B | E | L | E | M | Y | P | O | L | C | I | N | Y | S | J | I | V | I | C | O |
| G | O | R | J | A | M | E | S | B | U | C | H | A | N | A | N | A | T | L | L | B | V |
| H | R | A | F | N | H | O | S | S | W | P | D | A | O | R | M | M | D | G | L | E | E |
| A | H | H | A | N | D | R | E | W | J | O | H | N | S | O | N | E | O | A | I | U | R |
| I | T | A | F | P | J | O | S | V | E | D | E | L | P | O | M | S | S | I | A | Y | C |
| J | I | M | E | O | T | R | G | L | F | E | I | L | D | B | L | G | N | A | M | A | L |
| L | Y | L | T | D | O | S | R | G | L | H | O | D | Q | M | A | A | I | N | M | E | E |
| J | B | I | C | I | F | R | A | N | K | L | I | N | P | I | E | R | C | E | C | K | V |
| B | E | N | J | A | M | I | N | H | A | R | R | I | S | O | N | F | E | L | K | L | E |
| A | E | C | Q | U | L | U | T | N | E | R | P | Q | C | R | C | I | T | S | I | Q | L |
| I | Z | O | C | H | E | S | T | E | R | A | R | T | H | U | R | E | L | D | N | R | A |
| A | K | L | M | A | D | A | N | I | M | W | D | O | A | R | T | L | S | H | L | V | N |
| G | H | N | D | C | U | A | V | S | A | N | B | E | A | Y | D | D | A | H | E | I | D |
| A | T | H | E | O | D | O | R | E | R | O | O | S | E | V | E | L | T | I | Y | N | L |

Page 54

Skill: U.S. Presidents

## America's Leaders

Name ____________________

America is only as great as its people and its leaders! Circle 13 of America's presidents.

| | | | | | | | | | | | | | | | | | | | | | |
|---|---|---|---|---|---|---|---|---|---|---|---|---|---|---|---|---|---|---|---|---|---|
| D | W | I | G | H | T | E | I | S | E | N | H | O | W | E | R | Q | R | J | A | R | B |
| E | C | P | A | S | N | G | O | E | O | R | U | R | U | N | M | E | A | O | U | F | D |
| H | A | R | R | Y | T | R | U | M | A | N | S | A | T | H | I | E | G | H | M | R | L |
| U | L | S | N | H | A | N | V | E | P | N | A | T | R | U | O | S | T | N | B | W | C |
| R | V | A | L | E | D | O | E | D | U | T | M | A | E | W | N | V | E | K | O | A | L |
| U | I | O | R | O | N | A | L | D | R | E | A | G | A | N | O | T | I | E | C | R | E |
| S | N | U | S | T | M | A | O | N | S | T | U | L | Y | I | M | R | A | N | A | R | S |
| O | C | H | E | R | B | E | R | T | H | O | O | V | E | R | E | T | H | N | S | E | E |
| W | O | O | D | R | O | W | W | I | L | S | O | N | A | H | M | N | K | E | Q | N | B |
| C | O | T | S | A | S | H | E | W | R | G | T | I | F | H | E | I | C | D | E | H | U |
| L | L | Y | N | D | O | N | J | O | H | N | S | O | N | C | E | A | S | Y | T | A | B |
| R | I | C | H | A | R | D | N | I | X | O | N | O | A | R | H | N | B | O | E | R | S |
| T | D | E | L | I | O | N | Y | P | G | E | R | A | L | D | F | O | R | D | C | D | P |
| R | G | E | L | D | G | A | E | N | U | B | L | M | B | R | Y | E | T | T | N | I | W |
| S | E | D | E | O | T | R | J | I | M | M | Y | C | A | R | T | E | R | B | A | N | F |
| F | R | A | N | K | L | I | N | R | O | O | S | E | V | E | L | T | S | N | E | G | R |

Page 55

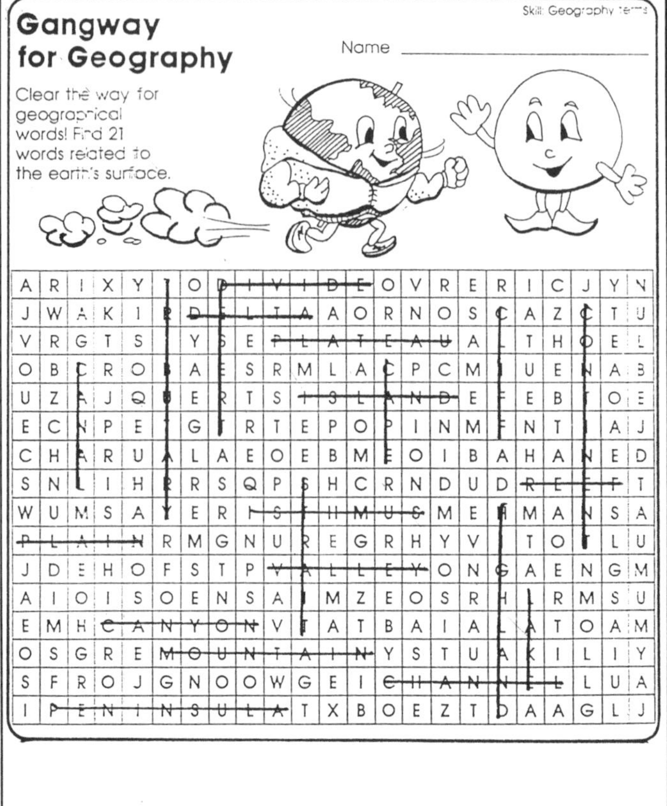

Skill: Geography terms

## Gangway for Geography

Name ____________________

Clear the way for geographical words! Find 21 words related to the earth's surface.

| | | | | | | | | | | | | | | | | | | | | | | |
|---|---|---|---|---|---|---|---|---|---|---|---|---|---|---|---|---|---|---|---|---|---|---|
| A | R | I | X | Y | T | O | D | I | V | I | D | E | O | V | R | E | R | I | C | J | Y | N |
| J | W | A | K | I | R | D | E | L | T | A | A | O | R | N | O | S | C | A | Z | C | T | U |
| V | R | G | T | S | I | Y | S | E | P | L | A | T | E | A | U | A | L | T | H | O | E | L |
| O | B | C | R | O | B | A | E | S | R | M | L | A | C | P | C | M | I | U | E | N | A | B |
| U | Z | A | J | Q | U | E | R | T | S | I | S | L | A | N | D | E | F | E | B | T | O | E |
| E | C | N | P | E | T | G | T | R | T | E | P | O | P | I | N | M | F | N | T | I | A | J |
| C | H | A | R | U | A | L | A | E | O | E | B | M | E | O | I | B | A | H | A | N | E | D |
| S | N | L | I | H | R | R | S | Q | P | S | H | C | R | N | D | U | D | R | E | E | F | T |
| W | U | M | S | A | Y | E | R | I | S | T | H | M | U | S | M | E | H | M | A | N | S | A |
| P | L | A | I | N | R | M | G | N | U | R | E | G | R | H | Y | V | I | T | O | T | L | U |
| J | D | E | H | O | F | S | T | P | V | A | L | L | E | Y | O | N | G | A | E | N | G | M |
| A | I | O | I | S | O | E | N | S | A | I | M | Z | E | O | S | R | H | L | R | M | S | U |
| E | M | H | C | A | N | Y | O | N | V | T | A | T | B | A | I | A | L | A | T | O | A | M |
| O | S | G | R | E | M | O | U | N | T | A | I | N | Y | S | T | U | A | K | I | L | I | Y |
| S | F | R | O | J | G | N | O | O | W | G | E | I | C | H | A | N | N | E | L | L | U | A |
| I | P | E | N | I | N | S | U | L | A | T | X | B | O | E | Z | T | D | A | A | G | L | J |

Page 56

# Answer Key

Skill: Plant terms
Dig Into These!
Name
Planted in this puzzle are 17 plant-related words. Dig them out and circle in green.


Page 57

Skill: Classifying animals
Be Wise—Analyze!
Name
Help this wise old owl find the 16 animal classification terms hidden in the puzzle.


Page 58

Skill: Abbreviations
The Long and Short of It
Name
Here are 15 abbreviations of words or phrases. Now, you find the words they are abbreviated for.


Page 59

Skill: Computer terms
Do You Compute?
Name
Are you computer wise? Sort through these letters and circle 18 words related to computers.


Page 60

 

# Answer Key

Skill: Measurement terms
Can You Measure Up?
Name
You can measure up by finding these 22 measurement terms. Circle them.


Page 61

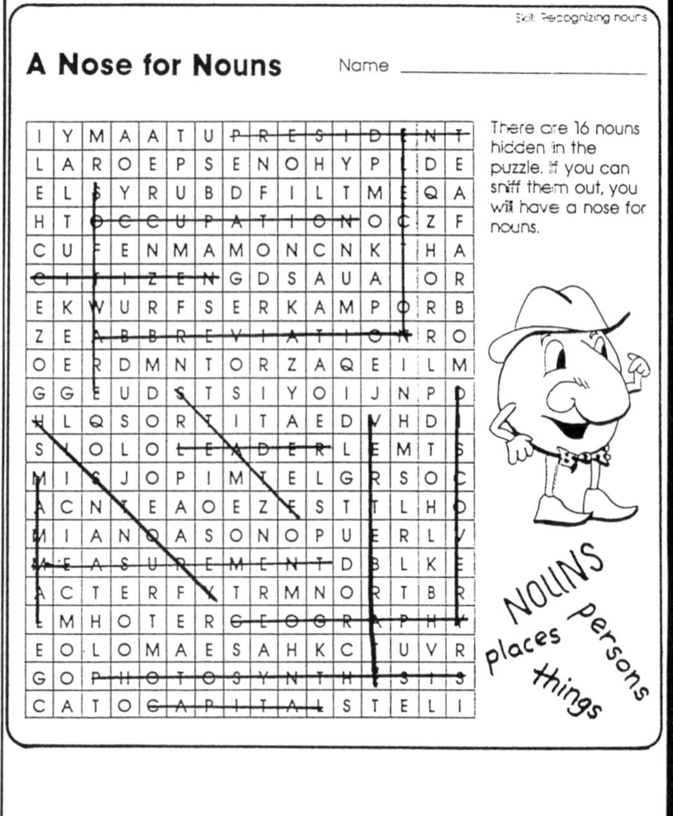

Skill: Recognizing nouns
A Nose for Nouns
Name
There are 16 nouns hidden in the puzzle. If you can sniff them out, you will have a nose for nouns.
NOUNS
persons
places
things


Page 62

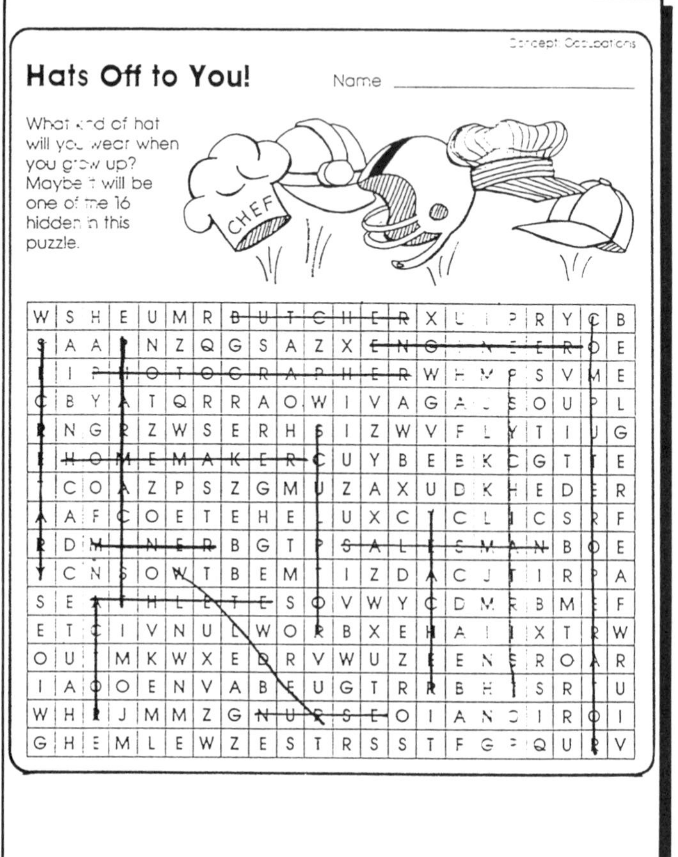

Concept: Occupations
Hats Off to You!
Name
What kind of hat will you wear when you grow up? Maybe it will be one of the 16 hidden in this puzzle.
CHEF


Page 63

Concept: Prominent Black Americans

## Prominent Blacks

Name

Find the 16 outstanding Black Americans hidden in this puzzle.

| | | | | | | | | | | | | | | | | | | | | | |
|---|---|---|---|---|---|---|---|---|---|---|---|---|---|---|---|---|---|---|---|---|---|
| S | R | C | O | N | S | T | A | N | C | E | B | A | K | E | R | M | O | T | L | E | Y |
| T | I | W | E | J | R | E | D | O | V | C | L | N | P | E | R | L | T | H | E | S | O |
| B | O | O | K | E | R | T | W | A | S | H | I | N | G | T | O | N | B | O | O | H | M |
| A | J | J | T | S | L | Y | N | G | P | A | L | T | Y | L | S | H | I | M | N | I | I |
| R | E | S | N | S | D | H | F | B | L | R | E | C | P | R | A | E | O | A | T | R | C |
| B | S | I | U | E | L | S | D | N | R | L | I | L | E | G | P | S | L | S | Y | L | H |
| A | S | M | F | O | R | N | T | O | D | I | M | O | R | T | A | F | S | B | N | E | A |
| R | E | P | C | W | E | M | L | A | F | E | R | C | F | H | R | T | E | R | E | Y | E |
| A | J | S | H | E | S | N | D | B | R | P | O | Y | M | E | K | I | P | A | P | C | L |
| J | A | O | M | N | A | L | R | M | T | R | U | P | H | D | S | C | T | D | R | H | U |
| O | C | N | A | S | N | O | L | U | N | I | H | I | T | V | B | R | O | L | I | I | A |
| R | K | A | M | U | H | A | M | M | E | D | A | L | I | J | E | T | F | E | C | S | C |
| D | S | P | O | N | S | A | N | D | R | E | W | Y | O | U | N | G | L | Y | E | H | K |
| A | O | L | G | L | P | C | E | M | L | O | M | P | E | R | T | D | G | C | P | O | S |
| N | N | R | T | H | U | R | G | O | O | D | M | A | R | S | H | A | L | L | A | L | O |
| U | M | A | R | T | I | N | L | U | T | H | E | R | K | I | N | G | J | R | T | M | N |

Page 64

# Answer Key

Concept: Prominent women

## You've Come a Long Way!

Name ______________________

There have been many outstanding women in history. Find the 15 hidden in this puzzle and circle them.

| | | | | | | | | | | | | | | | | | | | | | |
|---|---|---|---|---|---|---|---|---|---|---|---|---|---|---|---|---|---|---|---|---|---|
| C | F | L | E | L | E | A | N | O | R | R | O | O | S | E | V | E | L | T | O | R | M |
| O | B | R | M | A | R | G | A | R | E | T | M | E | A | D | K | O | T | R | M | S | O |
| R | I | T | I | M | O | N | T | R | A | K | E | M | L | P | Q | U | A | Z | E | U | T |
| E | H | E | L | E | N | H | A | Y | E | S | F | R | L | N | S | U | M | Y | C | S | H |
| T | E | F | Y | R | N | S | I | N | Y | C | T | A | Y | B | C | O | T | S | O | A | E |
| T | L | J | D | T | E | M | A | R | Y | L | O | U | R | E | T | T | O | N | T | N | R |
| A | E | C | I | V | M | E | C | L | B | R | E | A | I | Y | R | G | E | A | S | B | T |
| S | N | L | C | P | E | F | Y | R | L | G | O | L | D | A | M | E | I | R | M | A | E |
| C | K | V | K | F | O | L | S | W | Z | T | E | F | E | H | U | R | L | M | O | N | R |
| O | E | G | E | R | A | L | D | I | N | E | F | E | R | R | A | R | O | J | R | T | E |
| T | L | K | N | A | J | L | O | P | H | T | G | Z | Y | K | L | C | G | N | O | H | S |
| T | L | M | S | A | N | D | R | A | D | A | Y | O | C | O | N | N | O | R | G | O | A |
| K | E | G | O | M | Y | G | E | O | L | E | R | F | N | O | P | R | I | S | T | N | K |
| I | R | U | N | R | M | B | T | A | M | R | O | S | T | R | A | K | L | E | S | Y | F |
| N | T | S | P | H | A | R | R | I | E | T | T | U | B | M | A | N | T | C | U | R | L |
| G | B | R | G | Q | L | Y | A | L | T | H | E | A | G | I | B | S | O | N | F | G | O |

Page 65

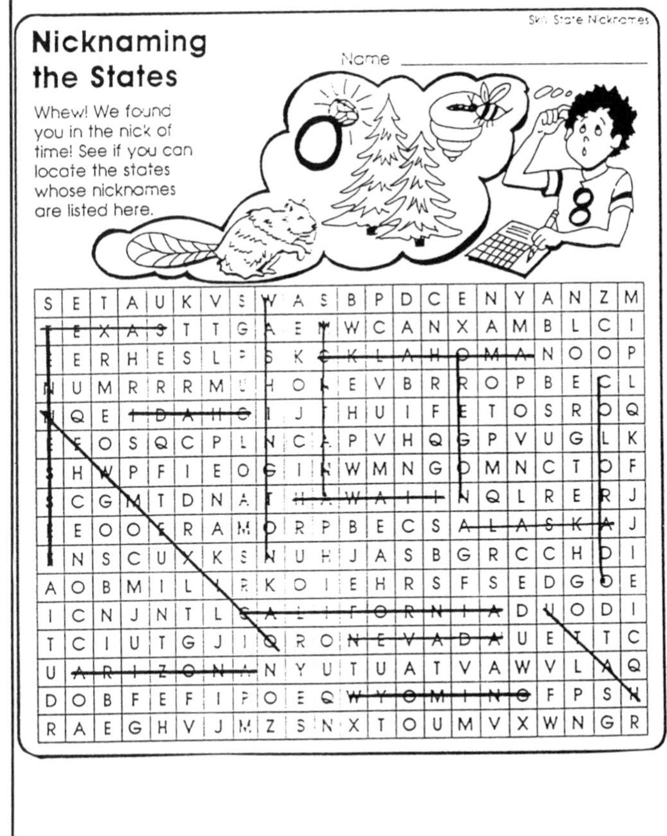

Skill: State Nicknames

## Nicknaming the States

Name ______________________

Whew! We found you in the nick of time! See if you can locate the states whose nicknames are listed here.

| | | | | | | | | | | | | | | | | | | | | | |
|---|---|---|---|---|---|---|---|---|---|---|---|---|---|---|---|---|---|---|---|---|---|
| S | E | T | A | U | K | V | S | W | A | S | B | P | D | C | E | N | Y | A | N | Z | M |
| T | E | X | A | S | T | T | G | A | E | M | W | C | A | N | X | A | M | B | L | C | I |
| E | E | R | H | E | S | L | P | S | K | O | K | L | A | H | O | M | A | N | O | O | P |
| N | U | M | R | R | R | M | U | H | O | N | E | V | B | R | R | O | P | B | E | C | L |
| N | Q | E | I | D | A | H | O | I | J | T | H | U | I | F | E | T | O | S | R | O | Q |
| E | E | O | S | Q | C | P | L | N | C | A | P | V | H | Q | G | P | V | U | G | L | K |
| S | H | W | P | F | I | E | O | G | I | N | W | M | N | G | O | M | N | C | T | O | F |
| S | C | G | M | T | D | N | A | T | H | A | W | A | I | I | N | Q | L | R | E | R | J |
| E | E | O | O | E | R | A | M | O | R | P | B | E | C | S | A | L | A | S | K | A | J |
| E | N | S | C | U | X | K | S | N | U | H | J | A | S | B | G | R | C | C | H | D | I |
| A | O | B | M | I | L | I | R | K | O | I | E | H | R | S | F | S | E | D | G | O | E |
| I | C | N | J | N | T | L | C | A | L | I | F | O | R | N | I | A | D | U | O | D | I |
| T | C | I | U | T | G | J | I | O | R | O | N | E | V | A | D | A | U | E | T | T | C |
| U | A | R | I | Z | O | N | A | N | Y | U | T | U | A | T | V | A | W | V | L | A | Q |
| D | O | B | F | E | F | I | P | O | E | Q | W | Y | O | M | I | N | G | F | P | S | H |
| R | A | E | G | H | V | J | M | Z | S | N | X | T | O | U | M | V | X | W | N | G | R |

Page 66

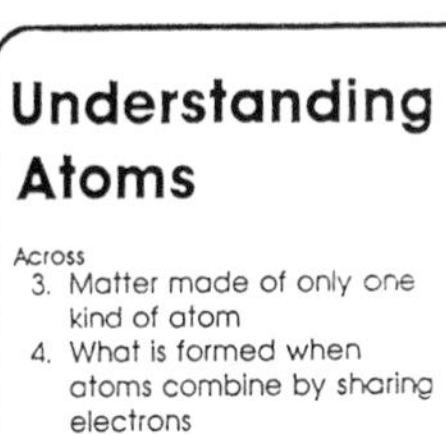

Skill: Atomic terms

## Understanding Atoms

Name ______________________

Across
3. Matter made of only one kind of atom
4. What is formed when atoms combine by sharing electrons
8. Positive electric charge within the nucleus of an atom
10. Small pieces of matter
11. Letter or letters
12. What a thing is made up of; it occupies space.

Down
1. An uncharged particle within the nucleus of an atom
2. Very tiny part that makes up matter
5. Tiny negative electrical charges that move around the nucleus of an atom
6. An atom that has lost or gained electrons
7. Characteristics or qualities of a thing
8. Chart that shows all of the elements classified by similar properties
9. Symbols put together to show the elements which make a compound

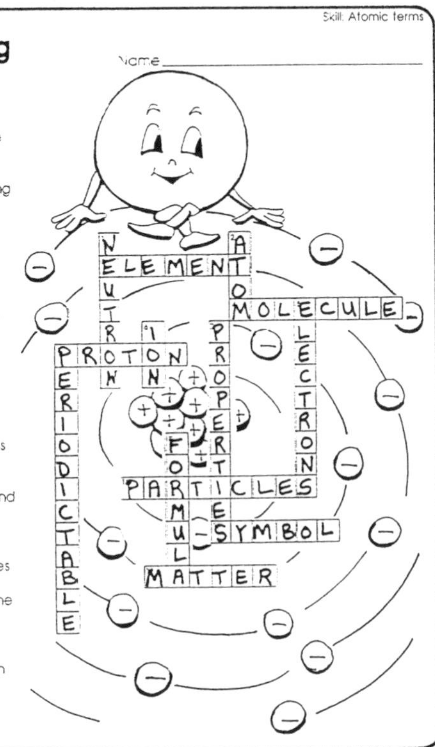


Page 67

Concept: Drug Awareness

## Put the Plug on Drugs

Name ______________________

Across
4. Drug used for relaxation and sleep, could cause drug dependence if misused
6. To use wrongly, misuse
8. Drug that produces altered sensations, or the seeing or hearing of things that do not exist
10. A dangerous, habit-forming drug made from opium
11. Narcotics are taken from this plant.

Down
1. A drug that may be prescribed by doctors to relieve tension or lower blood pressure
2. A stimulating drug present in coffee and tea
3. An unwanted effect in drugs
5. A drug that is capable of causing drowsiness, sleep, unconsciousness, or stupor
6. Drug used medically to increase the activity of the brain or some other part of the body
7. Food or drug that increases the activity of the brain or other part of the body
9. A depressant

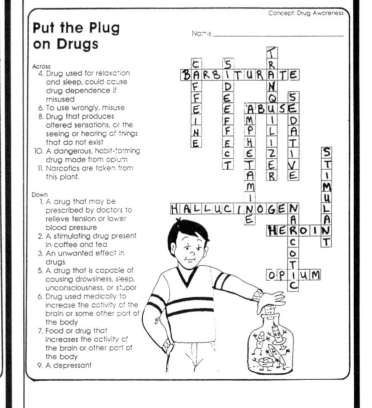

TRANQUILIZER
CAFFEINE
SIDE EFFECT
BARBITURATE
SEDATIVE
ABUSE
AMPHETAMINE
STIMULANT
HALLUCINOGEN
NARCOTIC
HEROIN
OPIUM

Page 68

# Answer Key

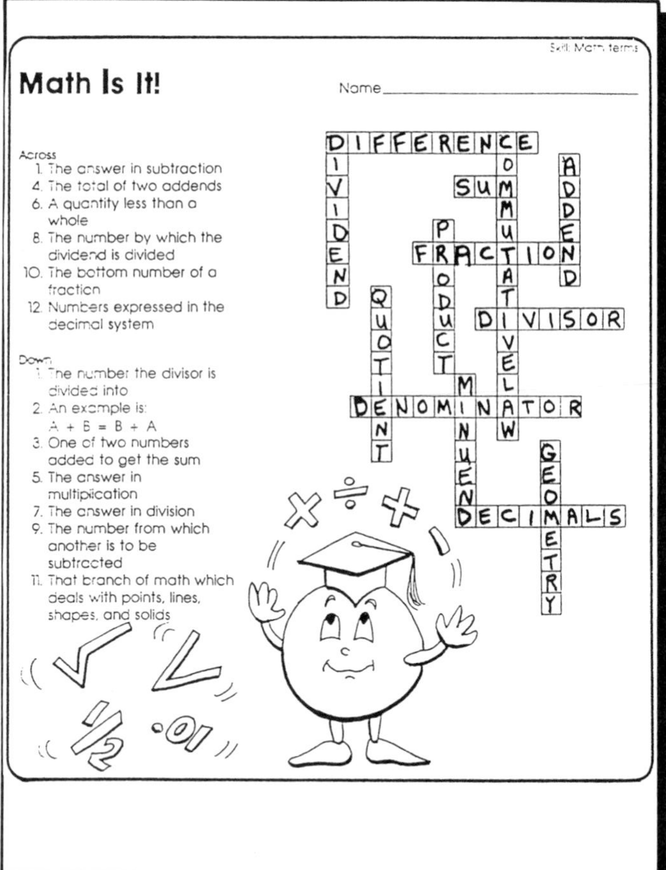

Skill: Math terms

## Math Is It!

Name

Across
1. The answer in subtraction
4. The total of two addends
6. A quantity less than a whole
8. The number by which the dividend is divided
10. The bottom number of a fraction
12. Numbers expressed in the decimal system

Down
1. The number the divisor is divided into
2. An example is: A + B = B + A
3. One of two numbers added to get the sum
5. The answer in multiplication
7. The answer in division
9. The number from which another is to be subtracted
11. That branch of math which deals with points, lines, shapes, and solids



Page 69

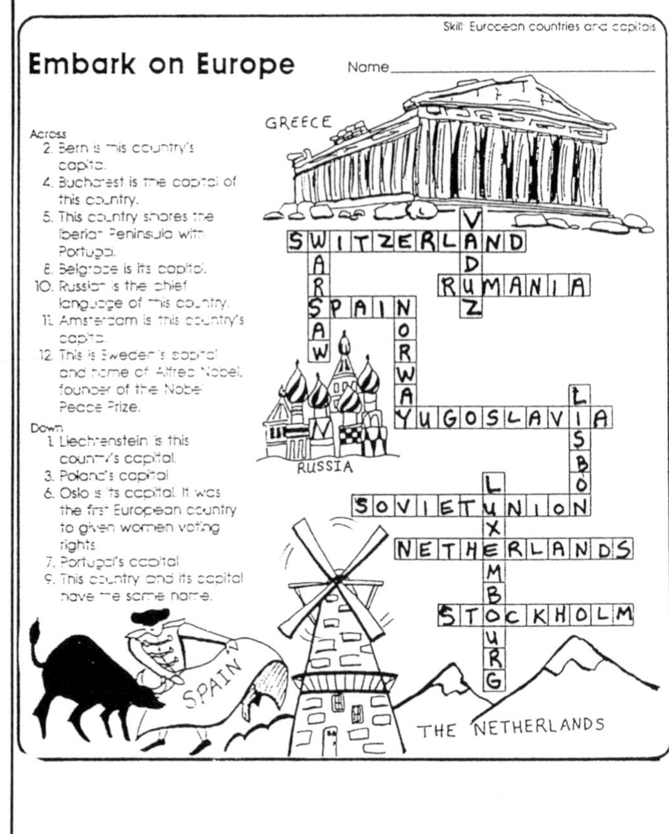

Skill: European countries and capitals

## Embark on Europe

Name

Across
2. Bern is this country's capital.
4. Bucharest is the capital of this country.
5. This country shares the Iberian Peninsula with Portugal.
8. Belgrade is its capital.
10. Russian is the chief language of this country.
11. Amsterdam is this country's capital.
12. This is Sweden's capital and home of Alfred Nobel, founder of the Nobel Peace Prize.

Down
1. Liechtenstein is this country's capital.
3. Poland's capital
6. Oslo is its capital. It was the first European country to given women voting rights
7. Portugal's capital
9. This country and its capital have the same name.



Page 70

Skill: Greek alphabet

## Gallantly Greek

Name

What Greek letters do these symbols represent?



Page 71

Skill: Prepositions

## Preposition Patch

Name

Find the preposition in each sentence.

Across
2. The dog ran after the cat.
6. The kite went above the trees.
7. The colt walked behind his mother.
8. The ladder leaned against the wall.
9. Do not go swimming without a buddy.
12. Look for the ball under the pile of leaves.
13. Harold and Sandy went to the store together.

Down
1. The child may not go beyond the gate.
3. Stacey went with her friend.
4. Your turn to bat is before his.
5. Pirates must have hidden the gold beneath this spot.
6. Jim just went around the corner.
10. Put the book upon the table.
11. Grandfather's farm is just over the next hill.
12. Practice your piano until the hour is finished.

with, after, over, to, above, upon, behind, around

BEYOND, AFTER, WITH, BENEATH, ABOVE, BEFORE, AROUND, BEHIND, AGAINST, WITHOUT, UPON, OVER, UNDER, UNTIL, TO

Page 72

 

# Answer Key

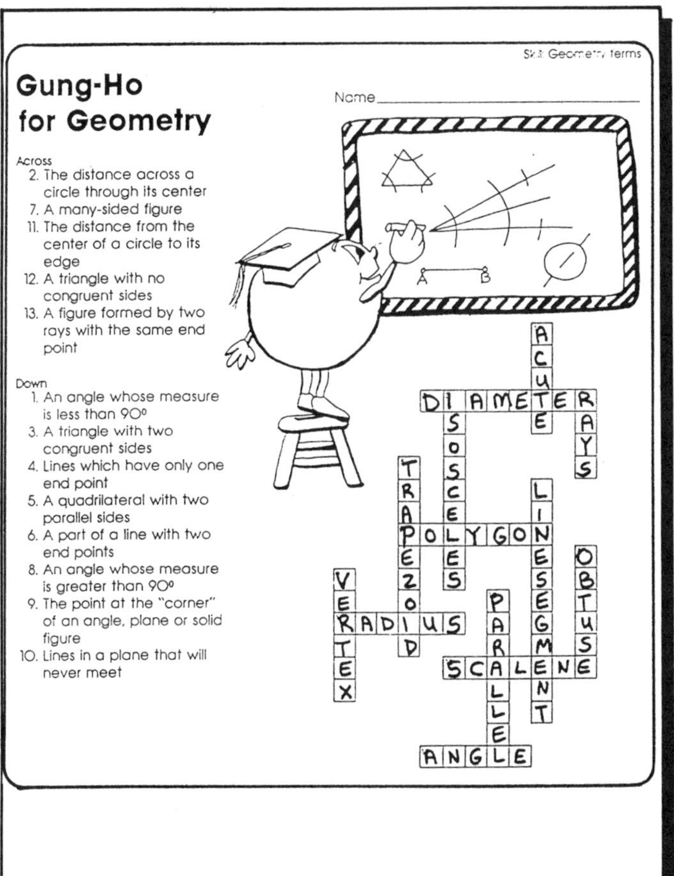
Skill: Geometry terms

## Gung-Ho for Geometry

Name ______________________

Across
2. The distance across a circle through its center
7. A many-sided figure
11. The distance from the center of a circle to its edge
12. A triangle with no congruent sides
13. A figure formed by two rays with the same end point

Down
1. An angle whose measure is less than 90°
3. A triangle with two congruent sides
4. Lines which have only one end point
5. A quadrilateral with two parallel sides
6. A part of a line with two end points
8. An angle whose measure is greater than 90°
9. The point at the "corner" of an angle, plane or solid figure
10. Lines in a plane that will never meet



Page 73

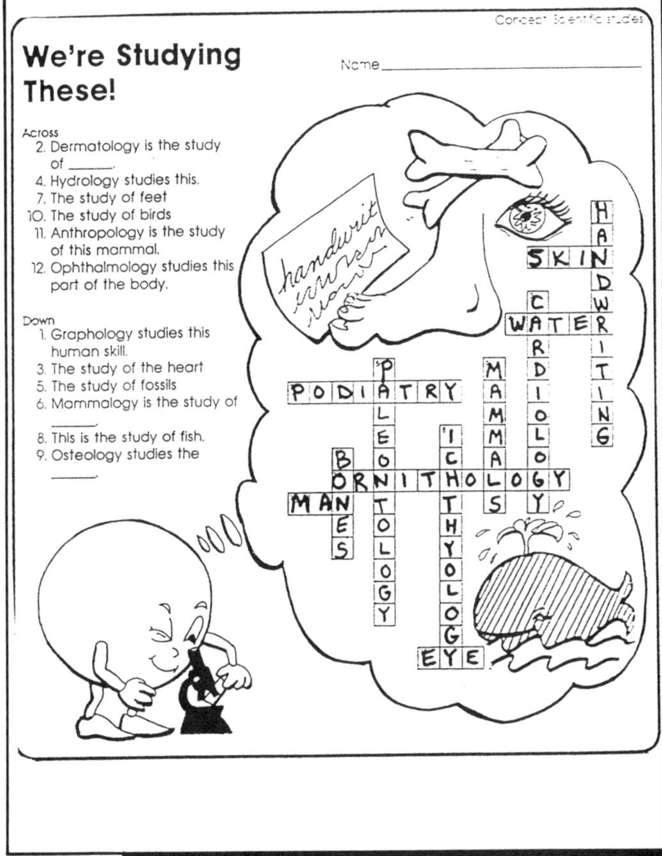
Concept: Scientific studies

## We're Studying These!

Name ______________________

Across
2. Dermatology is the study of ______.
4. Hydrology studies this.
7. The study of feet
10. The study of birds
11. Anthropology is the study of this mammal.
12. Ophthalmology studies this part of the body.

Down
1. Graphology studies this human skill.
3. The study of the heart
5. The study of fossils
6. Mammalogy is the study of ______.
8. This is the study of fish.
9. Osteology studies the ______.



Page 74

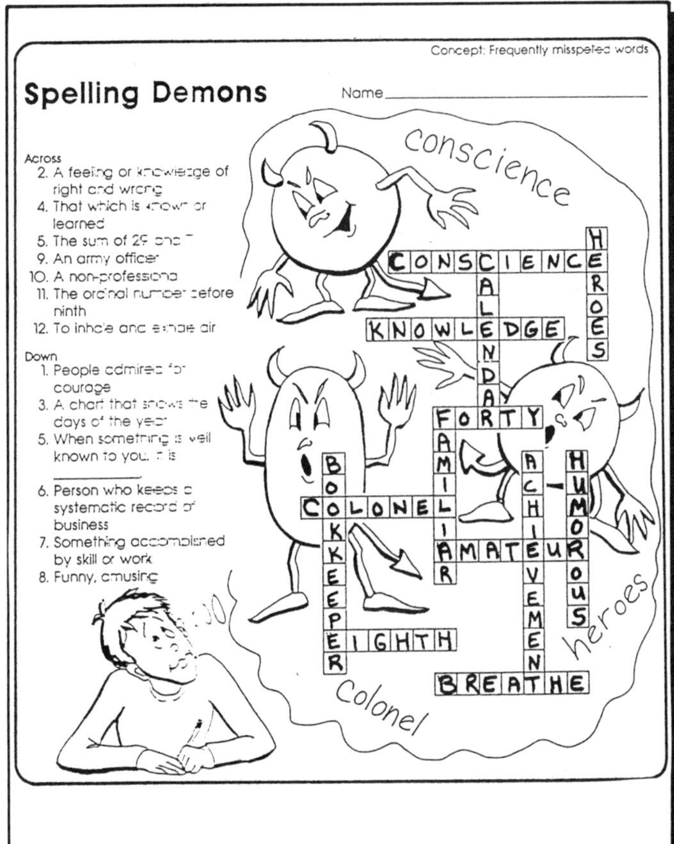
Concept: Frequently misspelled words

## Spelling Demons

Name ______________________

Across
2. A feeling or knowledge of right and wrong
4. That which is known or learned
5. The sum of 29 and 11
9. An army officer
10. A non-professional
11. The ordinal number before ninth
12. To inhale and exhale air

Down
1. People admired for courage
3. A chart that shows the days of the year
5. When something is well known to you, it is ______.
6. Person who keeps a systematic record of business
7. Something accomplished by skill or work
8. Funny, amusing



Page 75

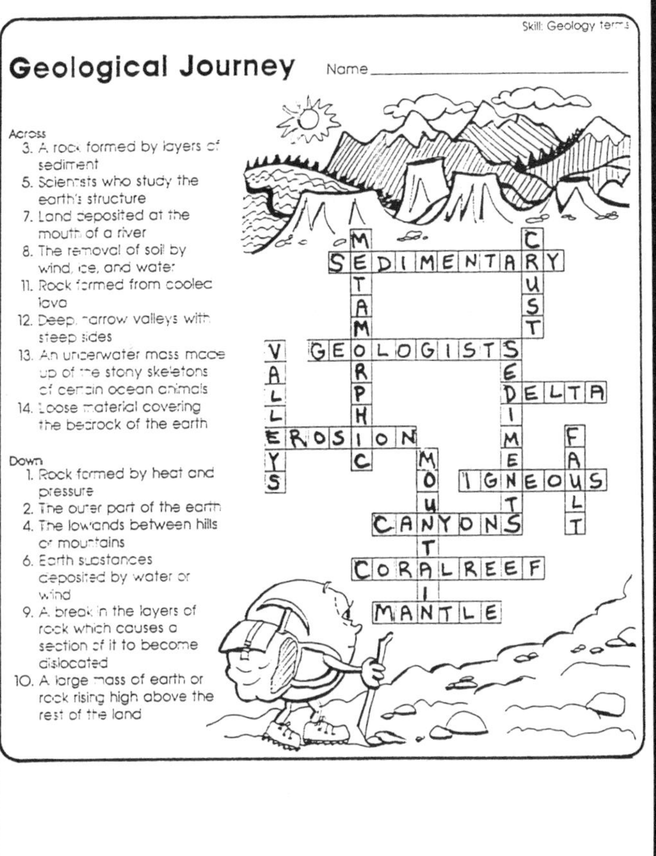
Skill: Geology terms

## Geological Journey

Name ______________________

Across
3. A rock formed by layers of sediment
5. Scientists who study the earth's structure
7. Land deposited at the mouth of a river
8. The removal of soil by wind, ice, and water
11. Rock formed from cooled lava
12. Deep, narrow valleys with steep sides
13. An underwater mass made up of the stony skeletons of certain ocean animals
14. Loose material covering the bedrock of the earth

Down
1. Rock formed by heat and pressure
2. The outer part of the earth
4. The lowlands between hills or mountains
6. Earth substances deposited by water or wind
9. A break in the layers of rock which causes a section of it to become dislocated
10. A large mass of earth or rock rising high above the rest of the land



Page 76

# Answer Key

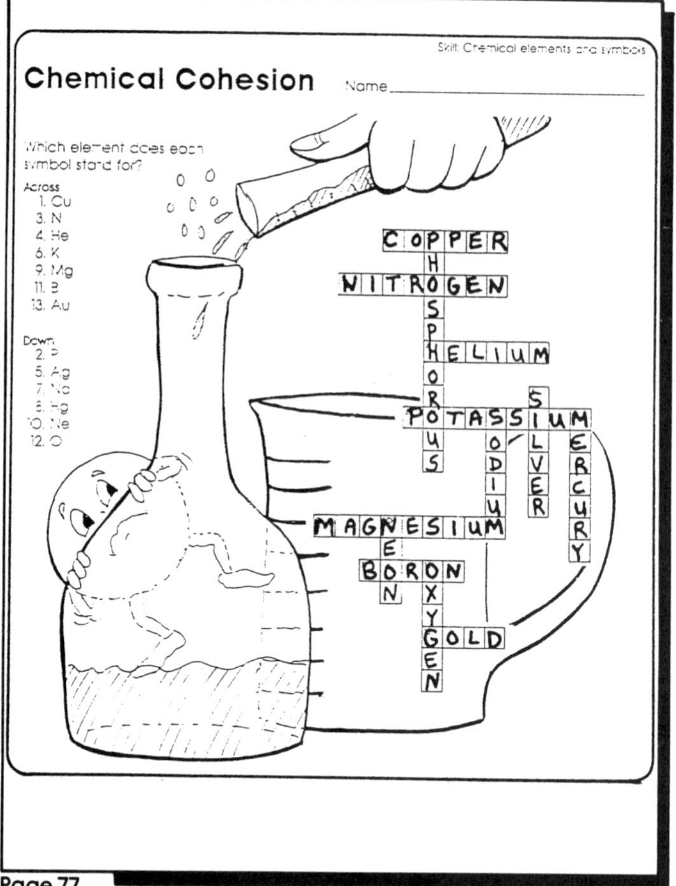

Skill: Chemical elements and symbols
Chemical Cohesion
Name
Which element does each symbol stand for?
Across
1. Cu
3. N
4. He
6. K
9. Mg
11. B
13. Au
Down
2. P
5. Ag
7. Na
8. Hg
10. Ne
12. O
COPPER
NITROGEN
HELIUM
POTASSIUM
MAGNESIUM
BORON
GOLD
PHOSPHORUS
SILVER
SODIUM
MERCURY
NEON
OXYGEN


Page 77

## Pick 'em Out

Skill: Parts of speech

Name ____________________

What part of speech is underlined?

**Across**

3. Jane went with Jim and her.
4. Geoffrey ate the apple.
7. Run for your life!
10. Happiness is two kinds of ice cream.
11. Cindy will help her mother.
12. Norma and Bruce live in Chicago.

**Down**

1. Suddenly, Aaron ran out of the house.
2. Wow! This is fun!
5. Those flowers are beautiful.
6. The broom closet is full.
8. Put the dishes in the dishwasher.
9. The chubby bear ate the marshmallows.

PRONOUN, ARTICLE, VERB, NOUNS, HELPINGVERB, CONJUNCTION, ADVERB, INTERJECTION, LINKINGVERB, ADJECTIVE, PREPOSITION, SUBJECT

is, the, her, fun, to, will, and, a, are

Page 78

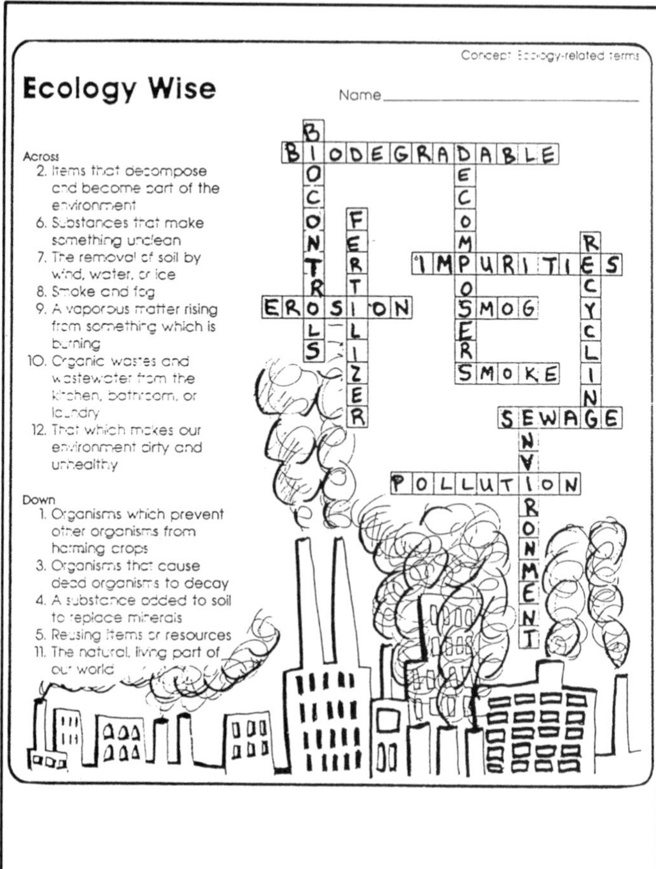

Concept: Ecology-related terms
Ecology Wise
Name
Across
2. Items that decompose and become part of the environment
6. Substances that make something unclean
7. The removal of soil by wind, water, or ice
8. Smoke and fog
9. A vaporous matter rising from something which is burning
10. Organic wastes and wastewater from the kitchen, bathroom, or laundry
12. That which makes our environment dirty and unhealthy
Down
1. Organisms which prevent other organisms from harming crops
3. Organisms that cause dead organisms to decay
4. A substance added to soil to replace minerals
5. Reusing items or resources
11. The natural, living part of our world
BIODEGRADABLE
IMPURITIES
EROSION
SMOG
SMOKE
SEWAGE
POLLUTION
BIOCONTROLS
DECOMPOSERS
FERTILIZER
RECYCLING
ENVIRONMENT


Page 79

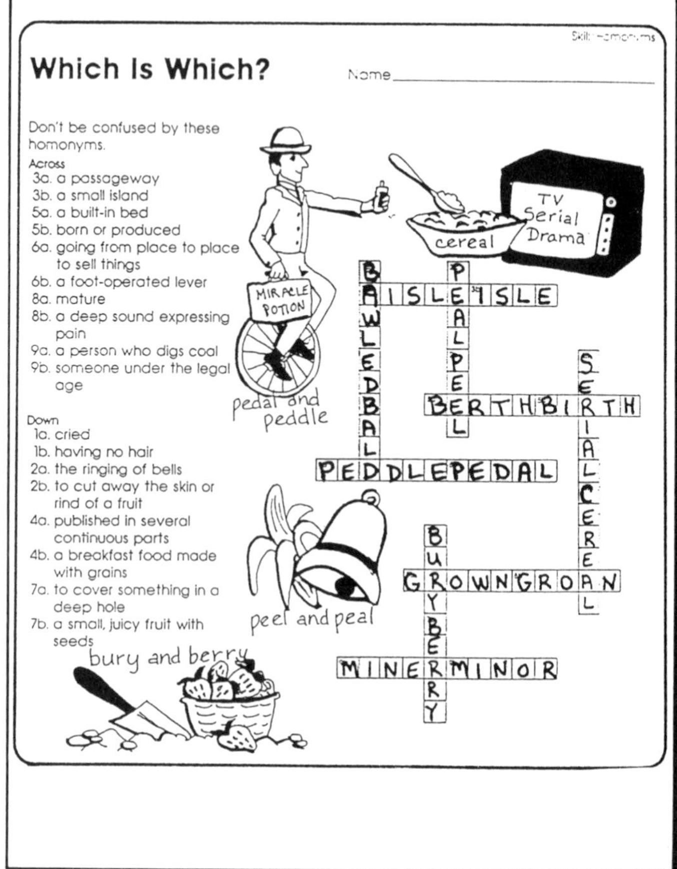

Skill: Homonyms
Which Is Which?
Name
Don't be confused by these homonyms.
Across
3a. a passageway
3b. a small island
5a. a built-in bed
5b. born or produced
6a. going from place to place to sell things
6b. a foot-operated lever
8a. mature
8b. a deep sound expressing pain
9a. a person who digs coal
9b. someone under the legal age
Down
1a. cried
1b. having no hair
2a. the ringing of bells
2b. to cut away the skin or rind of a fruit
4a. published in several continuous parts
4b. a breakfast food made with grains
7a. to cover something in a deep hole
7b. a small, juicy fruit with seeds
TV Serial Drama
cereal
MIRACLE POTION
pedal and peddle
peel and peal
bury and berry
AISLE ISLE
BERTH BIRTH
PEDDLE PEDAL
GROWN GROAN
MINER MINOR
BAWLED BALD
PEAL PEEL
SERIAL CEREAL
BURY BERRY


Page 80

# Answer Key

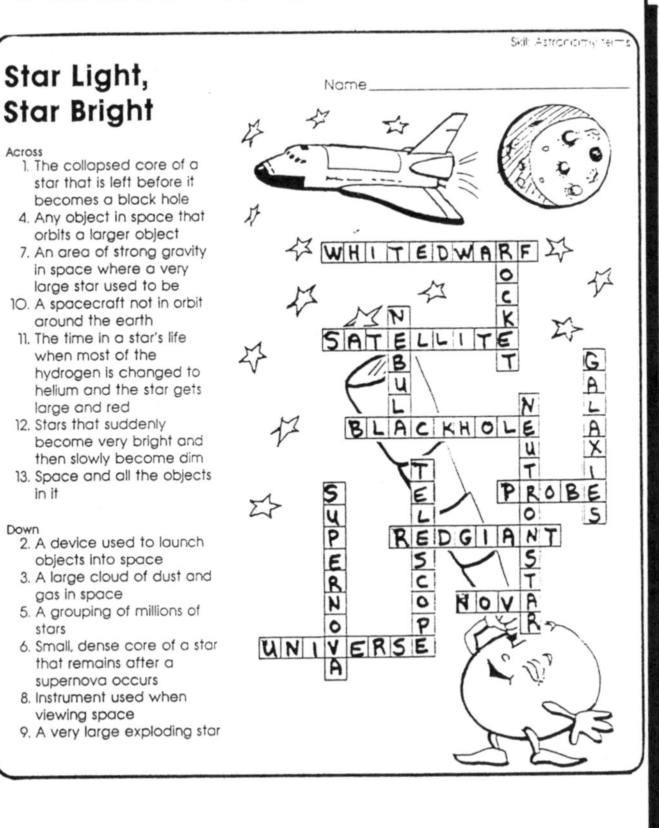

Skill: Astronomy terms

## Star Light, Star Bright

Name ____________________

Across
1. The collapsed core of a star that is left before it becomes a black hole
4. Any object in space that orbits a larger object
7. An area of strong gravity in space where a very large star used to be
10. A spacecraft not in orbit around the earth
11. The time in a star's life when most of the hydrogen is changed to helium and the star gets large and red
12. Stars that suddenly become very bright and then slowly become dim
13. Space and all the objects in it

Down
2. A device used to launch objects into space
3. A large cloud of dust and gas in space
5. A grouping of millions of stars
6. Small, dense core of a star that remains after a supernova occurs
8. Instrument used when viewing space
9. A very large exploding star



Page 81

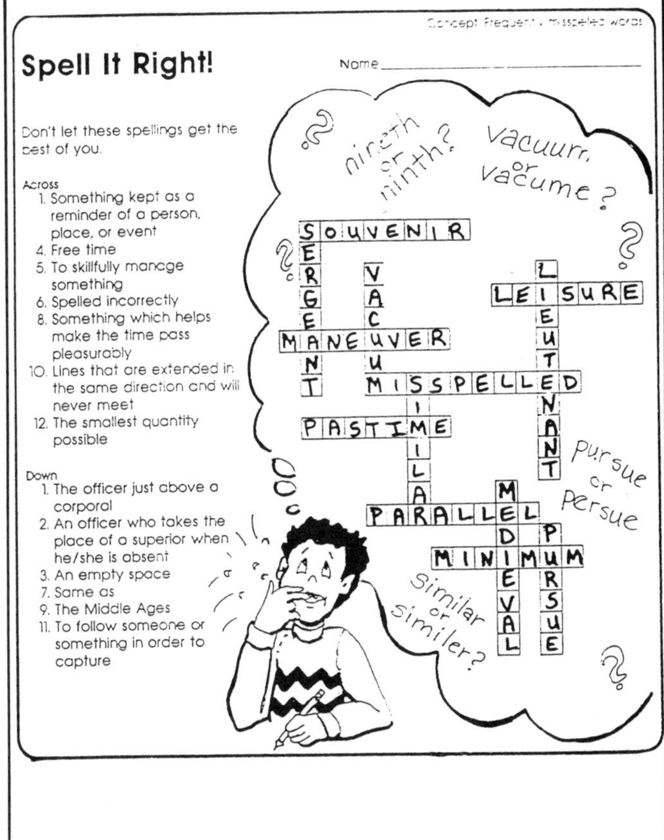

Concept: Frequently misspelled words

## Spell It Right!

Name ____________________

Don't let these spellings get the best of you.

Across
1. Something kept as a reminder of a person, place, or event
4. Free time
5. To skillfully manage something
6. Spelled incorrectly
8. Something which helps make the time pass pleasurably
10. Lines that are extended in the same direction and will never meet
12. The smallest quantity possible

Down
1. The officer just above a corporal
2. An officer who takes the place of a superior when he/she is absent
3. An empty space
7. Same as
9. The Middle Ages
11. To follow someone or something in order to capture



Page 82

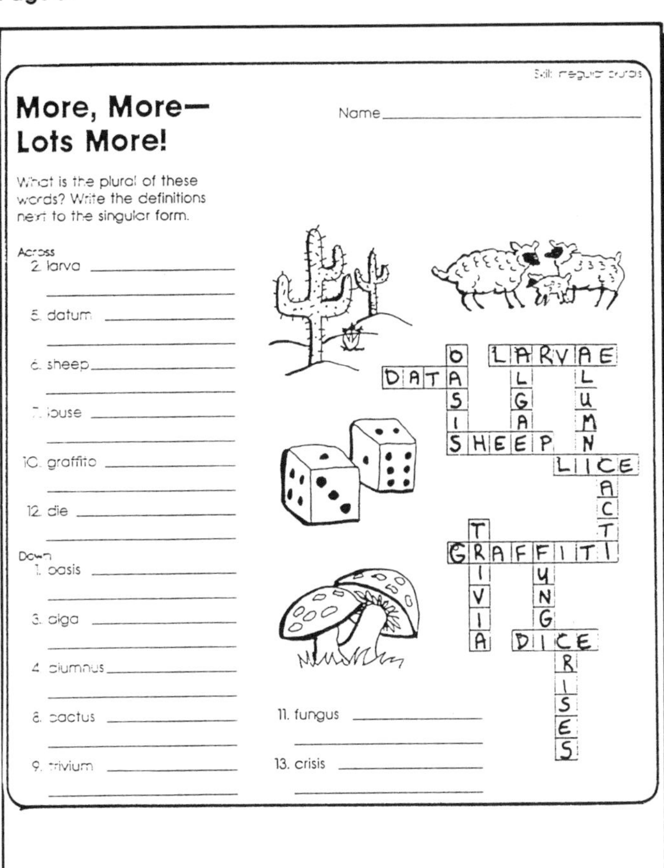

Skill: Irregular plurals

## More, More— Lots More!

Name ____________________

What is the plural of these words? Write the definitions next to the singular form.

Across
2. larva ____________________
5. datum ____________________
6. sheep ____________________
7. louse ____________________
10. graffito ____________________
12. die ____________________

Down
1. oasis ____________________
3. alga ____________________
4. alumnus ____________________
8. cactus ____________________
9. trivium ____________________
11. fungus ____________________
13. crisis ____________________



Page 83

Skill: Names of skeletal bones

## Find Those Bones!

Name ____________________

Across
2. toes or fingers
3. breastbone
4. collarbone
8. heel bone
9. wrist bones
12. ankle bones

Down
1. kneecap
4. tailbone
5. shorter forearm bone
6. shoulder bone
7. upper arm bone
10. larger forearm bone
11. thigh bone

PHALANGES, PATELLA, STERNUM, CLAVICLE, COCCYX, CALCANEUS, SCAPULA, HUMERUS, RADIUS, CARPUS, ULNA, FEMUR, TARSUS

Page 84

 

# Answer Key

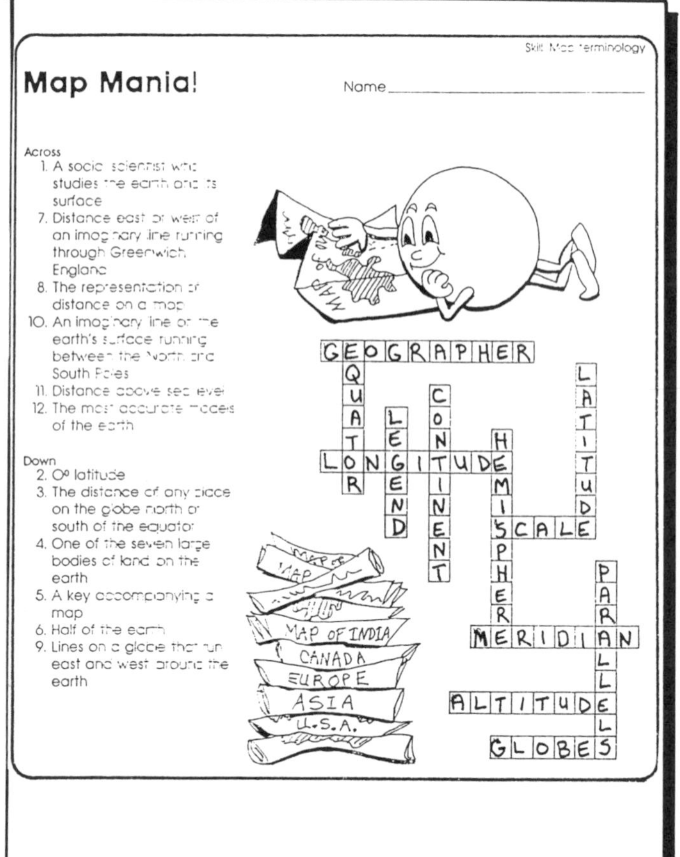

Skill: Map terminology

## Map Mania!

Name ____________________

Across
1. A social scientist who studies the earth and its surface
7. Distance east or west of an imaginary line running through Greenwich, England
8. The representation of distance on a map
10. An imaginary line on the earth's surface running between the North and South Poles
11. Distance above sea level
12. The most accurate models of the earth

Down
2. 0º latitude
3. The distance of any place on the globe north or south of the equator
4. One of the seven large bodies of land on the earth
5. A key accompanying a map
6. Half of the earth
9. Lines on a globe that run east and west around the earth



Page 85

Skill: Atomic terms

## Amazing Atoms!

Name ____________________

Atoms make up everything in this world. Locate and circle 17 terms related to the atom.

| I | R | I | L | N | E | R | N | S | A | S | M | A | P | O | R |
|---|---|---|---|---|---|---|---|---|---|---|---|---|---|---|---|
| N | E | D | E | I | S | P | A | R | T | I | C | L | E | S | I |
| H | A | S | L | N | K | S | Y | M | B | O | L | D | P | U | B |
| L | T | E | E | G | M | A | R | O | A | N | N | T | R | F | G |
| I | H | C | C | F | P | U | I | L | F | E | N | E | O | V | A |
| T | E | F | T | O | R | Y | E | E | M | N | I | T | P | E | T |
| S | P | E | R | I | O | D | I | C | T | A | B | L | E | N | B |
| O | V | L | O | N | T | P | T | U | E | N | A | M | R | R | M |
| C | T | E | N | Z | O | E | T | L | S | E | R | A | T | O | M |
| I | E | C | P | S | N | R | W | E | R | E | T | H | I | N | M |
| A | H | T | M | O | S | V | N | I | T | K | E | N | E | E | A |
| A | I | R | A | F | A | E | A | G | R | O | R | W | S | I | T |
| F | L | O | A | R | M | A | E | N | I | R | N | T | E | H | T |
| O | L | N | E | G | A | T | I | V | E | C | H | A | R | G | E |
| R | U | C | O | M | P | O | U | N | D | T | E | V | A | W | R |
| M | E | L | H | I | L | N | E | T | H | Y | I | R | E | Y | I |
| U | P | O | S | I | T | I | V | E | C | H | A | R | G | E | T |
| L | C | U | N | L | D | R | O | S | G | E | N | F | T | R | E |
| A | B | D | E | E | N | T | A | E | N | E | U | T | R | O | N |
| N | A | N | D | O | E | L | E | M | E | N | T | S | V | L | S |
| R | T | A | B | A | W | G | A | N | A | M | T | Y | T | E | N |

Page 86

Concept: Drug Awareness

## Drug-free is the Way to Be

Name ____________________

When you're happy about yourself, you don't need drugs to get high. Circle 19 drug-related words. Then, write 10 things you like about yourself.



| S | O | H | A | L | L | U | C | I | N | O | G | E | N | S | O | N | T | I | E | T | P |
|---|---|---|---|---|---|---|---|---|---|---|---|---|---|---|---|---|---|---|---|---|---|
| R | H | T | M | N | I | L | T | L | A | N | I | A | S | C | T | E | P | E | D | O | H |
| E | S | R | P | E | B | O | T | S | R | V | B | L | E | H | A | L | R | O | S | S | A |
| H | S | U | H | G | D | E | P | E | N | D | E | N | C | E | H | R | E | L | T | S | R |
| A | N | O | E | R | E | B | R | D | S | M | A | R | T | R | Q | U | S | U | I | I | M |
| B | A | C | T | L | R | I | H | A | T | S | E | Y | D | O | R | S | C | O | M | D | A |
| I | R | Y | A | D | D | I | C | T | I | O | N | L | R | I | Y | O | R | Y | U | E | C |
| L | C | E | M | I | H | E | R | I | R | A | O | M | A | N | E | R | I | E | L | E | Y |
| I | O | P | I | U | M | S | U | V | C | E | R | Y | H | T | H | E | P | O | A | F | V |
| T | T | R | N | P | L | A | C | E | B | O | F | A | U | K | S | A | T | I | N | F | L |
| A | I | F | E | S | O | B | T | R | M | U | N | H | A | N | L | T | I | L | T | E | L |
| T | C | F | H | A | R | U | N | O | R | M | A | O | H | V | A | I | O | B | I | C | Y |
| I | D | E | P | R | E | S | S | A | N | T | C | A | F | F | E | I | N | E | D | T | A |
| O | O | E | G | Y | C | E | Y | D | N | E | L | J | R | O | N | Y | Q | E | N | H | E |
| N | B | A | R | B | I | T | U | R | A | T | E | L | E | A | R | M | U | E | O | F | T |
| R | O | N | S | T | A | L | D | S | A | T | R | A | N | Q | U | I | L | I | Z | E | R |

Page 87

Skill: Math terms

## Math Counts Too!

Name ____________________

Circle the 20 math terms hidden in the puzzle. Be ready to explain what each term means.

| M | Q | R | E | M | A | I | N | D | E | R | L | A | U | W | M |
|---|---|---|---|---|---|---|---|---|---|---|---|---|---|---|---|
| P | U | O | Y | Z | B | O | B | R | P | C | E | S | I | Q | I |
| A | N | X | M | D | E | C | I | M | A | L | S | S | P | E | N |
| N | B | Q | U | O | T | I | E | N | T | I | L | O | D | U | U |
| U | C | W | L | F | R | A | C | T | I | O | N | C | D | D | E |
| M | U | L | T | I | P | L | I | C | A | N | D | I | E | E | N |
| E | A | W | I | C | A | M | S | S | M | P | I | A | O | N | D |
| R | N | V | P | E | G | R | E | F | E | N | F | T | I | O | E |
| A | J | D | L | R | E | T | L | O | U | T | F | I | U | M | S |
| T | K | A | I | T | O | A | O | T | T | L | E | V | F | I | M |
| O | A | C | E | A | M | D | D | N | A | T | R | E | R | N | T |
| R | R | I | R | A | E | R | U | O | A | M | E | L | E | A | R |
| L | G | B | H | D | T | N | R | C | T | W | N | A | A | T | O |
| W | D | I | S | N | R | A | A | H | T | H | C | W | L | O | O |
| T | I | V | T | A | Y | D | T | C | I | E | E | F | F | R | T |
| H | V | O | U | I | M | G | E | T | A | D | D | E | N | D | O |
| D | I | V | I | S | O | R | I | S | E | T | L | H | P | O | S |
| Y | D | C | O | M | M | U | T | A | T | I | V | E | L | A | W |
| S | E | U | S | Y | A | Z | N | C | E | E | X | T | A | K | T |
| U | N | S | T | A | S | U | B | T | R | A | H | E | N | D | O |
| M | D | I | S | T | R | I | B | U | T | I | V | E | L | A | W |

Page 88

# Answer Key

Skill: Prepositions
Preppy Prepositions
Name
Perfectly Preppy Peter prefers to prepare proper prepositions rather than practicing piano. Pacify him promptly by picking out the prepositions in this puzzle.
in
above
of
for
to
upon
behind


Page 89

Skill: Geometry terms
Dimensions in Space
Name
Circle the 18 geometric terms hidden in this wordsearch.


Page 90

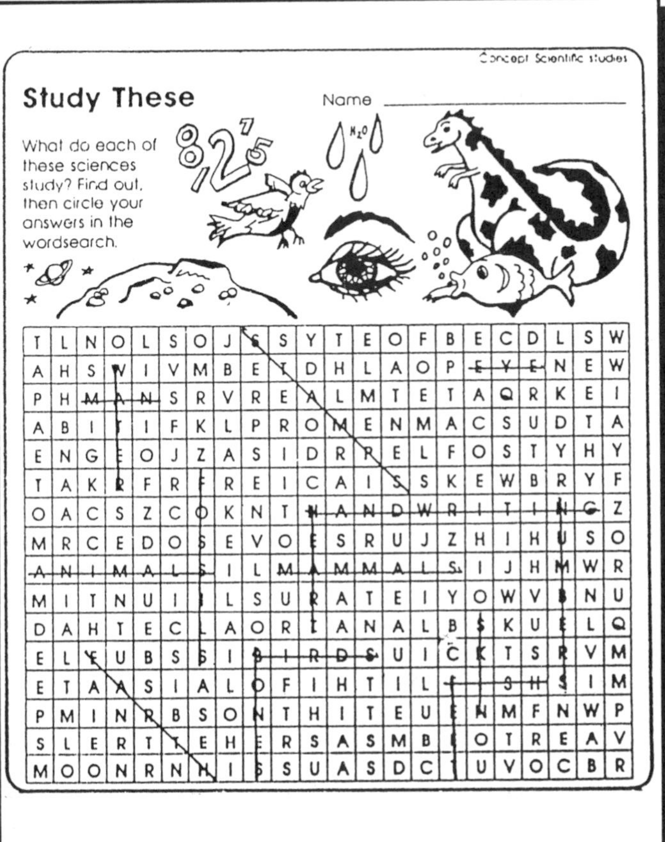

Concept: Scientific studies
Study These
Name
What do each of these sciences study? Find out, then circle your answers in the wordsearch.


Page 91

Concept: Frequently misspelled words

## Spelling Demons

Name

Beware... There are 16 frequently misspelled words hidden in this puzzle. Find and circle them. Proceed with caution.

ninth
similar
pursue

| W | Z | A | B | M | O | L | D | N | C | L | I | E | S | I | M | I | L | A | R | M | H |
|---|---|---|---|---|---|---|---|---|---|---|---|---|---|---|---|---|---|---|---|---|---|
| E | U | M | A | N | E | U | V | E | R | T | A | B | C | T | H | S | T | K | Q | U | O |
| H | R | I | W | N | A | T | E | K | V | A | S | F | O | D | G | O | D | L | U | U | Y |
| P | A | S | T | I | M | E | T | N | A | W | B | L | O | E | A | U | O | N | E | L | T |
| D | U | S | F | A | O | A | N | E | C | T | M | E | D | I | E | V | A | L | S | T | M |
| Y | V | P | X | E | P | I | W | O | U | H | O | I | S | E | T | E | S | L | T | G | A |
| I | T | E | B | I | A | R | E | Y | U | I | Z | S | A | V | C | N | R | O | I | A | E |
| I | U | L | D | H | R | Y | U | H | M | N | K | U | A | B | S | I | Y | S | O | S | T |
| D | A | L | B | L | A | B | O | R | A | T | O | R | Y | A | D | R | V | E | N | R | R |
| T | S | E | Y | W | L | A | P | T | S | K | T | E | C | E | W | I | A | R | N | F | N |
| Y | N | D | C | C | L | R | T | N | A | U | B | O | N | H | E | R | E | G | A | M | Q |
| S | O | M | Z | Y | E | O | C | A | N | O | E | I | I | T | A | W | P | E | I | N | U |
| O | N | G | A | T | L | I | E | U | T | E | N | A | N | T | E | L | T | A | R | A | P |
| H | A | C | H | A | V | S | R | N | E | R | B | U | T | G | R | A | U | N | E | O | A |
| U | M | I | N | I | M | U | M | O | H | S | D | L | H | U | K | T | M | T | O | W | D |
| U | M | J | R | K | E | L | S | W | M | W | A | H | N | O | J | L | E | S | A | W | Y |

Page 92

 

# Answer Key

Skill: Geology terms

## Geological Expedition

Name ____________________

| M | U | E | R | I | M | F | E | Y | E | C | D | R | E | A | N |
|---|---|---|---|---|---|---|---|---|---|---|---|---|---|---|---|
| I | P | S | T | R | I | A | T | I | O | N | P | Q | R | E | Y |
| N | R | S | E | T | O | D | N | U | D | H | L | E | O | P | M |
| E | M | E | T | A | M | O | R | P | H | I | C | U | S | Z | G |
| R | O | R | G | I | R | O | B | U | I | N | R | L | I | P | L |
| A | U | T | L | S | C | L | O | N | R | P | U | R | O | B | A |
| L | N | A | N | U | K | R | S | D | R | A | S | A | N | E | C |
| S | T | S | G | E | O | L | O | G | I | S | T | S | N | A | I |
| V | A | L | L | E | Y | S | M | R | G | R | A | N | I | T | E |
| T | I | T | E | S | E | T | U | E | B | I | N | L | E | B | R |
| S | N | B | O | E | S | I | E | P | R | A | K | I | Y | C | I |
| C | S | E | D | I | M | E | N | T | S | N | A | O | D | O | H |
| E | T | A | L | O | M | P | D | D | A | S | E | D | M | R | H |
| R | O | C | L | O | M | P | E | S | A | H | M | E | I | A | T |
| F | S | H | A | H | N | L | R | I | G | S | W | L | N | L | G |
| E | G | E | L | Y | S | E | D | I | M | E | N | T | A | R | Y |
| L | O | O | S | L | E | A | I | O | A | E | O | A | R | E | E |
| C | H | E | N | I | A | S | O | A | N | S | N | V | I | E | F |
| A | O | E | M | E | F | A | U | L | T | V | W | O | Y | I | K |
| I | E | R | A | C | S | N | M | L | L | E | F | L | E | T | D |
| T | C | M | E | H | M | I | G | N | E | O | U | S | L | C | A |

If you were a geologist, you would meet these terms in the study of the earth and its structure. Find the terms in the wordsearch and circle them.

Page 93

Skill: Chemical elements and symbols

## Chemical Connections

Name ____________________

| S | U | L | F | U | R | B | O | L | M | O | A | C | P | I | K |
|---|---|---|---|---|---|---|---|---|---|---|---|---|---|---|---|
| C | O | X | Y | G | E | N | T | W | S | C | I | A | E | E | T |
| N | M | D | O | C | H | L | O | R | I | N | E | R | W | I | T |
| L | E | V | I | S | R | I | T | R | L | Y | P | B | O | T | N |
| E | R | D | F | U | N | Q | S | O | Y | A | O | O | N | L | C |
| A | K | I | E | B | M | D | L | S | E | U | E | N | H | U | T |
| O | A | B | M | P | A | S | O | O | R | N | D | I | E | O | L |
| N | I | T | R | O | G | E | N | B | U | O | Y | P | V | O | E |
| E | J | N | G | E | N | E | T | H | Y | D | R | O | G | E | N |
| G | O | L | D | I | E | S | B | E | U | P | F | T | F | A | M |
| F | V | E | S | L | S | F | U | L | L | H | I | A | B | O | L |
| E | N | F | B | H | I | R | O | I | W | O | N | S | B | R | O |
| C | A | L | C | I | U | M | V | U | R | S | Z | S | E | T | S |
| M | O | U | G | Y | M | M | V | M | E | P | H | I | A | R | I |
| L | M | O | C | T | F | W | E | A | D | H | R | U | N | S | A |
| I | Y | R | E | X | H | O | R | R | I | O | C | N | I | C | E |
| I | S | I | L | I | C | O | N | E | C | R | Y | R | M | O | T |
| H | C | N | R | D | A | M | M | B | Y | U | A | O | S | P | I |
| I | Z | E | N | B | O | R | O | N | E | S | R | I | I | P | L |
| U | T | O | P | S | I | O | C | R | T | O | S | Y | O | E | L |
| M | H | A | L | U | M | I | N | U | M | B | H | Y | B | R | F |

The Clue Bank has the chemical symbols. You find the elements and circle them in the wordsearch.

Page 94

Skill: Parts of speech

## Sentence Sense

Name ____________________

| L | H | L | I | N | K | I | N | G | V | E | R | B | P | E | R |
|---|---|---|---|---|---|---|---|---|---|---|---|---|---|---|---|
| W | A | D | J | E | C | T | I | V | E | U | I | E | R | W | C |
| A | D | H | E | H | E | P | N | E | S | U | B | J | E | C | T |
| E | Y | U | T | A | T | N | I | O | E | I | L | E | P | V | A |
| S | E | T | C | E | L | A | E | R | H | D | A | V | O | E | P |
| A | R | T | I | C | L | E | R | V | H | S | E | L | S | E | O |
| T | B | H | A | M | E | L | U | H | E | P | M | E | I | V | S |
| G | O | P | O | I | E | C | E | A | U | R | B | O | T | F | S |
| W | C | I | N | W | E | S | C | S | E | O | B | T | I | L | E |
| C | O | N | J | U | N | C | T | I | O | N | Y | E | O | G | S |
| E | M | R | U | F | I | N | I | N | V | O | D | H | N | R | S |
| T | P | S | A | H | P | O | O | T | N | U | L | L | A | N | I |
| E | L | E | P | F | I | N | N | U | E | N | I | W | L | Y | V |
| K | E | D | P | A | E | S | T | Y | N | I | L | O | P | I | E |
| K | M | W | P | R | E | D | I | C | A | T | E | E | H | B | P |
| S | E | R | L | E | K | T | R | O | D | O | E | W | R | T | R |
| O | N | P | R | E | D | A | D | E | I | D | A | I | A | I | O |
| N | I | H | E | L | P | I | N | G | V | E | R | B | S | E | N |
| V | W | O | D | R | T | A | E | U | L | N | T | G | E | N | O |
| P | R | E | P | O | S | I | T | I | O | N | E | H | G | I | U |
| O | E | U | N | U | N | O | T | R | E | T | H | E | D | E | N |

Circle the parts of speech and words related to sentence structure!

verb
adverb
noun
subject
pronoun

Page 95

Concept: Ecology-related terms

## Clean It Up!

Name ____________________

| M | E | P | D | S | A | P | Y | E | S | M | N | D | C | H | T |
|---|---|---|---|---|---|---|---|---|---|---|---|---|---|---|---|
| B | I | O | D | E | G | R | A | D | A | B | L | E | T | A | F |
| E | O | L | U | W | Y | P | R | S | T | S | A | C | E | Z | Y |
| O | N | L | B | A | O | U | D | I | N | O | R | O | Y | A | I |
| N | O | U | C | G | S | A | K | A | E | B | R | M | A | R | S |
| N | H | I | D | E | R | I | A | U | D | I | L | P | R | D | V |
| C | G | I | E | R | A | H | T | R | A | O | U | O | T | O | E |
| E | W | O | Y | I | E | R | Y | O | R | C | U | S | E | U | E |
| C | O | N | S | E | R | V | A | T | I | O | N | E | G | S | E |
| O | H | I | S | M | O | K | E | H | M | N | T | O | S | W | N |
| L | V | Y | S | T | S | R | I | A | E | T | N | P | A | A | Y |
| O | S | T | P | M | I | G | S | E | T | R | C | I | F | S | I |
| G | C | W | Y | Y | O | U | T | P | D | O | I | R | H | T | R |
| Y | A | L | P | C | N | G | S | E | E | L | A | H | O | E | O |
| T | H | E | R | M | A | L | P | O | L | L | U | T | I | O | N |
| A | M | R | A | T | R | O | E | N | L | R | E | I | Y | X | M |
| R | T | O | H | L | O | Y | N | T | P | E | S | T | R | C | E |
| I | M | P | U | R | I | T | I | E | S | U | F | Z | O | L | N |
| O | N | N | S | R | E | C | Y | C | L | I | N | G | T | L | T |
| N | R | F | G | L | E | O | N | A | E | L | H | S | L | S | V |
| F | E | R | T | I | L | I | Z | E | R | R | I | E | Y | I | E |

Help America clean up. Circle all the words that have to do with ecology.

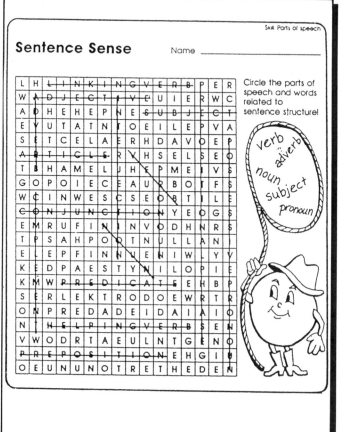

Page 96

# Answer Key

Skill: Homonyms
Homonym Hullabaloo!
Name
Confused by homonyms? Don't be! Find the homonyms for the words in the Clue Bank and circle them in the puzzle.
FLOUR
milk

Page 97

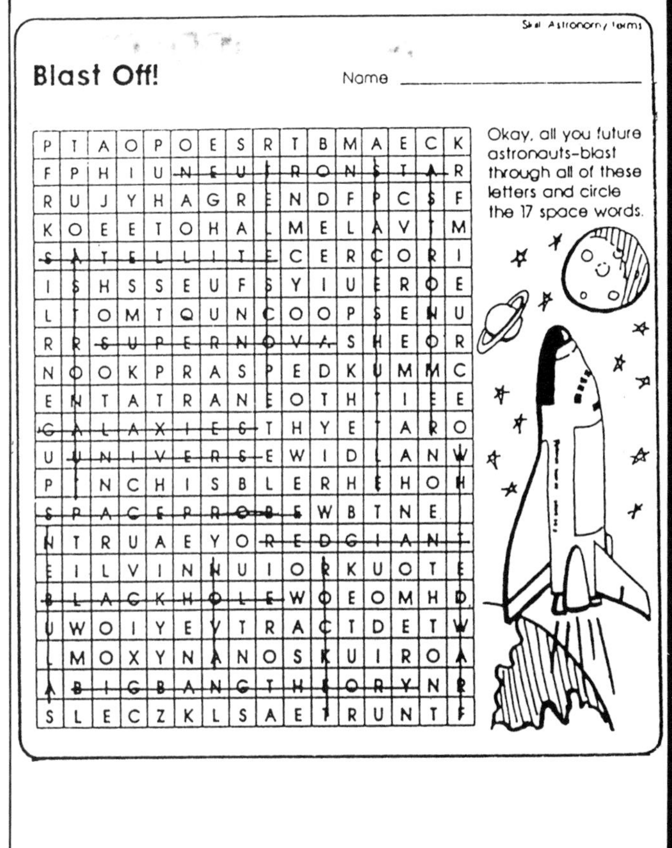
Skill: Astronomy terms
Blast Off!
Name
Okay, all you future astronauts–blast through all of these letters and circle the 17 space words.

Page 98

Concept: Frequently misspelled words
Spelling Gremlins
Name
Don't let these spelling gremlins scare you. Learn how to spell them correctly. Then circle them in the puzzle.

Page 99

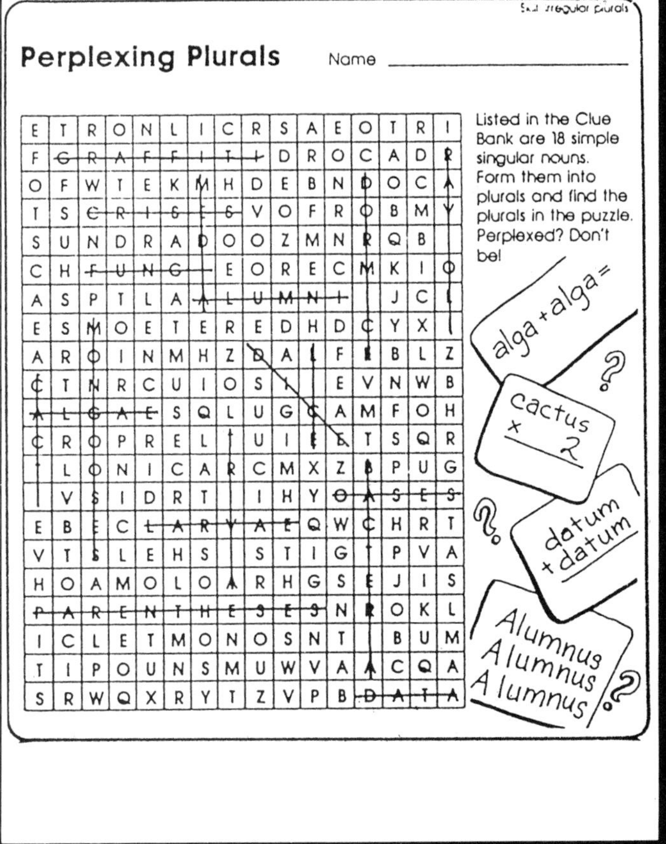
Skill: Irregular plurals
Perplexing Plurals
Name
Listed in the Clue Bank are 18 simple singular nouns. Form them into plurals and find the plurals in the puzzle. Perplexed? Don't be!
alga + alga =
cactus × 2
datum + datum
Alumnus
Alumnus
Alumnus

Page 100

Skill: Map terminology

## Mapping it Out

Name ____________

| | | | | | | | | | | | | | | | |
|---|---|---|---|---|---|---|---|---|---|---|---|---|---|---|---|
| N | C | O | N | T | O | U | R | L | I | N | E | S | P | N | T |
| H | A | I | O | P | R | E | H | I | S | E | O | T | R | S | H |
| O | L | O | N | G | I | T | U | D | E | T | E | S | I | A | G |
| T | W | R | S | H | E | L | T | G | H | I | N | H | M | A | R |
| O | H | I | S | T | N | A | H | L | O | L | E | G | E | N | D |
| P | I | C | E | M | O | R | I | O | W | Y | K | T | M | D | E |
| O | D | C | R | P | H | E | O | B | A | T | R | S | E | W | F |
| G | E | O | G | R | A | P | H | E | R | O | I | A | R | O | O |
| R | O | N | A | N | I | A | Y | S | N | H | O | T | I | I | R |
| A | I | T | H | A | T | R | Y | C | U | O | M | O | D | E | L |
| P | O | I | B | O | L | A | T | I | T | U | D | E | I | Y | R |
| H | D | N | O | L | O | L | R | B | U | A | K | L | A | O | U |
| I | G | E | E | R | A | L | A | P | E | A | N | G | N | Y | G |
| C | T | N | T | O | M | E | R | I | D | I | A | N | O | N | E |
| M | L | T | E | C | A | L | T | I | T | U | D | E | I | S | E |
| A | H | U | A | R | N | S | D | L | C | N | O | Q | I | D | I |
| P | A | O | S | I | C | U | O | L | I | T | H | U | A | T | B |
| S | E | T | L | E | R | N | M | A | R | S | C | A | L | E | W |
| A | R | H | O | M | O | S | T | E | O | K | U | T | A | E | U |
| H | E | M | I | S | P | H | E | R | E | R | L | O | M | A | R |
| T | U | J | E | N | L | I | N | T | V | Y | O | R | T | R | A |

Give this one a spin. Circle 16 terms related to the study of maps.



Page 101

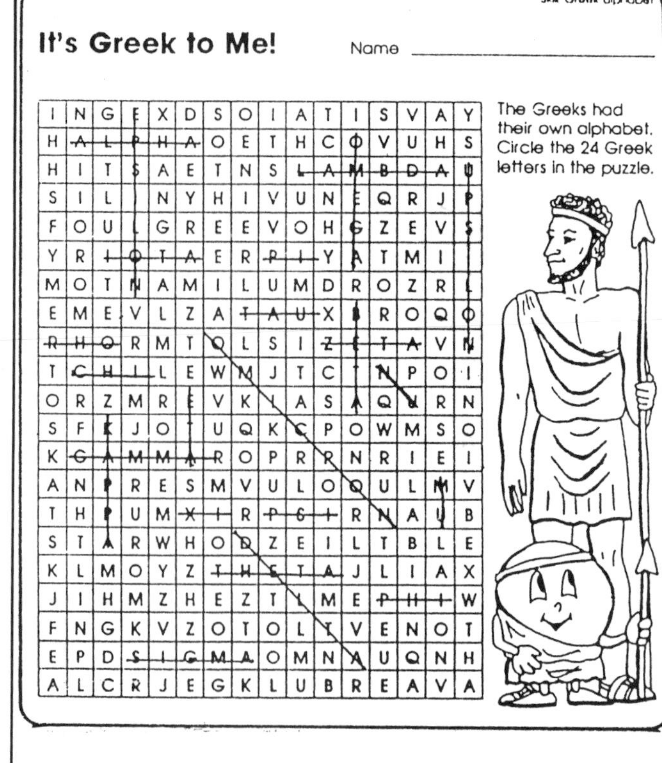

Skill: Greek alphabet

## It's Greek to Me!

Name ____________

| | | | | | | | | | | | | | | | |
|---|---|---|---|---|---|---|---|---|---|---|---|---|---|---|---|
| I | N | G | E | X | D | S | O | I | A | T | I | S | V | A | Y |
| H | A | L | P | H | A | O | E | T | H | C | O | V | U | H | S |
| H | I | T | S | A | E | T | N | S | L | A | M | B | D | A | U |
| S | I | L | I | N | Y | H | I | V | U | N | E | Q | R | J | P |
| F | O | U | L | G | R | E | E | V | O | H | G | Z | E | V | S |
| Y | R | I | O | T | A | E | R | P | I | Y | A | T | M | I | I |
| M | O | T | N | A | M | I | L | U | M | D | R | O | Z | R | L |
| E | M | E | V | L | Z | A | T | A | U | X | B | R | O | Q | O |
| R | H | O | R | M | T | O | L | S | I | Z | E | T | A | V | N |
| T | C | H | I | L | E | W | M | J | T | C | T | N | P | O | I |
| O | R | Z | M | R | E | V | K | I | A | S | A | Q | U | R | N |
| S | F | K | J | O | T | U | Q | K | C | P | O | W | M | S | O |
| K | G | A | M | M | A | R | O | P | R | R | N | R | I | E | I |
| A | N | P | R | E | S | M | V | U | L | O | O | U | L | M | V |
| T | H | P | U | M | X | I | R | P | S | I | R | N | A | U | B |
| S | T | A | R | W | H | O | D | Z | E | I | L | T | B | L | E |
| K | L | M | O | Y | Z | T | H | E | T | A | J | L | I | A | X |
| J | I | H | M | Z | H | E | Z | T | L | M | E | P | H | I | W |
| F | N | G | K | V | Z | O | T | O | L | T | V | E | N | O | T |
| E | P | D | S | I | G | M | A | O | M | N | A | U | Q | N | H |
| A | L | C | R | J | E | G | K | L | U | B | R | E | A | V | A |

The Greeks had their own alphabet. Circle the 24 Greek letters in the puzzle.

Page 102

**About the book . . .**

Crosswords and wordsearches have become popular means for teaching words, terms, and concepts. They've become popular for basically two reasons — they're enjoyable and they work. The topics in this collection cover the basic terms and concepts usually taught at this particular level.

Are the pages in this book "busywork" ? No. But they will keep your students busy learning.

**About the authors . . .**

Jan Kennedy and Barbra Glickstein are a team of elementary educators with advanced degrees and more than a quarter century of actual teaching experience.

Authors: Barbra Glickstein, Jan Kennedy
Editor: Jackie Servis
Artists: Colleen Sanders, Karen Caminata, Ann Dyer
Production: Ann Dyer, Pat Geasler
Cover Photo: Frank Pieroni
Art Consultant: Jan Vonk

 